Changing roles and contexts for health library and information professionals

Changing roles and contexts for health library and information professionals

Edited by
Alison Brettle and Christine Urquhart

facet publishing

Published by Facet Publishing,
7 Ridgmount Street, London WC1E 7AE
www.facetpublishing.co.uk

Facet Publishing is wholly owned by CILIP: the Chartered Institute of
Library and Information Professionals.

British Library Cataloguing in Publication Data
A catalogue record for this book is available from the British Library.
ISBN 978-1-85604-740-1

First published 2012
Reprinted digitally thereafter

Text printed on FSC accredited material.

Mixed Sources
Product group from well-managed
forests and other controlled sources
www.fsc.org Cert no. SA-COC-1565
© 1996 Forest Stewardship Council
FSC

Typeset from editors' files in 10/13 pt Garamond and Frutiger by
Flagholme Publishing Services.
Printed and made in Great Britain by MPG Books Group, UK.

Contents

About the editors

Alison Brettle BA(Hons) MSc PhD
Senior Lecturer/Information Specialist, School of Nursing, Midwifery and Social Work, University of Salford, UK
Alison has worked in health information for 18 years and has expertise in systematic review methodology, literature searching and evidence-based practice. A keen advocate of evidence-based library and information practice, she has published widely and carried out a range of systematic reviews and evaluations of library practice as well as undertaking a PhD on the Roles, Effectiveness and Impact of Health Information Professionals in Evidence-Based Practice. She is Editor of the journal *Evidence Based Library and Information Practice* and Chair of the 6th International Evidence-Based Library and Information Conference (EBLIP6) which took place in Salford, June 2011.

Christine Urquhart BSc MSc PGCE PhD FHEA
Senior Lecturer, Department of Information Studies, Aberystwyth University, UK
Christine initially graduated in Chemistry and has practised information science in a wide variety of organizations. After running a College of Nursing library for a couple of years, she took the chance of a research post working for Aberystwyth. She started lecturing at Aberystwyth in 1995, and since early 2009 has focused on research work for the Department of Information Studies. Her research interests are in health information management (value and impact work), information behaviour and systematic reviewing (for the Cochrane Collaboration). She has directed several research projects for the Joint Information Systems Committee (JISC) of the Funding Councils for Higher and Further Education, and various national and regional health service organizations in the UK.

List of contributors

Suzanne Bakker MSc
Library Director, Central Cancer Library, The Netherlands Cancer Institute, The Netherlands

Mandy Beaumont MSc
Knowledge and Library Services Manager, Lancashire Teaching Hospital NHS Foundation Trust, Preston, UK

Olwen Beaven BSc(Hons) MSc
Deputy Information Specialist Manager, BMJ Evidence Centre, BMJ Group, London, UK

Andrew Booth BA DipLib MSc MCLIP
Reader in Evidence-Based Information Practice and Director of Information, School of Health and Related Research (ScHARR), University of Sheffield, UK

Jackie Cheeseborough BA(Hons) DipLib FCLIP
Learning & Development Manager for Information & Knowledge Management, Royal College of Nursing, London, UK

Valentina Comba BA Masters
International Relations Project Leader, University of Bologna, Italy

Rachel Court MA MCLIP
Information Specialist, Warwick Evidence, University of Warwick, UK

Prudence Dalrymple PhD MS AHIP
The iSchool at Drexel, Drexel University, Philadelphia, USA

Katherine Dumenil MA
Head of Library and Knowledge Services, St Helens and Knowsley Teaching Hospitals NHS Trust, St Helens, UK

Joanna Dundon BA(Hons) Cert.Management ILM
Strategic Health Evidence Manager, Aneurin Bevan Health Board, Cwmbran, Wales,

UK and National Co-ordinator for Clinical Pathways, NHS Wales Informatics Service, Bridgend, Wales, UK

Neil Ford BSc MSc(Econ) MCLIP
Subject librarian, School of Health and Social Care, Bournemouth University, UK

Nunzia Bettinsoli Giuse MD MLS
Assistant Vice Chancellor for Knowledge Management, Professor, Biomedical Informatics & Medicine and Director, Eskind Biomedical Library, Vanderbilt University Medical Center, Tennessee, USA

Louise Goswami BA(Hons) MAMBA MCLIP
Head of Library and Knowledge Services Development, Kent, Surrey and Sussex Deanery, Tunbridge Wells, UK

Lotta Haglund BA Masters in Library and Information Science
Head of Information and Public Relations at Karolinska Institutet University Library, Stockholm, Sweden

Nicholas R. Hardiker RN PhD
Reader and Associate Head (Research), School of Nursing & Midwifery, University of Salford, Salford, UK

Rebecca N. Jerome MLIS MPH
Program Director, Eskind Biomedical Library and Knowledge Management
Assistant Professor, Department of Biomedical Informatics, Vanderbilt University Medical Center, Tennessee, USA

Lorie Kloda MLIS AHIP
Associate Librarian, McGill University, Canada

Taneya E. Koonce MSLS MPH
Associate Director for Research, Knowledge Management Team, Vanderbilt University Medical Center, Nashville, Tennessee, USA

Sue Lacey Bryant BA(Hons) DipLib MCLIP MSc
Associate Director of GP Consortia Development/Chief Knowledge Officer, NHS Milton Keynes, UK

Andrea Lane BA(Hons) MSc
Information Specialist Manager, BMJ Evidence Centre, BMJ Group, London, UK

Gareth Lawrence PGDip
Information Governance Manager, University Hospitals of Leicester, UK

Michelle Maden-Jenkins BSc MA
Clinical Information Specialist, Edge Hill University College, UK

Jessie McGowan BMus MLIS PhD
Library and Health Consultant, Toronto, Canada and Adjunct Professor, Departments of Medicine and Family Medicine, University of Ottawa, Canada

Kim Montacute BA(Hons) FCLIP
Knowledge Services Lead, NHS Yorkshire and the Humber, UK

Mike Raynor BSc PGDip
Information Specialist, National Institute for Health and Clinical Excellence, UK

Helen Seeley BA MSc PhD
Research Associate and Evelyn Project Manager, Academic Neurosurgery, Addenbrooke's Hospital, Cambridge, UK

Pat Spoor MA(Hons) MA
Faculty Team Leader, Health Sciences Library, University of Leeds, UK

Debra Thornton BA(Hons) MCLIP
Knowledge and Library Services Manager, Blackpool Teaching Hospitals NHS Foundation Trust, UK

Jenny Turner BA(Hons) DipLib MSc MCLIP
Trust Librarian, East Sussex Healthcare NHS Trust, St Leonards-on-Sea, UK

Ann Wales PhD
Programme Director, Knowledge Management, NHS Education for Scotland, UK

Anne Webb BSc DipIM MBA
Library Operations Manager, The Kostoris Library, The Christie NHS Foundation Trust, Manchester, UK

Annette M. Williams MLS
Associate Director, Eskind Biomedical Library and Knowledge Management, Vanderbilt University Medical Center, Tennessee, USA

Alison Yeoman BA MSc PhD
Department of Information Studies, Aberystwyth University, UK

Overview

Alison Brettle and Christine Urquhart

Introduction

Library and information professionals working in the health sector have faced challenges on many sides. Rapid developments in information technology and the provision of information coupled with constant organizational change in the public sector, the switch from local service provision to national agreements and the widespread adoption of evidence-based practice have ensured constant change for a number of years. How have library and information professionals met this challenge and how has this affected the roles they play? Will developments in electronic health information services render the hospital librarian obsolete? Is there a need for academic health librarians amongst the Google generation of students? Do health library and information professionals' skills and knowledge remain relevant?

A profession is 'a group of individuals who are recognized by the general public as having special knowledge, competencies and skills based on an extensive knowledge base, with extended education and training' (Cleveland, 2011). It is worth keeping this definition in mind if we are to look forward and ensure that we can answer these challenges and ensure a continued need for health library and information professionals. Alongside, we need to examine the context in which we work, as well as the roles we play, and question whether the skills we have are suitable for those roles and potential roles of the future. This book seeks to do just that. It aims to encourage and inspire health library and information professionals to take on new opportunities and ensure their continued development and recognition as valuable assets in the changing health care environment.

This book does not aim to predict the future, nor highlight all the potential roles available, rather it examines the different contextual factors that may affect how health library and information professionals might work. It showcases a range of roles, whilst examining the skills needed to perform them, both now and in the future.

Changing contexts

Whilst not limited to the UK, a book such as this cannot avoid reference to the UK National Health Service (NHS), which has been subject to continual organizational change for a number of decades. At the time of going to press this change is set not only to continue, but to intensify with the government's White Paper *Equity and*

Excellence: liberating the NHS proposing a radical structural overhaul, putting decision making in the hands of general practitioners and other front line staff, an increased focus on clinical outcomes (measuring success on survival and recovery rates) and putting patients in charge of decision making about their care (Department of Health, 2010, 1). These changes are undoubtedly worrying, and being made within difficult fiscal constraints that will inevitably affect libraries and library and information professionals. However, it is necessary to step back and look at the situation 'with a glass half full' rather than empty attitude (or perhaps with 'rose tinted glasses'!), and find potential opportunities. For example, to commission health care services: whoever is doing the commissioning will need information on which to base their decisions. If patients are to 'have more choice and control, helped by easy access to the information they need . . .' someone will have to provide that information (or easy access to it). Finally, if hospitals are to be measured on clinical outcome information, someone will have to collate and organize that information as well as provide evidence regarding what a 'successful outcome' looks like. Similar opportunities have been put forward in relation to hospital libraries in the USA regarding the government's emphasis on comparative effectiveness research, a focus on evidence-based practice and aligning reimbursement with better results, i.e. outcomes (Klein-Fedyshin, 2010). In other words as a range of governments are advocating a need for information on best practice, both in terms of service provision and for calling health care organizations into account, there will be a need for information specialists to be involved in a range of processes.

Similarly changes in education and publishing have been happening on a national and global scale, with reduced government funding for higher education, lower budgets and open access publishing models impacting on the traditional academic library. Libraries are being used differently in an internet age, and need to adapt their services accordingly to remain used and useful. They are increasingly focused on providing digital resources that are purchased through national consortia, developing teaching in information literacy and providing enhanced services to support researchers (Haines and Marshall, 2008). This means continued use of traditional skills as well as the development of new ones and an acceptance and adoption of technology that users are familiar with on a day to day basis.

We have identified several important contexts that impact on health library and information professionals. These include: the health context; education and publishing; information technology; and consumerism, governance and evidence-based practice. These are discussed in the first part of the book as a way of setting the scene for the second part, which focuses on roles.

Roles – problems or opportunities?

Roles are often tied up with competencies and skills and the second part of the book opens with a discussion on skills and competencies and how these are a necessary part of any discussion on roles.

There are some key concepts from sociology role theory that affect roles in the workplace, although much of sociology role theory covers general roles in everyday life (roles in the household, gender roles, for example).

1 Our social role is defined by a set of expectations, rights, duties, norms that we expect people in those roles to have, and which govern how they should act.

2 If we have division of labour in a society, then we expect work in an organization to happen through the interaction of people working in specialist roles. Sometimes it is more useful to look at the organization and then at the roles required (like an administrative hierarchy diagram), sometimes it is more useful to think of the organization as an abstract wrapper around lots of people interacting in different ways. The former perspective thinks of organizational culture as something the organization has, the latter views the culture as the outcome of all those interactions. These perspectives matter when we start thinking of role changes. In the first, changing role means stepping up or along a career ladder. In the second, roles appear to evolve organically, but there may be uncertainty about who does what in the interim phases, and a lot of mutual adjustment. This is the ad hoc (adhocracy) type of organizational structure (Mintzberg, 1979).

3 Our approval of certain roles is accompanied by a system of rewards (better performance than the norm merits a performance bonus) or punishments (delay in promotion, for example). Some of our ideas about role expectations may need to adjust to legislation on equality of opportunities and disability discrimination. Traditionally we expected people to be able to do certain things in certain roles for the sake of the organization, but under disability discrimination legislation the responsibility is on the part of the organization to ensure 'reasonable accommodation' or 'reasonable adjustment' to those with disabilities to ensure that they are not disadvantaged from participation.

4 Our ideas about what is acceptable in a particular role are governed by norms, and we accept and learn what is legitimate to do. Changes in the way work is organized, changes in technology and changes in society can affect the legitimacy of what some roles should and should not do. For example, with technology that is simple to use, a person with diabetes can use a monitor to transmit readings to their health care provider. Responsibility for taking the readings might have been a role only for the professional some years ago. Debate about extending a role often focuses on what is legitimate or safe for a member of staff to do in addition to their existing role.

5 Role conflict and role ambiguity. The basic hypothesis around role conflict and role ambiguity is that people who have several roles that compete for their time and attention, or roles that are fuzzy and not clearly recognized may become uncertain, anxious and stressed. Role conflict and role ambiguity have not, apparently, been researched much in the recent library literature. In fact, there are more articles (e.g. Eldredge, 2004; Harris, 2005) that examine the suitability of

new or expanding roles for health librarians, and welcome such developments. These two examples considered role expansion within reasonably confined settings. There could be problems in the future for health information and library professionals within larger organizational structures, as Meier (2010) suggests might happen with science and technology librarians in the USA, with too many responsibilities heaped on them.

Team role theory and collaboration

Although the word team has often been used in the health sector in the hope that the people designated as a team behave as one, and not necessarily as a description of what actually happens (West and Poulton, 1997), care pathways designed around patients mean that co-ordination and team working are more likely to happen, but there are other factors involved (Evans-Lacko et al., 2010). Meredith Belbin has researched the functioning of teams in organizations for many years and has identified the roles that emerge, as well as identifying the type of mix of team roles that produce dysfunctional teams (Belbin, 2010). The use of role here describes the behaviour and the contribution within the team, and the nine roles identified are plant (creative), monitor-evaluator (logical and impartial), co-ordinator, resource investigator (providing inside knowledge on the opposition), implementer, completer-finisher (the proofreader), team worker (flexible), shaper (the driver) and the specialist (with specialist knowledge).

Roles of the future

At a US symposium considering 'Transformational change in health sciences libraries: space collections and roles' (Lynn et al., 2011) it was suggested that librarians have three main areas of expertise that they can use to perform key roles within an institution: organizational expert and collaborator who brings people together to achieve institutional goals; information disseminator; and communicator and filterer, a neutral communication bridge between departments. Specific roles identified for the future include: e-science technology advisor, partner or collaborator; evidence-based medicine expert; information filterer; embedded informationist; educator integrated into the curriculum; open access and scholarly communicator; project co-ordinator; user-focused collection developer; designer of self- or on-demand instruction; and tool provider for the easier access of and the pushing of resources to where people will find them. Looking at the case studies provided in the second part of this book, it can be seen that health librarians have already taken on and developed these roles. This is a positive sign given the warning by Thibodeau: 'if librarians do not step into these roles, others will' (Lynn, FitzSimmons and Robinson, 2011). Within Part 2 of the book, the chapters describe: the librarian as information provider and educator; the librarian who analyses information and manages knowledge; the librarian within research and evidence-based practice; and finally the librarian as decision maker. Within each, a series of case studies illustrate how different health library and information professionals have performed roles in these areas. The majority of cases take the form of a diary or interview in which the authors provide an overview of the role, how they got there, the systems they use and the people they communicate with. Finally each author examines the challenges in the role and future possibilities.

It has been said that 'changing health care and the advent of sophisticated information technology are impacting on the way health information is generated, published, organized, accessed, communicated, shared and used' (Cleveland, 2011). This quote provides a useful summary of the book and explains the rationale of its arrangement in two parts. The first part of the book is about the context in which health librarians operate and the changes occurring within these contexts. It also seeks to explore how these changes are likely to impact on the professional roles of health librarians. The aim of this part is to help health library and information professionals 'to understand the environment in which they are working ... and become aware of the current events and trends and types of information needs which are being generated' (Cleveland, 2011). This, in turn, should help readers think about their roles and identify the challenges and opportunities they face.

Part 1 – Context
Part 1 provides an overview of the context in which health library and information professionals work. Contributors have drawn from the literature, their own research and their own experiences to describe the challenges which face them. To offer a range of perspectives, contributions have been drawn from varied countries and backgrounds.

Chapter 1 – The changing context of health for library and information professionals, Christine Urquhart and Suzanne Bakker
Provides an overview of the health and social care contexts in which library and information professionals work by describing the environment, trends, policies and the type of partnerships that may be involved. It also examines how roles have changed alongside these trends.

Chapter 2 – Changes in information generation and use, Jenny Turner and Louise Goswami, Neil Ford, Sue Lacey Bryant and Christine Urquhart
Provides an overview of information generation and use – and trends that are changing the way library and information professionals organize their role in educating health professionals via the NHS, higher education and primary care libraries.

Chapter 3 – Changing technology to meet clinicians' information needs, Nicholas R. Hardiker, Joanna Dundon and Jessie McGowan
Provides an overview of clinical information systems, how clinicians need and use information and how these might impact on the work of the library and information professional. These issues are illustrated by two projects described in more detail: Map of Medicine and the Just-in-Time question answering service.

Chapter 4 – The influences of governance, consumers and evidence-based practice, Gareth Lawrence, Alison Yeoman, Alison Brettle and Prudence Dalrymple

Within the NHS a number of factors that seek to improve quality, impact on health library and information professionals. These include the changing needs or demands of patients and how patients search for and access information, governance, clinical governance and quality requirements that trusts must adhere to, the movement towards evidence-based practice and changes in primary care.

Part 2 – Roles
Chapter 5 – Skills, competencies and knowledge, Christine Urquhart

It is difficult to talk about roles without discussing the skills and knowledge needed to perform those roles. This chapter provides a framework for the remainder of the book, which focuses on the roles librarians may play. Each chapter begins with an overview of the role, which is illustrated by a range of case studies that highlight various aspects of each role using a diary or interview format.

Chapter 6 – The librarian as information provider and educator, Pat Spoor and Debra Thornton

Information provider and educator roles include organizing, classifying and ordering, and providing access to information as well as information literacy training: teaching people to access information for themselves.

The cases described are:

1 Clinical Information Specialist: Michelle Maden-Jenkins.
2 A librarian's role in e-learning: Valentina Comba.
3 Liaison Librarian: Lorie Kloda.
4 The librarian as information broker, educator and change manager in primary care: Sue Lacey Bryant.

Chapter 7 – The librarian who analyses information and manages knowledge, Christine Urquhart

These roles include analysing information and using technology and systems to manage the knowledge base.

The cases described are:

1 NHS Evidence Specialist Collections: Rachel Court.
2 Setting up and managing an organizational repository: Anne Webb.
3 Strategic development of library services: Mandy Beaumont.
4 Information Specialist: Mike Raynor.
5 Co-ordinator Clinical Pathways: Joanna Dundon.

Chapter 8 – The librarian within research and evidence-based practice, Alison Brettle

Librarians can both support research and evidence-based practice as well as becoming involved in a range of ways.

The cases described are:

1 Reader in Evidence-Based Information Practice: Andrew Booth.
2 Information Specialists: Olwen Beaven and Andrea Lane.
3 Lecturer/Information Specialist: Alison Brettle.
4 The health information professional role in a clinical research setting: Helen Seeley.
5 The integration of informationists into advanced roles: Rebecca N. Jerome, Taneya Y. Koonce, Annette M. Williams and Nunzia Bettinsoli Giuse.

Chapter 9 – The librarian as decision maker, Jackie Cheeseborough

Librarians manage and make decisions on behalf of their libraries and staff. They also ensure that visible, high quality services are provided that meet the needs of users.

The cases described are:

1 Head of Library and Knowledge Services in Primary Care: Katherine Dumenil.
2 Programme Director for Knowledge Management: Ann Wales.
3 Knowledge Services Lead: Kim Montacute.
4 Head of Information and Public Relations: Lotta Haglund.

Conclusion

The first part of the book describes some of the changes that are taking place in education and in the health service (the contexts). The case studies presented in the second part of the book provide some transferable lessons for library and information professionals working in different settings (the roles). Librarians offer both transferable skills and specialized knowledge that can be applied in a wide range of situations. However, we need to be prepared to change and adapt and consider how our skills can be used in different ways.

A number of authors have noted that the only constant is change, and changing contexts are the theme of the first part of the book. Drawing on the views of a number of change theorists, Weiner (2009) suggests that change is more likely to be successful if either organizations or individuals are committed or prepared to change (described as 'readiness to change'). He notes a number of reasons for being committed to change: wanting to change, having to change or being obliged to change, with wanting to change likely to lead to the most success. Whatever the reasons for change, health library and information professionals need to become familiar with change. Put simply, in the continued changing context, it is likely that health library and information professionals need to continually rethink what they do and how they do it in order to develop as professionals (wanting to change) and survive as a profession or as professionals within an organization (having to change). This book provides food for thought to help library and information professionals do just that.

References

Belbin, M. (2010) *Management Teams: why they succeed or fail*, 2nd edn, Butterworth-Heinemann.

Cleveland, A. D. (2011) Miles to go Before we Sleep: education, technology, and the changing paradigms in health information, *Journal of the Medical Library Association*, **99** (1), 61–9.

Department of Health (2010) *Equity and Excellence: liberating the NHS*, The Stationery Office.

Eldredge, J. D. (2004) The Librarian as Tutor/Facilitator in a Problem-based Learning (PBL) Curriculum, *Reference Services Review*, **32** (1), 54–9.

Evans-Lacko, S., Jarrett, M., McCrone, P. and Thornicroft, G. (2010) Facilitators and Barriers to Implementing Care Pathways, *BMC Health Services Research*, **10**, 182m, DOI:10.1186/1472-6963-10-182.

Haines, M. and Marshall, J. G. (2008) Future of Academic and Health Libraries: personal perspectives, *Health Information and Libraries Journal*, **25** (suppl. 1), 94–5.

Harris, M. R. (2005) The Librarian's Roles in the Systematic Review Process: a case study, *Journal of the Medical Library Association*, **93** (1), 81–7.

Klein-Fedyshin, M. (2010) It was the Worst of Times, it was the Best of Times: positive trends influencing hospital libraries, *Journal of the Medical Library Association*, **98** (3), 196–9.

Lynn, V. A., FitzSimmons, M. and Robinson, C. K. (2011) Special Report: symposium on transformational change in health sciences libraries: space, collections, and roles, *Journal of the Medical Library Association*, **99** (1), 82–7.

Meier, J. J. (2010) Are Today's Science and Technology Librarians being Overtasked? An analysis of job responsibilities in recent advertisements on the ALA joblist web site, *Science and Technology Libraries*, **29** (1-2), 165-75.

Mintzberg, H. (1979) *The Structure of Organisations*, Prentice-Hall.

Weiner, B. J. (2009) A Theory of Organizational Readiness for Change, *Implementation Science*, **4** (67), DOI:10/1186/1748-5908-4-67.

West, M. A., and Poulton, B. C. (1997) A Failure of Function: teamwork in primary health care, *Journal of Interprofessional Care*, **11** (2), 205-16.

Part 1
Context

1

The changing context of health for library and information professionals

Christine Urquhart and Suzanne Bakker

Introduction

This chapter looks forward and examines the changing context of health care and how this may affect health information professionals. It also reflects how health has changed over the last 15 years and the corresponding changes that health information professionals have made.

THE HEALTH CONTEXT
Christine Urquhart

Introduction – future changes in health care

Trying to predict the future is always difficult. For health care, we have some help from a report produced by the Foresight Panel established to predict health care trends for 2020, and provide recommendations for action by the UK government (Department of Trade and Industry, 2000). By the end of 2010, we should be able to judge how far we have progressed, and whether there have been other changes in science, technology or the socio-economic environment that now need to be considered. Most of the key recommendations would have some implications for the work of health information professionals but some have a direct impact, or might have had, if political and economic events had not overtaken the changes. The panel recommended that independent and publicly accountable bodies be formed to help regulate the privacy, availability, sourcing and accuracy of health information, as well as the access that should be granted to certain users of that information from patient records. These are not problems with easy solutions, as the Health 2.0 Debate (December 2010) in *The Economist* (online edition) indicates (The Economist Debates, 2010). Nevertheless, there is still strong support for the idea that patients should have more control over the health information that belongs to them. In the UK, the White Paper published in 2010 (Department of Health, 2010a) suggests that patients should have control of their health records, that patients should be able to determine who else can access their records, and should be able to see what changes have been made to their records. Sharing of records with organizations such as support groups should be possible if that enables patients to manage their condition better. Aggregated (and anonymized) patient data should be made available in a standard format to allow accredited intermediaries to analyse this for research, for presentation of data to patients and patient groups. For this to happen, levels of trust in the systems need to be high and, at the same time, we need to remember how the changes in genomics mean that consumers may be very reluctant to share their genomic information with others – who wants to advertise that their genetic data indicates the possibility of 'criminal tendencies', for example? A special report on the human genome (Anon, 2010) points out that the benefits of DNA information being freely available probably outweigh the disadvantages, but certainly the problems of predictive genomics worry a lot of people.

The Foresight Panel also suggested that there would be a sharp increase in the number and range of systems and organizations that supply information to support health care – infomediaries – that would guide both patients and professionals. Members of the public would be able to gather information on any health subject, and information available to professionals would also be available to lay people. The panel suggested that by 2020 patients would be using decision support systems, and that websites would gather information from experienced patients rather than experts.

Empowering patients and the public

In 2010, in the UK, patients and the public have the NHS Choices website that contains information on local health services, some comments from users of local hospitals, a link to NHS communities (blogs, forums and advice services), tools that include mole self-assessment and a body mass index (BMI) healthy weight calculator. This suggests some progress towards decision support and information provided by experienced patients. There are other online services (often commercially sponsored), such as BabyCentre, offering expert advice, as well as a large number of support group websites for advice and information sharing. In the USA, the MEDLINEPlus service provides information on health topics, drugs and supplements with a videos and 'cool tools' part of the site containing interactive tutorials, calculators and quizzes. Other European countries are providing national health information services, online, for the general public. In Finland, for example, the medical society Duodecim has a portal for professionals and a portal for patients and the public, which contain articles that provide more information on certain conditions, and advice for patients on whether to seek professional advice about a condition. Such changes could be seen to empower patients and the public – or to reduce the amount of face to face contact time required with expensive health professionals. For health care to remain affordable, some type of 'cyber physician' care, as the Foresight Panel described it (Department of Trade and Industry, 2000, 18), is probably necessary, but there will be profound changes in the way health care is staffed, and how we view cost-effectiveness options for health care.

Libraries have traditionally championed access to information for all – and putting health services online disadvantages those without easy access to the internet or skills to use the services successfully. A Pew Internet survey (Pew Internet & American Life Project, 2010a) found that between April 2009 and May 2010, social networking use among American internet users aged 50–64 grew by 88% – from 25% to 47%, and that during the same period, use among those aged 65 and older grew 100% – from 13% to 26%. The increase is impressive but from a low base, and another study (Pew Internet & American Life Project, 2010b) found that 80% of higher income Americans researched medical information online, whereas only 54% of lower income Americans search for medical information online. Clearly libraries need to help bridge this gap. A report by Sally Middleton outlines some of the approaches taken in Gloucestershire to developing public library services that worked with the health service to tackle some of the social inclusion problems and promote community networking for older adults – particularly those that are housebound. Another strand of services targeted those with mental health problems (in prisons) and people who might benefit from the Books on Prescription scheme (Middleton, 2005). The social inclusion development officer responsible for developing these services was not a library or information professional, but had a background in social and community work. It is hard to know for sure what the effect of a different skill set was, but it is not just the health professionals who need to rethink how they react to changing consumer behaviour for accessing and using health information. Consumers are uncertain what to expect from public library staff (Harris et al., 2010) when looking for guidance in selecting and using health information resources. A systematic review of bibliotherapy services for mental health service users (Fanner and Urquhart, 2008) concluded that basic bibliotherapy services appeared to be cost-effective in supporting the treatment of a wide range of mental health conditions, but that evidence to guide development of more sophisticated bibliotherapy services was very limited. The associated survey of psychiatric libraries (Fanner and Urquhart, 2009) found that more training and support for mental health service library service staff would be desirable if innovative services – and the necessary joint working across a range of professionals and sectors – are to develop successfully. With pressure on resources even more constrained at present, some very creative thinking will be required to find solutions. Consumer health is discussed in more detail in Chapter 4.

The data deluge

Some of the solutions will be assisted through technology, and the world of bio-informatics includes not just the genome data mentioned earlier but also the manipulation of large data sets. Medical equipment produces large amounts of data and, with suitable algorithms, that data can be processed to monitor changes in health status. The 2010 conference proceedings of the IEEE Engineering and Medicine in Biology (IEEE, 2010) contains papers on motor function assessment using wearable sensors, biological network modelling, decision support, analysis of heart rate dynamics using mathematical models and robotics inside the body, as well as techniques for smart homes, to help people live independently, but under the watchful eye of monitors set up to detect harmful changes in condition. Much of this presumes that monitoring, and feedback to patients (and professionals) on changes in the condition, will actually contribute to better health outcomes. More knowledge might simply make patients more anxious or turn them into nervous iPhone hypochondriacs.

Integrating health and social care – for better quality care

For health services themselves the ability to analyse patient data to reveal more detail about patient outcomes, and quality of care, has been important – but difficult to achieve. For the English NHS, for example, the Centre for Health Economics at York University estimated that between 2003/4 and 2007/8, productivity has increased (since 2004/5) in the secondary and primary care sector, with increases in the number of patients treated, improvements in the quality of care patients received and less reliance on agency staff (and a slowdown in staff recruitment) (Street and Wood, 2009). In the English NHS, the Quality, Innovation, Productivity and Prevention (QIPP) programme aims to support quality improvements and efficiency savings. One of the workstreams, Technology and Digital Vision, is intended to support the other workstreams, as well as promoting interoperability of IT systems. Other home countries in the UK have taken slightly different approaches to improving health care, but a common theme is the focus on the patient and the public, with greater public involvement a key objective.

For most patients, integration of health and social care seems a sensible objective but separate funding, delivery structures and staffing have complicated many efforts at joint working across health and social services in the UK. Initiatives such as personal budgets for people with social (and health) care needs may help to leverage greater integration, and the vision for social care in England envisages more personalization of services, a greater emphasis on prevention (to keep people independent for longer) and partnership (among various agencies that contribute to social care) (Department of Health, 2010b). In the USA the Kaiser Permanente health maintenance organization has offered a vision of what is possible when health care does not have sharp boundaries between community, primary and secondary care. The report on the NHS Beacon Sites (Ham, 2010) confirmed that partnership working, and the expected benefits (such as reduced use of hospital beds) were easier to implement when the sites had previous experience of joint working across health and social care. That made it easier for sites to establish integrated care organizations and promote intermediate care to pre-empt hospital admissions.

Implications for information providers

The themes of personalization, greater choice and more control are present in a consultation document on the information services and systems to support the proposed changes in health and social care (in England) (Department of Health, 2010c). This echoes the previous policy documents, with emphasis on the need for information that is based around patient needs and service user consultation (rather than administrative needs), with a move 'away from the Government being the main provider of information about the quality of services to a range of organizations being able to offer service information to a variety of audiences'.

Personalization of health care requires personal health records, owned and controlled by individuals. There are two main competing commercial providers – Google Health and Microsoft HealthVault, and both will pay their way through advertising or by selling data that consumers are prepared to share, or other similar services. The Microsoft product has been adopted for the Mayo Clinic Health Manager (Kolakowski, 2009). What consumers might expect from a personal health record, personally controlled, may include the ability to update it easily, share information with selected health providers and link self-reported data with clinical data (Weitzman, Kaci and Mandl, 2009). Others note that bathroom scales can be Wi-Fi connected to Google Health (Ray, 2010) – good news for the confectionery suppliers or the diet food industry?

All these changes to health care mean that existing staff need to be trained and updated to help change their practice. Unsurprisingly (and as discussed in more detail in Chapter 2) technology is providing part of the solution through e-learning. An evaluation of over 5000 learners using e-learning modules based on National Institute for Health and Clinical Excellence (NICE) guidelines showed that the programme (devised by NICE in collaboration with BMJ Learning) was effective in promoting change in practice (Walsh et al., 2010).

National and international perspectives

The contribution by Suzanne Bakker that follows in this chapter tracks the history of medical librarianship and how organizations such as the European Association of Health Information and Libraries (EAHIL) have helped health librarians to discuss common problems and reach solutions.

In the early days of computing, information systems had to be designed to suit the computer, but with later developments in storage capacity and processing speed it became possible to provide services and systems that met the needs of health staff, health students and – increasingly – patients and the public. Suzanne Bakker provides an overview of the changes that are apparent in health library and information services. The guiding principle has been user orientation, but Suzanne also stresses how health information professionals have developed solutions to information problems. Given a particular 'problem setting', the information professionals have framed the problem as one that can be resolved wholly or partly with an information solution. For example, health students needed to learn how to use bibliographic databases successfully – and the teaching role for health librarians was born (discussed in more detail in Chapters 2 and 6). It is much easier to create data now, but much more difficult to manage that data and manage the knowledge created within a health care organization or network. There are new roles in research data management for health information and library professionals and new roles in knowledge management (see also Chapter 7).

In her conclusion Suzanne Bakker reminds us that technological challenges also bring changes in the legislation as policy makers try to control the ramifications of new technology for the mutual benefit of producers and consumers. In Chapter 2,

Jenny Turner and Louise Goswami consider how some of the technological changes can alter service design and delivery, and remind information professionals of the importance of monitoring such changes. We need that evidence, so that the health librarians can advocate successfully for beneficial changes in copyright legislation.

Suzanne Bakker has witnessed how EAHIL has helped health librarians throughout Europe learn from each other, sharing knowledge and transferring lessons learned in one country to another, and making necessary adaptations. One of the recurrent themes in this book is the development of new roles, to meet new changes in the delivery of health and social care. Economic constraints mean that information professionals need to be aware of the ways in which the taxation regime of their country affects information service delivery (e.g. different rates of value added tax (VAT) for electronic and print versions of the same product). Health library and information professionals can learn useful lessons from colleagues in other countries but it is probably wise to be aware of the distortions different regulatory environments may have on information service design and delivery.

HEALTH LIBRARY AND INFORMATION PROFESSIONALS IN EUROPE
Suzanne Bakker

Introduction
The European Conference of Medical Libraries in Brussels in 1986 was the first of a series of annual meetings of medical librarians in Europe (Forrest et al., 1987). The founding of the EAHIL a year later in Brighton provided the infrastructure and platform for professional development and further co-operation in Europe, in line with the intentions of the founders of EAHIL who had met at first far from home at the International Congress on Medical Librarianship (ICML) in Tokyo in 1985 (Walckiers et al., 1987).

These were the years before fax machines came into use. Online literature searching was introduced in the medical libraries by terminals connected to mainframe computers by modems and dial-up phone lines. Host computers in Stockholm (Medical Information Centre of the Karolinska Institute) and Cologne (Deutsches Institut fuer medizinische Dokumentation und Information – DIMDI) provided access to copies of the Medical Literature Analysing and Retrieval System (MEDLARS) database. The MEDLARS produced by the National Library of Medicine (NLM) in Bethesda, Maryland, USA, was brought online and became known as MEDLINE. The system itself was developed for production of the *Index Medicus*, the bibliography of articles published in medical journals. The hosted MEDLINE databases were made accessible for online literature search and retrieval by librarians. By introducing computer technology, the work of health library and information professionals changed and continues to do so, with arrival of the internet, Web 2.0 and other IT developments. The internet and electronic journal publishing in the last decade replaced the tons of paper on miles of shelves and stacks and changed the libraries. Today more and more medical and university libraries are offering mobile access to their digital collection with applications for smartphones and tablets (Obst, 2008). Customized access is offered by smart toolbars for installation in your personal browser (Van den Brekel and Bauer, 2010).

Echoing developments in the health context, library work in the medical field is more than ever user oriented; the main focus has less to do with collection development and cataloguing but the more so with supporting the users: clinicians, medical students, nurses and researchers, to name the major groups. The availability of MEDLINE/PubMed increased the demand for user education by librarians (Colaianni, 1985). Some examples of a user-oriented approach, which describe the changing roles of health librarians and the factors that have affected these changes, are reflected in the following sections.

Information needs of clinicians leads to librarians in the clinic

The growth of the literature contributes to the need for summarizing and translating research into practice, which is at the heart of evidence-based medicine (described further in Chapter 4). Making use of the best available evidence for clinical decisions is the day to day challenge for physicians (Giuse et al., 2005). The Cochrane Collaboration is working on systematic reviews and meta-analyses, and medical information professionals are in charge of identifying, selecting and collecting the evidence in a broad variety of bibliographies and databases. Critical appraisal of the literature is part of the job for a growing number of colleagues working in medical librarianship.

In the last decade we have seen a revival of clinical librarianship (CL). Although the concept of CL was introduced in 1975 by Gertrud Lamb, Brian Haynes and David Sackett, it propagated the concept of evidence-based medicine as *the* method of decision making in the clinic (Sackett et al., 2000). The success of the UK Clinical Librarian Conference, with the 5th International Conference in Birmingham on 13–14 June 2011, illustrates how a close co-operation between librarians and clinicians impacts on health care.

Information needs of medical students leads to librarians as teachers

Information literacy is an essential tool for academics and medical professionals. New technologies arising and the many resources published on the internet resulted in the need to include literature retrieval and information management in the curricula (Haines and Horrocks, 2006). Ways in which this has been achieved are discussed in Chapter 6.

Information needs of nurses leads to librarians as consultants

Development of clinical pathways and practice guidelines by nurses and the responsibility for patient control by nurse practitioners brought a stronger emphasis on the use of the medical literature by nurses. In many cases the librarian has a consultant role by retrospective subject searching and providing supporting documentation for critical pathways in the clinic (Middleton and Roberts, 2000). Increasingly there is a need for librarians to be involved in medical and nursing education and professional development programmes for nurses (Dozier and Brown, 2009; Kelly, 2009) such as those described in Chapters 6 and 8.

Information needs of authors leads to librarians as reference managers

The use of personal database management systems for organizing piles of photocopies and reprints or the digital equivalents (portable document formats (PDFs) and Word documents) has increased exponentially. The different styles in referencing and the requirements for publishing and the respective instructions to authors are easy to handle by specific applications. Librarians are involved in introductory training and application support for reference management software, such as EndNote, Reference Manager, ProCite and RefWorks. Librarians are faced with new questions, issues and concerns given the new workflows and pathways that new generations of web-based reference and PDF manager programs require (Mead and Berryman, 2010).

Information needs of researchers leads to librarians in scientometrics

Research funding depends in many areas on the quality and impact of former work by the research group or institute. Scientometric data of citation analysis and impact factors are important in comparing the scientific output of research institutes. Funding bodies require this data from applicants; staff members need this data for tenure. Although these analyses were never designed for evaluating and measuring the performance of individuals or small research groups, funding bodies do request these data and the (medical/science) librarian is in the position to collect and analyse them and to present the appropriate listings and figures. In addition to analysing, an explanation and annotation of these data can be very helpful in developing publication strategies in order to increase the visibility of publications and the overall citation counts. Librarians offer courses in strategic publishing (Gerritsma, 2010a, 2010b). Further descriptions on librarians' roles in research are covered in Chapter 8.

Information needs of patients leads to identification and provision of patient information material by librarians

Patient education evolves from the receipt of information leaflets towards empowerment and shared decision making. Patient associations are actively involved in organizing relevant resources on their websites and in their publications (e.g.

'Nothing about us without us' (www.ecpc-online.org)). Patient information centres in hospitals as well as health information sources provided by public libraries are responding to the increasing demand from patients who seek to be well informed (Trzan-Herman and Rozic, 2010), themes that are described in more detail in Chapter 4. Advice and consultation from informationists, such as that described in their case study in Chapter 8 by Rebecca Jerome and colleagues, are an extension of the librarian on rounds as described by Gertrud Lamb (Spatz, 2009).

Conclusion

These are only a few examples of the different roles for medical librarians. Together these illustrate how the health library and information service is user oriented. It is no longer the physical space of the library, nor the digital equivalent, but the value added by the librarians that make the difference.

Nevertheless, some of the traditional roles are still of interest, especially in the European context, such as the maintenance of national bibliographies and indexing systems. Within EAHIL there is a special interest group (www.eahil.net/subgroups.htm) active in exchanging information and experience on MeSH (Medical Subject Headings) translations and subject indexing in the medical field. Keeping up with technological developments found in information and communication technology (ICT) tools, networks, web-based and mobile applications is a challenge; medical librarians are eager enough to implement new features in their services. But the new technologies create other challenges as well: the publishing industry is monitoring the electronic reuse and copying of copyrighted material. Library laws regarding interlibrary loan differ in Europe. Traditionally in several countries (Germany and The Netherlands, at least, but maybe in more) no payment for clearance was involved in cases of personal, non-commercial use for library-provided and delivered documents such as print photocopies. But the European directive on databanks and electronic resources has changed library practice. Publishers no longer sell subscriptions to their journals as they did with printed versions, but instead licensed access to e-journals is mainstream nowadays for medical, health and sciences libraries. Librarians must know about the copyright issues for their resources, regarding the different publishing formats and interlibrary loans. Today it is the agreement with publishers that sets the rule and restricts access and distribution (Subito, 2008).

With open access publishing, the creative commons and intellectual property rights are still applicable, so librarians could advise on publishing issues, fees and management of rights. (See, for example, the Zwolle Principles and University Copyright Policies at http://copyright.surf.nl/.)

After 25 years of EAHIL, medical librarians in Europe have a strong professional network and share job-related knowledge and experiences. The present day European medical library is a library without walls, medical librarianship is a profession without boundaries. Budget cuts and legal restrictions are a threat, technology a challenge. Service orientation, efficiency, evidence-based medicine and user support are the key factors in the context and practice of medical informationists, in Europe and elsewhere.

References

Anon (2010) Special Report on the Human Genome, *The Economist*, 17 June.

Colaianni, L. A. (1985) Medlars III - Improved Services for Medical Libraries Worldwide. Medical Libraries - One World: resources, cooperation, services. In *Proceedings of 5th International Congress on Medical Librarianship, 30 September - 4 October, Tokyo, Japan*, 116–119.

Department of Health (2010a) *Equity and Excellence: liberating the NHS*, www.dh.gov.uk/en/Healthcare/LiberatingtheNHS/index.htm.

Department of Health (2010b) *A Vision for Adult Social Care: capable communities and active citizens*, www.dh.gov.uk/en/Publicationsandstatistics/Publications/PublicationsPolicyAndGuidance/DH_121508.

Department of Health (2010c) *A Revolution for Patients: consultations on an information revolution and greater choice and control*, www.dh.gov.uk/en/Consultations/Closedconsultations/DH_120080.

Department of Trade and Industry, Foresight Health Panel (2000) *Health Care 2020*, Department of Trade and Industry.

Dozier, M. and Brown, F. (2009) The Librarian as a Collaborator in Teaching and Learning, EAHIL Workshop 2009 (slides and abstract), www.eahil.net.

Fanner, D. and Urquhart, C. (2008) Bibliotherapy for Mental Health Service Users Part 1: a systematic review, *Health Information and Libraries Journal*, 25 (4), 237–52.

Fanner, D. and Urquhart, C. (2009) Bibliotherapy for Mental Health Service Users Part 2: a survey of psychiatric libraries in the UK, *Health Information and Libraries Journal*, 26 (2), 109–117.

Forrest, M., Godbolt, S., Tabor, R. and Valentine, P. (1987) First European Conference of Medical Libraries, 22–25 October 1986, Brussels, *Health Libraries Review*, 4 (1), 43–6.

Gerritsma, W. (2010a) Publish, be Cited or Perish, Videotaped interview on the role of the information specialist in an academic library environment, www.youtube.com/watch?v=6rZKKPzSZQw.

Gerritsma, W. (2010b) Publishing for Impact (slides), www.slideshare.net/Wowter/publishing-for-impact.

Giuse, N. B., Koonce, T. Y., Jerome, R., Cahall, M., Sathe, N. A. and Williams, A. (2005) Evolution of a Mature Clinical Informationist Model, *Journal of the American Medical Informatics Association*, 12 (3), 249–55.

Haines, M. and Horrocks, G. (2006) Health Information Literacy and Higher Education: the King's College London approach, *Library Review*, 55 (1), 8–19.

Ham, C. (2010) *Working Together for Health: achievements and challenges in the Kaiser NHS Beacon Sites programme*, University of Birmingham Health Services Management Centre, HSMC policy paper no.6.

Harris, R., Henwood, F., Marshall, A. and Burdett, S. (2010) 'I'm not Sure if That's What Their Job is': consumer health information and emerging 'healthwork' roles in the public library, *Reference & User Services Quarterly*, 49 (3), 239–52.

IEEE (2010) IEEE Engineering in Medicine and Biology Society Annual Conference 2010, http://ieeexplore.ieee.org/xpl/mostRecentIssue.jsp?punumber=5608545.

Kelly, K. (2009) Information Literacy Competencies in Health Sciences Curricula in Ireland, EAHIL Workshop 2009 (slides and abstract), www.eahil.net.

Kolakowski, N. (2009) Microsoft's HealthVault a challenge to Google Health?, *E-Week*, 22 April, www.eweek.com/c/a/Health-Care-IT/Microsofts-HealthVault-A-Challenge-to-Google-Health-711489/.

Mead, T. L. and Berryman, D. L. (2010) Reference and PDF-manager Software: complexities, support and workflow, *Medical Reference Services Quarterly*, 29 (4), 388–93.

Middleton, S. (2005) *Working with Health: one public library authority's story - the Gloucestershire model*, www.idea.gov.uk/idk/aio/1053294.

Middleton, S. and Roberts, A. (2000) *Integrated Care Pathways: a practical approach to implementation*, Butterworth-Heinemann.

Obst, O. (2008) Evaluation of the PDA-project at the Branch Library Medicine at Münster, *GMS Medizin Bibliothek Information* 8, doc16, www.egms.de/de/journals/mbi/2008-8/mbi000113.shtml.

Pew Internet & American Life Project (2010a) *Older Adults and Social Media*, www.pewinternet.org/Reports/2010/Older-Adults-and-Social-Media.aspx.

Pew Internet & American Life Project (2010b) *Use of the Internet in Higher Income Households*, www.pewinternet.org/Reports/2010/Better-off-households.aspx.

Ray, B. (2010) Bathroom Scale Plugs into Google Health. Share your weight with Mountain View, www.theregister.co.uk/2010/01/29/wiscale/.

Sackett, D. L., Straus, S. E., Richardson, W. S., Rosenberg, W. and Haynes, R. B. (2000) *Evidence-based Medicine - How to Practice and Teach EBM*, Churchill Livingstone.

Spatz, M. A. (2009) Personalized Health Information, *American Journal of Nursing*, 109 (4), 70–2.

Street, A. and Wood, P. (2009) *NHS Input and Productivity Growth 2003/4 - 2007/8*, www.york.ac.uk/che/pdf/rp47.pdf.

Subito (2008) Urheberrecht/Copyright Law - Informationen zum Gesetz/Information to the Copyright Law and Lawsuit filed by Börsenverein against Subito, www.subito-doc.de/index.php?pid=Urheberrecht2.

The Economist Debates (2010) Health 2.0: this house believes that any loss of privacy from digitising health care will be more than compensated for by the welfare gains from increased efficiency, *The Economist*, www.economist.com/debate/debates/overview/189.

Trzan-Herman, N. and Rozic, A. (2010) Public Libraries for Public Health: the contribution of an innovative project in Slovenia, *Journal of EAHIL*, 6 (1), 8–10.

Van den Brekel, G. and Bauer, B. (2010) Innovative Information and Communication Systems for Scientific Libraries: 10 questions about practice and experience covering Web 2.0 to emerging technologies, *GMS Medizin Bibliothek Information*, 10, doc20, www.egms.de/static/en/journals/mbi/2010-10/mbi000203.shtml.

Walckiers, M., Hausen, U., Comba, V., Deschamps, C., Wright, D. and Nicolaysen, A. (1987) *Newsletter to European Health Librarians*, (2), 3.

Walsh, K., Sandars, J., Kapoor, S. S. and Siddiqi, K. (2010) Getting NICE Guidelines into Practice: can e-learning help?, *Clinical Governance*, 15 (1), 6–11.

Weitzman, E. R., Kaci, L. and Mandl, K. D. (2009) Acceptability of Personally Controlled Health Record in a Community-based Setting: implications for policy and design, *Journal of Medical Internet Research*, **11** (2), e14.

2
Changes in information generation and use

*Jenny Turner and Louise Goswami, Neil Ford,
Sue Lacey Bryant and Christine Urquhart*

Introduction

This chapter provides an overview of the way changes in publishing (in the widest sense) and information use are affecting library and information services in the NHS and higher and further education, and points to the way the health services aimed at greater patient and client choice will affect how primary health care services (and social care services) will be organized. Library and information services are changing and will change even more, with different models of service delivery likely to emerge. In the first section, Jenny Turner and Louise Goswami present the perspective from the NHS, discussing the implications of continuing professional development for a much wider range of staff, the needs of students on placement, and the way e-resources and open access publishing will change the ways in which staff access materials. Such open access ideals often fall foul of NHS firewalls, however. The next contribution, from Neil Ford, discusses some of the changes from the higher education perspective. Assumptions that all incoming students will be Millennials and digital natives need to be tempered by the fact that many students entering degree courses in the health professions are mature students. In many ways, such mixed groups are more rewarding to teach and support, but it is not possible to make sweeping assumptions about the information and IT literacy of the student cohort. We are still collecting good evidence about the effectiveness of various models of information literacy support, but it is likely that excellent liaison with academic staff and a support programme that is suited to many different levels of skills and knowledge is likely to be more effective than the library operating on its own. As Neil Ford points out, evidence-based practice means something to health students, and if information literacy programmes are not seen to contribute to evidence-based practice then they may not seem relevant. It is also important to remember, as Sue Lacey Bryant points out, that the existing evidence that is needed to make a decision about commissioning may be hard to find. The evidence may not come already prepared, it may need to be put together from multiple sources, and that includes sources that are not published in the traditional sense of books, journals or reports. And the information on costs is more vital than ever.

CHANGES IN INFORMATION GENERATION AND USE: THE EFFECTS ON NHS LIBRARY STAFF ROLES
Jenny Turner and Louise Goswami

Changes in education of health staff

Technology has driven rapid change in the way information can be generated and accessed, modifying both the information-handling behaviour and the expectations of library users (or non-users) in a health care setting. Information behaviour and expectations in turn drive and influence library developments.

Many factors interplay with library and information provision in the health care sector, including UK government policies on education, funding decisions, health and social policies, new drugs and devices, and social priorities. As in all library sectors, health library staff are working to identify existing trends to determine their future roles, and the skills and the knowledge they will need to provide pertinent services.

As a result of the previous UK Government's education policy there are more students, more higher education providers and more diversity in both (Scott, 2010). Larger numbers suggest a higher demand on library services and resources generally. Diversity in the student body can translate into a range of ability in information and study skills, and a particular requirement for information skills training from the libraries. There is some evidence for all of this (Davies, 2008; Mittrowann, 2009), although the picture is mixed. Information behaviour is complex and the internet and mobile technologies add to the complexity.

The future for higher education (HE) is currently unfolding (Browne, 2010), but the trends are likely to reverse; fewer HE students, fewer physical but more virtual HE organizations, greater specialization and less money. The diversity and overall number of learners using health care libraries is unlikely to decrease; with vocational training underpinning non-professional roles, apprenticeships, lifelong learning and continuous professional (personal) development (CPD).

Nursing has joined midwifery and other clinical specialties to become an all graduate profession, with around 50% of the course delivered on placement in clinical areas. Health care assistants increasingly follow vocational qualifications based in the workplace.

Paramedicine is also now a graduate profession. The implication is that the academic nature of health care courses and workplace (rather than university classroom) teaching will mean health care libraries remain vital. Mobile technologies will have an impact. In Surrey, for example, an NHS librarian is exploring the information needs of ambulance crews, and has arranged to ride in the ambulance to test delivery of point-of-care resources.

Learner numbers and the trend towards teaching and learning on placement will (despite mobile technology) put the emphasis on the physical NHS library, as a place for study, group work and internet access. Placements are likely to be in any organization delivering NHS clinical care, so each library's client base will remain defined by geography not by organization. This requires some clear thinking from NHS library funders, and is a challenge for managing e-resources. Many commercial suppliers of e-resources link payments to organizations (see also Chapter 6).

E-learning and social networking

Methods of delivering education are also changing rapidly. Smart classrooms and managed, virtual learning environments are increasingly used (Sevendik, 2010). Web 2.0 enables dynamic learning as students interact with teachers and each other via e-mails and online communities (blogs, wikis, etc.). Libraries are already adapting traditional roles to the virtual environment. Many health care libraries already use blogs and Facebook to interact with their users rather than just providing 'static' information about opening times, services and resources and this is set to develop further. A librarian, for example, can be 'embedded' in a fully online course (Konieczny, 2010) delivering library services through interaction with an online community. Konieczny likens this to the 'clinical librarian' and 'outreach librarian' in concept. The impact for health care libraries may be both in actual roles (embedded electronically in e-learning communities) and in the changing expectations, experiences and information behaviour of library users as they emerge from HE.

Libraries working behind NHSnet firewalls increasingly have trouble making use of social networking (as do all the NHS staff). Many NHS organizations, balancing security with access, and prioritizing demands on bandwidth, block social networking sites or standardize desktops that cannot cope with newer web technology. Using social networking tools extensively will be difficult for NHS libraries unless they establish their own routes for internet access, or the NHS network infrastructure develops sympathetically. Several NHS libraries have wireless internet access outside NHSnet to ensure they remain key providers. The roles as 'cybercafé' and e-learning centre may be effected by mobile technologies, but this is balanced by the need for protected (and quiet) spaces to actually access the internet and work with the information retrieved.

E-portfolios are used for CPD in many health care professions. E-learning is replacing face to face teaching in health care organizations, with mandatory and statutory training, for example, offered online through E-Learning for Healthcare (ELH; www.e-lfh.org.uk/). The library's role once again may be to provide areas for internet access, training for those struggling with IT or a quiet space to study (as discussed in Chapter 6).

There is evidence that newer generations, also described as 'Millennials' and 'internet natives', demonstrate different information behaviours (Brynko, 2006; Cullen, 2008). One aspect is the dynamic interaction with information providers, with an expectation to share knowledge rather than just receive information (Wikipedia demonstrates this idea in action). Another aspect is that nuggets and summaries of information are readily available on the internet and can be easily browsed, swiftly read and linked together. This expectation of the way information is presented and synthesized will add to the need for library staff to have critical appraisal skills. The preference for summarized evidence rather than primary research has already been observed by health professionals (Brookman et al., 2006; Barley, Murray and Churchill, 2009), although experience and time constraints as well as learning habits and styles play a role.

Changes in publishing

The traditional print publishing models for books and journals currently exist alongside the new models made possible by technology. Initially the availability of full-text documents online, and online buying, seemed destined to sideline libraries and high street retailers. Commercial publishers began to directly target end-users, some adopting purchasing options and technical solutions that excluded libraries. NHS health libraries, sitting behind NHS network firewalls, had particular problems with access managed by Internet Protocol (IP) address.

Emerging models include options for libraries and other institutions to purchase and oversee resources on behalf of their users, much as before, often using third parties to manage the access, such as Athens or Shibboleth. The trend here is towards centralized buying of online resources by libraries working in collaboration. This suggests the knowledge and skills required for resource management may be centralized also, with fewer information professionals taking that role.

Open access publishing, if adopted as the main publication model for academic and research papers, would impact on library roles around journal licence management and also on the traditional library role of document delivery. Open access publishing enables direct downloading by the end-user as it is free at the point of use. BioMed Central, for example, charges the author to publish in its online journals, but also gives the option for institutions to pay on their authors' behalf. There could be a role for libraries in managing the research output of their organizations (see for example Anne Webb's Kostoris Library case study in Chapter 7).

Anyone who generates or disseminates information can make use of Web 2.0 technology like Really Simple Syndication (RSS) feeds and automatic e-mail alerts. In theory this puts the ability to manage current awareness into the end-users' hands, without the need for library input. The role for libraries could be more around training clients to use tools as they emerge. It will be a challenge, but a necessity for library staff to keep their skills in new technologies and software up to date.

A series of discussions and focus groups with NHS libraries in Kent, Surrey and Sussex suggested that the use of e-books was currently low. A decline in the use of textbooks has been identified in American academic libraries (Cox, 2008). The evidence in the UK is less clear: statistics for 2008/9 on the Library and Information Statistics Unit website (LISU; www.lboro.ac.uk/departments/dils/lisu/) show an increase in issues per full-time student from 2003/4. Increasing sales of e-readers may rapidly change the picture, with predicted sales of 6 million in 2010 (Dougherty, 2010).

This may translate into fewer books on shelves, and fewer loans (which can be managed by Radio Frequency Identification Device (RFID) or self-issue systems). There are also indications from America that enquiry desk questions are falling. A survey in

2008 of 191 academic librarians found 44% seeing a drop in enquiries (Banks, 2008). In the UK, however, five-year comparison LISU statistics show academic 'satisfied enquiries' up, although enquiries were down in public libraries. Once again the picture is difficult to determine.

Responding to change

How might all this change the library staff roles? In public and academic libraries the library assistants are less bound to their service desks, walking the floor to offer help on the spot. Professional staff based off-site, answer the more complex information enquiries. IT help desks and enquiry desks have merged to form a single enquiry point staffed by non-professionals. Health care libraries, however, tend to be small, and already operate in this way. The change could be to utilize the professional staff in clinical librarian and outreach roles, leaving the non-professional staff to manage the day to day library duties. This model is already appearing in NHS libraries in Kent, Surrey and Sussex.

The way we manage document delivery and interlibrary loans in NHS libraries does not yet reflect the changes in publishing models. We use different tools, accepting the request by e-mail, and returning a PDF (licence permitting), but the process is much the same. Each library works with its own client base within geographical and funding boundaries. If e-resources are handled and administered centrally and remotely then the likelihood is that document supply will follow.

For the services and resources that can be delivered electronically, perhaps specific libraries will pick up tasks for a wide area, and not every librarian will need all the professional technical library skills. In NHS libraries staffing levels tend to be low, so maintaining the capacity to deliver the full range of services and resources effectively need not translate to less staff, or even less physical libraries (as trends suggest we need the physical space also).

What may change are the overall management of NHS libraries and the allocation of some tasks across service points (when physical location is irrelevant). There may be more specialists and less generalists. Certainly every member of library staff will need a high level of IT expertise as standard, and be constantly updating it to match the swift emergence of new technologies (Booth, 2007). Instead of advising on a referencing format, for example, library staff will be advising how to use bibliographic software.

Published information enabled for mobile devices supports the trend for library roles outside the physical library, which may increase the capacity to provide outreach training and clinical (or otherwise embedded) librarians (as described by Jessie McGowan in Chapter 3 and Michelle Maden-Jenkins' case study in Chapter 6).

Digitization and powerful retrieval tools (like Google) are transforming archiving, and influencing OPACs (Online Public Access Catalogues). This seems like a change of tools not of roles, although the technical knowledge and skills required for archiving will be different. Collaboration on projects between all sector libraries will be required.

In our information driven economy the need for library skills is increasingly important. The trends in education for health care staff indicate that physical library space will still be required. Some roles and tasks could become more specialist, centralized and shared when publishing models and technology make location irrelevant. NHS libraries are actually well placed to deliver this mix of local, regional and national services given appropriate funding models and reflecting health care delivery reconfigurations. We should be driving the development of NHS libraries to make best use of what we have, and ensuring the diversity of library needs is met.

TAKING ADVANTAGE OF CHANGE: HOW HEALTH LIBRARY AND INFORMATION PROFESSIONALS ARE SHAPING THE HIGHER EDUCATION EXPERIENCE
Neil Ford

Introduction

HE is in the midst of a period of drastic change. Bradwell's recent statistics, showing that 40% of students in HE are now part-time, 59% are mature students and 15% are from overseas (Bradwell, 2009), are stark indicators of the effect of government efforts to widen participation in HE. The recent Browne Report, in addition to outlining radical changes to the way education in the UK is funded, also acknowledges that students are increasingly diverse (Independent Review of Higher Education and Student Finance in England, 2010).

But does this demographic shift come as such a surprise to *health* education? Even a decade ago, studies identified that the mean age of students entering a pre-registration nursing course was 27, almost half of the entrants were mature students and they came from a diverse range of educational backgrounds (Kevern, Ricketts and Webb, 1999). A body of literature has emerged, investigating the specific challenges that health students face such as childcare, employment, financial commitments and time spent away from their university on placements. Universities have started to understand how courses can accommodate these factors to improve the student experience and reduce attrition rates on health programmes (Lauder and Cuthbertson, 1998).

It is interesting to note that efforts to widen participation in health education came from a need to recruit more people to the health professions *before* the broader agenda of the government to widen participation in HE, outlined in *The Future of Higher Education* (Department for Education and Skills, 2003a) and implemented with *Widening Participation in Higher Education* (Department for Education and Skills, 2003b).

Alongside this shift in demographic, we have also seen a change in focus. As nursing and midwifery, allied health and social work evolve into *evidence-based professions* that place a greater emphasis on 'research in practice' (Kelson, 2004), part of the challenge is to enable students to find and use evidence at any time and from anywhere.

With challenge comes opportunity. Changes in publishing towards increased availability of networked electronic information allow us to provide access irrespective of time and location. Developments in educational technology mean that, as well as providing online information, we can also support its use over the internet. The emergence of open access (OA) and institutional repositories allow us to play a role in disseminating our own research and learning materials.

As Bradwell comments on the need for HE to 'embrace' technology to meet the increasingly diverse needs of learners (Bradwell, 2009), are there lessons to be learnt from the recent experience of health education in catering for 'non-traditional' (Kevern, Ricketts and Webb, 1999) learners?

The following sections will outline the changes, ongoing trends and challenges in health education and will give examples of how Bournemouth University (BU) is harnessing technology to exploit changes in the publishing cycle in meeting these challenges.

What are the changes in HE?
Increase in HE
The last two decades has seen a radical change in the pedagogy of health education. In the early 1990s, Project 2000 moved nurse education from nursing schools attached to hospitals into Higher Education Institutions (HEIs) and placed a greater emphasis on theory to allow nurses to 'quickly acquire competencies which had previously been gained through much longer clinical practice' (Davies et al., 2000, 408). This trend is set to continue with the Nursing and Midwifery Council's (NMC) moves towards degree-only registration. Recent figures show a 20% year on year increase in the number of nursing degree students as universities prepare for degree-only entry to the register (Dean, 2009). Whilst some have commented that an all degree profession may exclude those who don't have the academic qualifications necessary to study for a degree (*Nursing Times*, 2008), others have pointed out that a degree enables nurses to 'think and to critically evaluate information' (Gagan, 2010, 16). In practical terms, this means developing students from a wider range of educational backgrounds to degree standard, as students who previously may have opted for an advanced diploma now aim for a degree.

In a climate of cuts in public sector spending, the challenges for librarians are manifest. We will need to provide information to more students for less, ensuring that our information provision is as cost-effective as possible. We will also have to develop the information skills of students from increasingly diverse backgrounds to the advanced levels of finding and evaluating information needed at degree level.

Preparing students for an evidence-based profession
One of the main drivers of increased HE for health and social care students is the evolution of the health professions into evidence-based professions. *Evidence-based* is significant. Health education now has to prepare students to critically assess real world situations and then base their professional practice on the evidence available to them

(Howard, Mcmillen and Pollio, 2003). This greater emphasis on finding and evaluating information to support decision making is recognized in the standards that professional bodies expect from graduates. The latest revision of *Standards of Proficiency for Pre-registration Nursing Education* sets a context in which registered nurses deliver 'nursing practice (care) that is appropriately based on research, evidence and critical thinking' (Nursing and Midwifery Council, 2010a).

The implication for librarians is an increased role in developing the information literacy involved in finding and evaluating information, but also an increased role in developing the academic skills of critical thinking.

Increase in lifelong learning

Alongside professionalism comes CPD. As the health and social care sector is increasingly professionalized, we are also seeing an increase in lifelong learning opportunities. *The NHS Knowledge and Skills Framework* very clearly sets out career progression through ongoing skills development for all NHS employees (Department of Health, 2004) and professional bodies also have a requirement that members continue to develop; the NMC, for example, specifies that to remain on the register, professionals must evidence over 35 hours of learning every three years (Nursing and Midwifery Council, 2010b). The changes to HE that the Browne Report heralds may also drive an increase in lifelong learners, as one of its aims is to reduce the financial barriers to part-time study by providing the same funding model for part-time courses as for full-time (Independent Review of Higher Education and Student Finance in England, 2010). With a reduction in government funding for education will there be more incentive to 'earn while you learn'?

Changes to publishing cycle

The changes above suggest that we are likely to see even more students who spend large amounts of time studying away from our institutions. Whilst we are already aware of the difficulties of providing information to health students who spend up to 50% of their time away from their university on practice placements (Baird, Peacock and Dobbins , 2006), these challenges are set to amplify as more students take degree courses and barriers to part-time or distance learning are removed. When this happens in parallel with an increased use of academic literature by health students as their professions place a greater emphasis on evidence-based practice, we will need to find ways to provide more academic literature to more students regardless of their location.

From collection development to support

Fortunately, the changes in education and the health professions are coincident with changes in the way information is published. Whilst some have commented that managing the progression from print to electronic resources is one of the greatest challenges the information profession faces (Crudge and Hill, 2006, 88), the availability of electronic resources, which can be accessed from anywhere, represents a great opportunity to overcome some of the problems that health students face when accessing information. Information provision for students on placement is generally achieved in partnership between university and NHS libraries (Childs and Dobbins, 2004). Here in 2011 we are approaching a tipping point, where enhanced electronic access to academic literature may lead us to review the nature of these partnerships. In the past, efforts have focused on replicating the print material that students need in NHS collections, but there is increasing evidence to suggest that this is not an ideal model. A number of studies (Baird, Peacock and Dobbins, 2006; Mailer, 2006) have concluded that, whilst access to information on placement is incredibly important to health students, the location, opening hours and stock levels of health care libraries are all barriers to accessing print materials (Mailer, 2006). Improving access to e-resources is a solution to the barriers of accessing physical stock (Baird, Peacock and Dobbins, 2006). That is not to say that the partnership between NHS and university libraries is not still incredibly important, just that the emphasis needs to shift towards user support – both in terms of the skills that students need to access e-resources and also in providing access to learning spaces and IT equipment on practice placements.

Because e-resources can be accessed at any time and from anywhere, they are ideal for health students. The great irony here is that the IT and information literacy skills of health students are still perceived as being relatively poor (Bond, 2009) and, with regards to developing these skills, there is often a 'lack of any structured way of ensuring this [is] achieved' (Bond, 2009). Changes to publishing allow us to change the way we interact with our users through our collections but we also have a duty to support the development of the information literacy needed to find, access and evaluate online information.

Collection development

At BU, the use of e-resources is integral to our working culture. The Library Collection and Access Development Plan states that 'given current and future requirements, the predominant medium will be electronic' (Bournemouth University Academic Services, 2007). This is a working document that includes a number of measures to promote and facilitate the use of networked electronic information. This commitment to e-resources is based on evidence of their usefulness for both staff and students. Longitudinal data from action research studying the impact of e-resources at BU found a marked increase in e-resource use year on year. Quantitative data from the study showed, for example, a startling 600% increase in Athens logins by BU health students between 2002/3 and 2005/6 (Beard, Dale and Hutchins, 2007) and this was backed up with qualitative data from both staff and students, endorsing the library's 'heavy investment in e-resources' (Beard, Dale and Hutchins, 2007).

Our collections are not developed in isolation but in partnership with our academic colleagues. Whilst our collection development and access plan enables us to select electronic as a preferred medium whenever it is available, there is also a role here in academic liaison to foster open dialogue between library staff and academics to communicate the importance of selecting resources that are available electronically. Academics are acutely aware of the difficulties students have in accessing print resources. Explaining the ways that electronic texts can overcome some of these access issues, and making them aware of the resources that are available electronically, enables academics to factor how accessible learning resources are when deciding whether to recommend them. At BU, academics are actively encouraged to make use of e-books and e-journals (Dale and Cheshire, 2009).

Availability of electronic information

A key determinant of how well librarians can acquire and promote electronic information is its availability. The Google generation has grown up with a great deal of the information they need to live their lives available freely on the internet, and they sometimes expect that this also applies to academic literature. Unfortunately this is not always the case. In the public library sector, the recent adoption of e-book lending services like Overdrive have led publishers to place restrictions on the availability of e-books (Misener, 2011). This highlights the underlying concern of the publisher: potential loss of earnings from print sales due to users accessing library e-books. Whilst most publishers do make their content available electronically there is a vast array of access and pricing models (Silberer and Bass, 2007). Finding a business model that allows publishers a return on their investment in intellectual property and represents good value for libraries is one of the major challenges we face. Open dialogue between library and publishing communities is essential to avoid communication breakdown and tension points (Fialkoff and Kenney, 2010).

At Bournemouth, the experience of working with publishers to make content available electronically has been mixed. In the past, providers have been reluctant to make core material (i.e. textbooks) available (Crowley and Spencer, 2011). Recent developments may indicate a paradigm shift. One example of this is through Demand Driven Acquisition (DDA), where books are added to the library catalogue but are only purchased when a library patron accesses them (Hyams, 2011). BU are currently piloting a number of patron programmes to evaluate the benefits as a potential alternative to paying for titles in subject collections that may never get used. The role for subject librarians is to provide a subject profile, ensuring that relevant titles are added to the catalogue for library users to choose from.

With regards to textbooks we have also been working closely with publishers such as Elsevier who are starting to make core titles available as e-books. Despite evidence that e-availability can actually drive print sales (Ernst and van der Velde, 2009), publishers are keen to protect revenue from students buying personal copies of books. As a result, the pricing model for core textbooks tends to be an annual subscription based on full-time equivalent (FTE) student population. There are three roles for subject librarians here: the first is to apply diligence in determining which titles to subscribe to, working with our academic colleagues to ensure that not only is this expensive content useful, but that it is core to what they will be teaching. Secondly, we need to promote and monitor use to ensure that we are getting best value from these resources (highlighting the electronic availability of core reading when marketing courses is one way that we can get added value from such materials). Thirdly, there is a strategic role in talking to publishers to ensure that their pricing models accurately reflect the way e-books are used in HE.

Open access

As libraries and publishers work to find mutually beneficial means of access to electronic information, OA and repositories offer alternative solutions to the 'issues of production, ownership, dissemination, use, and preservation' (Morgan, 2007). Raising awareness and facilitating access to OA research is explicitly mentioned in BU's collection development plan (Bournemouth University Academic Services, 2007, 2). A key tool in this, as well as in the broader dissemination of BU research, is our institutional repository: Bournemouth University Research Online (BURO). Whilst the library manages and facilitates use of the repository, the success of the repository, in terms of data collection, relies on researchers depositing their own outputs. The role here for librarians is in advocacy, raising awareness of the institutional and personal benefits for researchers entering their outputs on BURO, and, if possible, in full text (Holland et al., 2011). This approach has been successful. BURO now contains over 11,600 items making it one of the largest repositories in the UK and placing it in the top 200 of the World Ranking Web of Institutional Repositories (Holland, Denning and Crowley, 2011). BURO has already played its part in raising the research profile of the institution and, in a climate of limited funding for research, it will also play a key role in the Research Excellence Framework (REF) (Crowley et al., 2009). In the longer term, BURO has the potential to become a publishing platform. The potential for the repository to store full text is perhaps of particular relevance to health. As UK funding for health research often mandates open access to research findings (Morgan, 2007) we can expect to see a wealth of health research eligible for uploading in full text to institutional repositories. As well as raising the profile of BU research externally, BURO also gives us an opportunity to make our research more visible to students, especially as results are now indexed in BU's discovery service (see below). In a sector that recognizes the value of linking research to practice, it is no surprise that the School of Health and Social Care are particularly positive about the benefits of a vibrant institutional repository (Crowley et al., 2009).

Resource discovery

Systems

As well as developing our e-resource collections through policy and advocacy, there is also a role for our systems to make it easy to find and use e-resources. This concept is not new; the British Nursing Index (BNI) (developed in partnership between Bourne-mouth University and local NHS libraries) was born out of recognition of the need for nurses, midwives and students to be able to locate articles reflecting UK health practice, published in journals readily available to them. Its evolution from the print-based Nursing and Midwifery Index (NMI) through to the birth of the BNI in 1997 as an online database demonstrates an early awareness of health care students' needs for networked information (Beard, 1997).

These principles are still in evidence today. In recent developments, our reading list system (Talis List) is now embedded within the Virtual Learning Environment (VLE) at unit level so that when a student accesses unit materials on the VLE, they see a link to the reading list for that unit of study, which has led to a dramatic increase in the use of reading lists (Dale and Cheshire, 2009). Taking this forward, we are set to pilot the next generation of reading list system – Talis Aspire. From the experiences of other institutions it is hoped that this will make it easier for academics to select electronic resources for reading lists and integrate these with the VLE, as well as driving efficiencies in the workflows between an academic selecting a resource to it being accessed by a student (Talis Education, 2010).

Capitalizing on the shift from print to electronic publishing is not just about selecting e-resources, it is also about facilitating and supporting their use. It is well established that ease of use is a key factor in determining the degree to which technology is accepted by users (Davis, Bagozzi and Warshaw, 1989). Recent developments with Bournemouth University's federated search tool, mySearch, have involved moving to the EBSCO Discovery Service (EDS). EDS aims to allow users 'fast, simple access to all of the library's full-text content (electronic and print)' (EBSCO, 2010), and because the majority of the metadata is hosted within the discovery service, the performance is noticeably faster than federated search, which calls out to linked databases when searches are made. As well as providing a better user experience it also means that students are more likely to discover material based on its quality rather than the speed with which it is returned from a database (Lederman, 2010). Initial results show a marked increase in the use of academic literature. Full-text downloads from the Cumulative Index to Nursing and Allied Health Literature (CINAHL), for example, have increased by 53%, abstracts viewed by 112%, and link-outs from CINAHL to full text hosted elsewhere are up by 47%. These early results suggest that making systems quicker and easier to use can have dramatic results on health student's use of evidence from the literature. These results are for a full-text database that is fully integrated into the discovery service. Such a startling correlation between ease of access (particularly of full text) suggests that we should be considering the platform very carefully when selecting resources. It has always been essential to ensure that our databases have good coverage of relevant subject areas, but these early results also suggest that it is essential to select resources that can be integrated with the discovery service and are therefore easily discovered.

Given the direction published information is moving in, and the fact that the NHS is increasingly moving towards e-resources funded centrally or by local consortia (Marriott, 2008), it is inevitable that, in their professional life, today's student will need to know how to make use of online evidence. The resource discovery solution we have found is very close in concept to NHS Evidence, which aims to provide a single, simple interface to the e-resources available to NHS employees (NHS Evidence, 2010). In a sense, we are failing our students if we do not teach them to overcome the IT skills barriers associated with e-resources.

Support and skills development
Supporting e-resource use with CHAT
Evidence suggests that health care students (and in particular placement students) find accessing support a challenge (Baird, Peacock and Dobbins, 2006; Mailer, 2006; Callaghan et al., 2008). Limited access to IT means that students on placement need immediate answers to problems as they arise and they are reluctant to call help desks – particularly those that use voicemail (Bond, 2007). At Bournemouth we have an integrated CHAT (virtual enquiry service) and Telephone Enquiry Service (TES). This enables users to enter an internet CHAT with librarians between 9:00am and 9:00pm during term time. The key point here is that it is a live system and for most simple enquiries students will receive an immediate answer and are able to continue their studies. The CHAT widget is embedded within the VLE, library web pages, databases and mySearch so that support is provided at the point of need. Partly, this is a systems solution, with the library's CHAT service embedded in the form of a prominent widget in library resources – but it is also a very human solution, with scripted answers on the enquiry service tailored to the specific needs of health students. Embedding a CHAT widget in resources (rather than just on the library home page) may be significant in how well it is used. A recent survey of HEIs using virtual enquiry found evidence to suggest that users are more likely to use virtual enquiry if it is accessible at the point of need (Geeson, 2011). Although we are using the technology to support those students who need it, this comes with the recognition that one size most certainly does not fit all. Many enquiries can be dealt with instantly but for those that need it the CHAT/TES provides access to more detailed support from our online academic skills community, or tutorials and workshops with a subject librarian.

From quick enquiry to skills support
It is increasingly the case that we are not guaranteed face to face contact time with our students. Some of our health students on CPD or distance learning courses rarely or never visit the university and even full-time students may need to fit academic skills development in around work placements and find it hard to attend workshops or tutorials during the normal working week. There is a real need to provide support for academic skills development that students can access at the time they need it and from anywhere. At Bournemouth University we have developed an Academic Skills Community within the VLE, containing a wide range of materials designed to enable students to develop their study skills, including information literacy. The community allows us to take a graduated approach to academic skills development, providing a single location for online materials for independent learners, but also providing a

point of contact with the Library and Learning Support team for workshops and tutorials. This blended approach to academic skills support enables us to use our resources efficiently: by providing online materials for independent learners, we are able to focus more individual support on those students who really need it.

An important feature is that the Academic Skills Community includes traditional academic skills like critical thinking alongside language support and information skills material. Where some educationalists may draw a line between these skills, in our experience, students rarely make any distinction. For health students preparing for an evidence-based profession, it makes perfect sense to see materials on search strategy next to support for essay writing.

CHAT provides valuable support for quick enquiries and our skills community provides a home for self-managed learning activities. Future development in this area will be to look at how a blend of similar technology can be used to provide more substantial support for skills development. As more information is available electronically, teaching the skills needed to access this material becomes extremely important. In this case, technology provides us not only with a reason to develop skills (to capitalize on the benefits of e-resources), it also provides a potential solution with the emergence of web conferencing software. Features such as Voice over IP (VoIP), video, desktop sharing, white board, file sharing and chat can all be used to move beyond merely answering enquiries or hosting self-managed activities, to delivering teaching over the internet (Glassman et al., 2009). Learners and teachers being able to see what each other are doing (using desktop sharing) whilst at the same time having a conversation (through VoIP or video) offers the level of interactivity needed from a teaching environment. One of the challenges will be to find the right blend of functionality coupled with technical considerations, such as browser compatibility or compliance with NHS firewalls (Glassman et al., 2009).

Conclusion

As we support more health students to a higher standard of education for professions that place a greater emphasis on research evidence, technology offers us solutions. Changes to the publishing cycle allow HEIs to develop their collections and provide networked electronic information to move beyond the barriers that placement students have with accessing print materials, but this comes with a greater need for support. The role for NHS libraries may shift more towards providing supportive learning environments whereas for academic libraries there are a number of new roles.

Working with publishers to advocate electronic publishing and driving the OA movement through managing and facilitating use of institutional repositories is essential to increasing the availability of electronic information. Our relationship with academics is crucial to ensuring that electronic availability is considered during resource selection but we also have a duty to support the use of that information by the end-users. Ensuring that our systems facilitate simple discovery of e-resources and access to full text is one way of doing this whilst, now more than ever, we need to help students to develop the skills in finding and using e-resources that they need for careers in evidence-based professions.

Electronic publishing enables us to provide information in ways that are ideal for the lifestyles and learning needs of health students, but technology also allows us to facilitate the use of that information. Embedding quick enquiry support within e-resources, catering for self-managed skills development in our online communities and developing interactive online teaching allows us to break free from the buildings and opening hours of our institutions and into the 24/7, networked lives of our users.

INFORMATION GENERATION AND USE: A PRIMARY CARE PERSPECTIVE
Sue Lacey Bryant

Introduction

Health is a knowledge-based industry. Moving through the 2010s the information needs of primary care are changing – partly in response to the reconfiguration of health services in the UK as the NHS seeks to address the growing demands on health care from older and sicker patients. With the integration of community health services into hospitals, the shift of public health into the remit of local authorities and the focus on delivering care across the health and social care divide, totemic organizational barriers that hold neither meaning nor value for patients become redundant.

The speed of change, and the harsh economic environment in which it is being effected, further raise the stakes for health library and information professionals as public servants whose skill set remains poorly understood by the clientele they serve. As NHS managers take responsibility for shaping new-style health care organizations that must innovate to provide efficient, productive, leaner and patient-focused services, knowledge becomes an ever more vital asset for the NHS.

Evidence for decision making in primary care

Decision making in primary care is driven by a range of factors. The evidence base is of paramount importance – all along the pipeline from diagnosis to treatment, within the selection of one therapy in preference to another, underpinning self-management of long-term conditions, at the heart of the design of the patient pathway, informing both the commissioning and contracting of health care and disinvestment to meet fiscal challenges, as well as in funding decisions on requests for exceptional expensive treatments for individuals, and not forgetting our everyday choices about lifestyle.

The best evidence is derived data (on activity, cost and quality as described above), research evidence, and the experience of both health care professionals and patients. Hence, it needs to be trawled and aggregated from multiple sources to be brought to bear on decision making. The production and presentation of evidence is a team effort;

in no sense the province of any one discipline. Yet, both the mindset and skill set of librarians fit them well to take a leading role in working with other disciplines to enable usage of a broad spectrum of information.

Public health intelligence offers an understanding of the social stratification of our changing community as well as mortality and morbidity. Business intelligence brings analyses of activity (e.g. the referrals patterns between practices with comparable demographics) alongside an understanding of drive times to particular providers. Performance managers track activity and highlight hot spots. Financial analysts monitor spend and interpret evidence of cost-effectiveness. Complaints managers highlight concerns. Public and patient involvement yields insights into local health services. Knowledge officers (librarians by any other name) undertake a range of desk-retrieved research evidence and guidelines founded on clinical consensus (which may be used to inform the choice of treatments, define the optimum specification for a service and set clinically safe thresholds for elective surgery). By applying a combination of information searching skills, networking and sheer sleuthing, primary care information professionals also surface models of service being tried out elsewhere.

The need for customer focus
Diverse teams and individuals need information and many librarians are most familiar with visible front line staff: general practitioners (GPs), the primary health care team, community nurses, allied health professionals – even social care workers. As services change many of these professions find themselves spanning organizational boundaries within integrated care teams for the first time. Historically, health library services have been unduly preoccupied with the front line, making far less effort to get into the minds of either the top corridor or of those many backstage players for whom evidence is critical. For instance, working matrix-style with planners, intelligence analysts, procurement managers, finance leads, clinicians (including public health consultants), commissioners work at population level, reaching and implementing decisions that impact on the shape, type and cost of health service provision available to each and every patient.

Primary health care customers require information in multiple settings – in practice, in community-based clinics, at the bedside in hospital wards, at NHS and council offices, and when working from home. They face practical barriers at every turn – multifarious passwords, a lack of interoperability between systems and difficulties in moving between newer and older versions of common software packages all hamper flexible working. These hurdles lie atop of other well recognized barriers to getting evidence into practice: time, skills, medical hierarchies, the power of the status quo, parking . . .

For the NHS, organizational change is a constant. Some library managers fall foul of the illusion that it is only the deckchairs that move – such that their services (and hence the application of evidence-based practice in primary care that these support) are at risk of being washed overboard in heavy weather. Inevitably each wave of change brings fresh opportunities and challenges for knowledge services. A model of medical library service provision focused on collections management to support educational needs can still be espied here and there, yet it misses the target for the majority of health professionals by a long way. The trick for durability is to understand and realign to new organizational profiles and priorities, redesign roles and service provision, launching new information products to support the information needs of a different balance of user groups. The ability to 'read' and optimize the prevailing political alliances between NHS stakeholders to maximize funding streams is crucial. The need to court influential champions, and to evaluate and promote the impact of the service never changes and is unlikely to in the near future.

Across the country there are examples of NHS librarians that have felt the winds of change and used their currents to become fully fledged members of the health care team, making a difference to the future of health care (see for example, case studies in Chapters 6 and 7). They have looked afresh at potential customers, profiled their information needs, defined priorities and set a new course to drive evidence-based practice in primary care. It is time for more library and information professionals to step up to the plate, changing their own roles in order to bring knowledge to bear so that best evidence can jostle for its place alongside the many drivers of decision making in primary care.

CHANGES IN INFORMATION GENERATION AND USE: REFLECTIONS ON THE EFFECTS ON ACADEMIC AND NHS INFORMATION SERVICES
Christine Urquhart

In the first section of this chapter, Jenny Turner and Louise Goswami have mentioned some of the developments that affect work for those in academic library and information services. For higher and further education institutions in the UK, the Joint Information Systems Committee (JISC) of the Funding Councils has led and supported many of the developments. The message on the JISC website front page on 24 April 2011 was that 'Through the effective use of technology, we [JISC] keep the UK at the forefront of global education and research and save the sector millions of pounds every year.' JISC aims to support the sector in several ways: better institutional management (improved management information systems), reducing costs (perhaps a more recent emphasis since the financial crisis), research excellence (preparing institutions for the next research assessment, in the form of the research excellence framework), the student journey (recruitment, learning and skills for employment) and sustainable futures (reducing carbon footprints, digitization). It is very difficult to make sweeping statements about the differences between library and information services that mainly serve NHS staff (and students) and the academic library and information services, but there are some traditional differences that affect how the libraries and information services have developed and may develop in the future. First, the obvious factor of size – universities and colleges tend to have much larger libraries, much larger 'information services' and they are organized around the needs of academic staff and students for learning and research. Second, there are differences in the links between the library services, learning technology services, and the IT services responsible for the networks, hardware and software support. Universities and colleges do not always have converged information services that include learning technology, IT and the library, but there is a tradition that this is an accepted way of organizing things, and that has an impact on the way staff, as library and information professionals, see their roles. And as a final afterthought, there are other organizations that are neither officially NHS, nor officially 'academic' where health library and information professionals work. Public libraries, charities, voluntary groups, agencies, social enterprises could all have roles for information professionals, and Sue Lacey Bryant has discussed the challenge for primary care earlier in the chapter. Cross-sectoral working, collaboration between the NHS or academic institutions, and these other organizations may offer solutions that are cheap and effective for some health and social care problems.

It is apparent that new ways of working are required for many librarians in universities and colleges. JISC's digital libraries programmes have supported methods for resource discovery, library management systems and an infrastructure for resource discovery, so that a range of institutions, not just academic libraries, can exchange information about resources according to agreed metadata standards. The vast mass of resources available to students and staff do not just require better tools for searching. Guidance is required for students and staff on how to evaluate and use the information resources effectively in their work (Haines and Horrocks, 2006).

Liaison systems

Many universities operate a 'subject librarian' liaison system (such as that described by Lorie Kloda's case study in Chapter 6, and discussed earlier by Neil Ford in this chapter), which is intended to foster links between academic staff and the library service. For academic staff, one of the main changes to their working practice over the past ten years has been the introduction of virtual learning environments (learning management systems), and other types of technology support for teaching and learning administration. The way in which the virtual learning environment is organized and administered may affect how the subject librarian can provide guidance and support for students. A 2008 survey of subject librarians in seven UK universities (Corrall and Keates, 2011) found that many subject librarians struggled to get access to the virtual learning environment (as course tutors controlled access to module areas) and therefore the support that could be offered to students was often limited. Where support through the virtual learning environment was established, most provided electronic links to resources and many provided subject specific information literacy support within the VLE. Corrall and Keates (2011) also note that the subject librarians largely learn the skills for such educational support on the job, with some internal training programmes, exchange of information with colleagues in similar settings, and, in future, Web 2.0 technologies such as RSS feed, blogs and wikis were identified as having the potential to make resources more relevant and accessible to students.

There are some academic institutions where the health subject librarians have been able to work with learning technologists, to provide innovative support for health science students (e.g. Dale and Cheshire (2009) mention use of blogs within a module that required students to work together on critical appraisal (within a problem-based learning curricular approach)), and Neil Ford mentions several of the projects at BU.

An important strand of the current JISC programmes is digital repositories. For many academic institutions the repository is a showcase for the research done by staff and research students. Librarians are involved in the establishment, organization and maintenance of the repository, leading to new roles for librarians in more direct support of the research activities. Increasingly, work on digital repositories is leading into data curation, and librarians may be extending their roles into management and stewardship of research data (see Chapter 7). Ball (2011) summarizes some of the events at the 2010 Digital Curation Conference. If data curation is to become a function of its own, and something librarians could be entrusted to do, with appropriate training, then it must be funded, rather than being something that academic researchers are expected to do as an add-on activity.

Open access

Related to the work on digital repositories is the pressure for open access to the biomedical literature. The National Institutes for Health public access policy has had an impact on the work of academic libraries supporting biomedical research (e.g. Stimson (2009) describes training programmes for researchers in submission). In other institutions the training associated with open access is also bound up with training on the use of the institutional repository. In 2010, the Wellcome Trust announced that four more European research funders have agreed that the research outputs from projects funded by them should go into the UK PubMed Central.

Some may be better placed to take advantage of new opportunities, and many might envy the set-up in one UK university of academic liaison teams (Neal, Parsonage and Shaw, 2009). These require members of the team to obtain a teaching qualification, for their work in supporting learning, including development of the virtual learning environment, but, more unusually, the team also cover a range of other work including, critically, research support. As the authors title their article – 'It's all up for grabs'!

References

Baird, I., Peacock, D. and Dobbins, S. (2006) Exploring Health Pre-registration Students' Use of Learning Resources Whilst on Clinical Placement: replication of a case study at

Northumbria and Teesside Universities, UK, *Health Information and Libraries Journal*, **23** (4), 286–90.

Ball, A. (2011) International Digital Curation Conference 2010, *Ariadne*, www.ariadne.ac.uk/issue66/idcc-2010-rpt/.

Banks, J. (2008) Reference Desk Staffing Trends, *Reference and User Services Quarterly*, **48** (1), 54–9.

Barley, E., Murray, J. and Churchill, R. (2009) Using Research in Mental Health: user-rating and focus group study of clinician's preferences for a new clinical question-answering service, *Health Information Libraries Journal*, **26** (4), 298–306.

Beard, J. (1997) British Nursing Index: the UK's most comprehensive nursing index launch, *Health Libraries Review*, **14** (2), 124.

Beard, J., Dale, P. and Hutchins, J. (2007) The Impact of E-resources at Bournemouth University 2004/2006, *Performance Measurement & Metrics*, **8** (4), 7–17.

Bond, C. (2007) Nurses' Requirements for Information Technology: a challenge for educators, *International Journal of Nursing Studies*, **44** (7), 1075–8.

Bond, C. S. (2009) Nurses, Computers and Pre-registration Education, *Nurse Education Today*, **29** (5), 731–4.

Booth, A. (2007) *New Breed or Different Species: is the 21st century health information professional generic or specific?*, www.bm.cm-uj.krakow.pl/Conferences/E.AHIL/proceedings/oral/Booth%20A.pdf.

Bournemouth University Academic Services (2007) *Library Collection and Access Development Plan 2007-2012*, www.bmth.ac.uk/library/using_the_library/documents/collection_access_plan.pdf.

Bradwell, P. (2009) *The Edgeless University: why higher education must embrace technology*, Demos report, www.demos.co.uk/files/Edgeless_University_-_web.pdf?1245715615.

Brookman, A., Lovell, A., Henwood, F. and Lehmann, J. (2006) What do Clinicians Want From Us? An evaluation of Brighton and Sussex University Hospitals NHS Trust clinical librarian service and its implications for developing future working patterns, *Health Information Libraries Journal*, **23** (suppl. 1), 10–21.

Browne, J. (2010) *Securing a Sustainable Future for Higher Education: an independent review of higher education funding and student finance*, http://hereview.independent.gov.uk/hereview/report/.

Brynko, B. (2006) Of Millennials and Mashups, *Information Today*, **29** (4), 29.

Callaghan, L., Doherty, A., Lea, S. J. and Webster, D. (2008) Understanding the Information and Resource Needs of UK Health and Social Care Placement Students, *Health Information & Libraries Journal*, **25** (4), 253–60.

Childs, S. and Dobbins, S. (2004) Partnerships in Practice: partnership working in health library information services, *Health Information and Libraries Journal*, **21** (suppl. 1), 1–2.

Corrall, S. and Keates, J. (2011) The Subject Librarian and the Virtual Learning Environment: a study of UK universities, *Program*, **45** (1), 29–49.

Cox, J. (2008) Making Sense of E-book Usage Data, *The Acquisitions Librarian*, **19** (3-4), 193-212.

Crowley, E. J. and Spencer, C. (2011) Library Resources: procurement, innovation and exploitation in a digital world. In Dale, P., Beard, J. and Holland, M. (eds), *University Libraries and Digital Learning Environments*, Farnham, Ashgate.

Crowley, E. J., Northam, J., Petford, N. and Johnstone, P. (2009) BURO: A bespoke repository for the UK Research Excellence Framework & beyond, *ARMS 2009 - 11th Annual Conference of the Australasian Research Management Society, Christchurch Convention Centre, Christchurch, New Zealand,* http://eprints.bournemouth.ac.uk/11216.

Crudge, S. E. and Hill, M. L. (2006) Electronic Journal Provision in a Health-care Library: insights from a consultation with NHS workers, *Health Information & Libraries Journal,* **23** (2), 87–94.

Cullen, J. (2008) Professionalizing Knowledge Sharing and Communications: changing roles for a changing profession, *Business Information Review,* **25** (1), 53–7.

Dale, P. and Cheshire, K. (2009) Collaboration Between Librarians and Learning Technologists to Enhance the Learning of Health Sciences Students, *New Review of Academic Librarianship,* **15** (2), 206–18.

Davies, C., Stilwell, J., Wilson, R., Carlisle, C. and Luker, K. (2000) Did Project 2000 Nurse Training Change Recruitment Patterns or Career Expectations?, *Nurse Education Today,* **20** (5), 408–17.

Davies, K. (2008) Job Hunting in the UK Using the Internet: finding your next information professional role in the health care sector and the skills employers require, *Health Information and Libraries Journal,* **25** (2), 106–15.

Davis, F. D., Bagozzi, R. P. and Warshaw, P. R. (1989) User Acceptance of Computer Technology: a comparison of two theoretical models, *Management Science,* **35** (8), 982–1003.

Dean, E. (2009) Profession's Popularity on the Rise Ahead of Graduate-only Entry, *Nursing Standard,* **24** (8), 7.

Department for Education and Skills (UK) (2003a) *The Future of Higher Education,* Cm 5735, www.bis.gov.uk/assets/biscore/corporate/migratedd/publications/f/future_of_he.pdf.

Department for Education and Skills (UK) (2003b) *Widening Participation in Higher Education,* DfES/0301/2003, www.bis.gov.uk/assets/biscore/corporate/migratedd/publications/e/ewparticipation.pdf.

Department of Health (UK) (2004) *The NHS Knowledge and Skills Framework (NHS KSF) and the Development Review Process,* www.dh.gov.uk/en/Publicationsandstatistics/Publications/PublicationsPolicyAndGuidance/DH_4090843.

Dougherty, W. (2010) E-Readers: passing fad or trend of the future, *Journal of Academic Librarianship,* **36** (3), 254–6.

EBSCO (2010) *EBSCO Discovery Service (EDS),* www.ebscohost.com/discovery/eds-about.

Ernst, O. and van der Velde, W. (2009) The Future of eBooks? Will print disappear? An end-user perspective, *Library Hi Tech,* **27** (4), 570–83.

Fialkoff, F. and Kenney, B. (2010) *Dear Publisher: an open letter about e-books and libraries,* www.schoollibraryjournal.com/slj/printissuecurrentissue/887170-427/dear_publisher_an_open_letter.html.csp.

Gagan, M. (2010) The Future of Nursing: positive spin required, *Journal of Community Nursing,* **24** (3), 16.

Geeson, R. (2011) Virtual Advice Services. In Dale, P., Beard, J. and Holland, M. (eds), *University Libraries and Digital Learning Environments*, Farnham, Ashgate.

Glassman, N. R., Habousha, R. G., Minuti, A., Schwartz, R. and Sorensen, K. (2009) Let Me Show You How it's Done! Desktop sharing for distance learning from the D. Samuel Gottesman Library, *Medical Reference Services Quarterly*, **28** (4), 297–308.

Haines, M. and Horrocks, G. (2006) Health Information Literacy and Higher Education: the King's College London approach, *Library Review*, **55** (1), 8–19.

Holland, M., Denning, T. and Crowley, E. J. (2011) Making the Repository Count: lessons from successful implementation. In Dale, P., Beard, J. and Holland, M. (eds), *University Libraries and Digital Learning Environments*, Farnham, Ashgate.

Howard, M. O., Mcmillen, C. J. and Pollio, D. E. (2003) Teaching Evidence-based Practice: toward a new paradigm for social work education, *Research on Social Work Practice*, **13** (2), 234–59.

Hyams, E. (2011) Interview: e-books procurement – a disruptive business, *Update*, April, 20–2.

Independent Review of Higher Education and Student Finance in England (2010) *Securing a Sustainable Future for Higher Education*, Independent Review of Higher Education & Student Finance in England, www.bis.gov.uk/assets/biscore/corporate/docs/s/10-1208-securing-sustainable-higher-education-browne-report.pdf.

Kelson, J. (2004) Special Topic (H) Determining the Information Needs of Practising Nurses Post-registration in the UK from 1990 to 2003 (Evidence Digest). In Booth, A. and Brice, A. (eds), *Evidence-based Practice for Information Professionals: a handbook*, London, Facet Publishing.

Kevern, J., Ricketts, C. and Webb, C. (1999) Pre-registration Diploma Students: a quantitative study of entry characteristics and course outcomes, *Journal of Advanced Nursing*, **30** (4), 785–95.

Konieczny, A. (2010) Experiences as an Embedded Librarian in Online Courses, *Medical Reference Services Quarterly*, **29** (1), 47–57.

Lauder, W. and Cuthbertson, P. (1998) Course-related Family and Financial Problems of Mature Nursing Students, *Nurse Education Today*, **18** (5), 419–25.

Lederman, S. (2010) *Beyond Federated Search Bias*, Federated Search Blog, www.federatedsearchblog.com/2010/11/23/beyond-search-result-bias/.

Mailer, L. (2006) The UK's SMARTAL Project: St MARTin's College health students Access to Learning resources whilst on placement, *Health Information & Libraries Journal*, **23** (2), 110–17.

Marriott, R. (2008) Let's Stick Together: collaborative purchasing of electronic journals in the National Health Service, *Health Information and Libraries Journal*, **25** (3), 218–24.

Misener, D. (2011) *HarperCollins Sets Checkout Limits on Library E-books*, CBC News, www.cbc.ca/news/technology/story/2011/03/08/f-vp-misener-ebooks.html.

Mittrowann, A. (2009) Strategic, Digital, Human: the library of the future. A view on international developments by a German library supplier, *Public Library Quarterly*, **28** (3), 193–203.

Morgan, P. (2007) Alive and Kicking: a progress report on Open Access, institutional repositories, and health information, *Health Information on the Internet*, **58**, 6–8.

Neal, C., Parsonage, H. and Shaw, H. (2009) It's All Up for Grabs: developing a new role for the academic liaison team at NTU, *Sconul Focus*, **45**, www.sconul.ac.uk/publications/newsletter/45/

NHS Evidence (2010) *About NHS Evidence*, www.evidence.nhs.uk/aboutus/Pages/AboutNHSEvidence.aspx

Nursing and Midwifery Council (2010a) *Pre-registration Nursing Education: statutory requirements: context*, http://standards.nmc-uk.org/PreRegNursing/statutory/competencies/Pages/context.aspx.

Nursing and Midwifery Council (2010b) *CPD and Practice*, www.nmc-uk.org/Employers-and-managers/Your-responsibilities/CPD-and-practice/.

Nursing Times (2008) Call for Nursing Diplomas to Remain, www.nursingtimes.net/whats-new-in-nursing/call-for-nursing-diplomas-to-remain/752408.article.

Scott, P. (2010) *UK Higher Education in the Twenty-first Century: a changing picture? (QAA 360 09/10)*, Gloucester, The Quality Assurance Agency for Higher Education.

Sevendik, T. (2010) Future Learning Environments in Health Education: the effects of Smart classrooms on the academic achievements of the students at a health college, *Telematics and Informatics*, **27** (3), 314–22.

Silberer, Z. and Bass, D. (2007) Battle for eBook Mindshare: it's all about the rights, *IFLA Journal*, **33** (1), 23–31.

Stimson, N. F. (2009) National Institutes of Health Public Access Policy Assistance: one library's approach, *Journal of the Medical Library Association*, **97** (4), 238–40.

Talis Education (2010) *Case Study: Talis Aspire improves the student experience: the University of Manchester and Nottingham Trent University choose Talis Aspire to manage their resource lists*, www.talis.com/aspire/documents/aspire_cs.pdf.

3
Changing technology to meet clinicians' information needs

Nicholas R. Hardiker, Joanna Dundon and Jessie McGowan

Introduction

Information technology has dramatically changed all our lives over recent years. For those working in the health sector, this has been no exception. This chapter begins with an overview by Nicholas Hardiker of the information needs of clinicians and the technology and information systems that may be used to answer them. This is followed by two examples of that technology in action: the first is a description of the Map of Medicine clinical information system by Joanna Dundon, and the second, by Jessie McGowan, describes a project which uses personal digital assistants (PDAs) to bring clinical information directly to the clinicians who need it.

CLINICIANS' INFORMATION NEEDS
Nicholas R. Hardiker

Clinicians face important decisions every day. They must be able to answer, sometimes immediately, a range of questions: 'What is the accepted assessment process for a particular group of patients?'; 'What is the most likely diagnosis given a set of signs and symptoms?'; 'What is the most effective treatment for a particular condition?'; 'What are the potential adverse effects of a particular medicine?'; and so on. The process of asking and answering clinical questions has been summarized as: (1) recognizing uncertainty; (2) formulating a question; (3) pursuing an answer; (4) finding an answer; and (5) applying the answer in practice. Most questions go unanswered – clinicians do not always pursue answers to their questions, perhaps because of doubt that an answer actually exists. And where clinicians do pursue answers, the answers cannot always be found, perhaps due to lack of time, an inability to access appropriate resources or an inability to navigate a particular resource (Ely et al., 2005). Potential solutions rest with clinicians themselves – selecting the most appropriate resource, formulating questions to match particular resources and using more effective search terms. Other solutions concern clinical information resources and systems that seek to make relevant information more accessible at the point of care – anticipating questions that may arise in practice and providing clearer, more explicit and actionable answers (Ely et al., 2007). An understanding of clinical information needs is an important precondition to the development of clinical information resources and systems (Smith, 1996). The focus of this chapter is on the resources and systems themselves.

Clinical information resources and systems

Clinical information resources and systems provide a foundation for (computer-based) clinical decision support. Clinical decision support provides to clinicians or patients 'clinical knowledge and patient-related information, intelligently filtered, or presented at appropriate times, to enhance patient care. Clinical knowledge of interest could include simple facts and relationships, established best practices for managing patients with specific disease states, new medical knowledge from clinical research, and many other types of information' (Osheroff et al., 2005, x).

Clinical decision support may take the form of:

- A standardized list of proposed actions for patients with a particular condition (sometimes referred to as an order set).
- Alerts or warnings, for example to notify a clinician of an abnormal laboratory result or to warn a prescriber of an unusual prescribed dose for a particular medicine.
- Reference clinical information, which may or may not be synthesized.
- Information for patient education (Sittig et al., 2010).

The increasing adoption and use of clinical information systems provides an opportunity to use these and other approaches to provide novel ways of delivering clinical knowledge and other information to clinicians and patients where and when they need it.

Clinical information systems increasingly are delivered with order sets and alert logic 'built in'. Alternatively they may be developed and maintained 'in-house' (Rocha et al., 2006); or they may draw on knowledge that has been synthesized by external content developers – a kind of plug-and-play approach to clinical decision support.

Synthesized information

Patient education information, once restricted to relatively static information sheets, can now be generated more dynamically, to present timely information that more closely meets the needs of individual patients; information prescriptions draw together information from different sources to inform a patient about their condition, medicines or other treatments, where to find further information and support, etc.

The Map of Medicine, which is discussed later in this chapter, is an example of an application that delivers synthesized clinical knowledge and other information to clinicians and patients. Other examples of synthesized knowledge include clinical knowledge summaries (National Health Service, 2010a) and resources provided via subscription-based proprietary products. These synthesized sources may be brought together with non-synthesized sources and delivered to clinicians and patients via portals, which usually include a form of accreditation or review to assure quality (National Health Service, 2010b).

Electronic sources of clinical knowledge are poorly utilized by clinicians; their use has not matched advances in information and communication technology. Reasons cited include lack of time and the volume of material available (Dawes and Sampson, 2003). While the use of electronic resources appears to be increasing, the preference is still for text-based sources and colleagues (Davies, 2007). The use of PDAs, in a way described below by Jessie McGowan, may well prove to reduce some of these barriers.

Infobuttons

Several authors have described work on 'infobuttons' that seek to make access to clinical knowledge faster and more convenient (Del Fiol, Rocha and Clayton, 2006; Maviglia et al., 2006; Cimino, 2007). Infobuttons link patient-specific and context-sensitive clinical information to external web-based knowledge resources such as PubMed, or other proprietary resources, in order to deliver clinical knowledge at the point of care (i.e. when activated by users, infobuttons use clinical information that is entered into a clinical information system to generate automatically queries that are then sent to an online knowledge resource). Infobuttons might be used to return a guideline for a particular condition, to report the dosage, adverse effects or toxicity of a medicine, or to provide general information on a clinical topic. In evaluation studies, infobuttons tend to be positively received by clinicians, they generally provide answers to clinicians' questions and appear to have a significant impact on decision making (Maviglia et al., 2006). However, despite the fact that they are designed specifically to meet information needs conveniently and quickly at the point of care, infobuttons are infrequently used (Maviglia et al., 2006). Attempts have been made to increase utilization, for example through reminders (Cimino and Borovtsov, 2008).

Challenges for clinical information

While it is clear that clinical decision support has great potential, it is yet to achieve widespread acceptance, and a number of challenges remain. In addition to the need to develop a greater number of 'recommendations' and distribute effort and the results of development work, there is clearly a need to improve existing clinical decision support. Current challenges include:

- Summarization of key patient data, to provide the information needed for optimal decision making in a particular context without overloading the clinician.
- Delivery of recommendations to clinicians in a way that supports their usual way of working. For example, alerts should warn a clinician of a potential hazard but should not cause the current process to be aborted.
- Management of competing influences and prioritization and filtering of recommendations to prevent information overload and alert fatigue.
- Consideration of co-morbidities and the combination of recommendations – current guidelines tend to focus on particular conditions in isolation (Sittig et al., 2010).

Information specialists or 'infomationists' (Oliver and Roderer, 2006) who have training in both information and clinical science clearly have a significant role to play. Many of the roles outlined later in this book demonstrate how health librarians use technology and, indeed, how health librarians have played key roles in the examples described below.

Examples of library and information professional involvement in clinical information systems

The Map of Medicine – Joanna Dundon

As noted above, as an application that delivers synthesized clinical knowledge, the Map of Medicine is an online evidence-based clinical pathways tool that is available across England and Wales, Queensland, Australia, and Denmark. The Map of Medicine comprises 'a collection of evidence-based, practice-informed care maps which connect all the services and knowledge around a clinical condition' (www.mapofmedicine.com).

Figure 3.1 shows a screenshot of a pathway on the Map, and in particular one of the references (links to evidence) within the pathway. Users can click on an 'i' icon to access the information and evidence at each stage of the pathway.

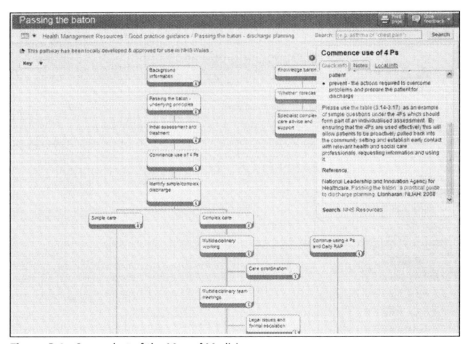

Figure 3.1   *Screenshot of the Map of Medicine*

The need for the Map of Medicine

The Map of Medicine was developed by clinicians as part of a team at The Royal Free Hampstead NHS Trust in London, UK in 2001. The hospital was under pressure to reduce clinic waiting times in the face of increasing referral numbers and the team found that the quality of referrals had a major impact on waiting times. The Map was developed as a tool to improve dialogue between primary and secondary care by making specialist knowledge available to all clinicians to improve referrals (www.mapofmedicine.com).

Use of the Map of Medicine

By providing synthesized, evidence-based information, the Map of Medicine allows clinicians to understand where they fit into the patient's journey and how they can collaborate on the best care with the resources they have. This means that clinicians have to think about their roles working with people in other specialties and across boundaries rather than in isolation on a ward, department or service. The clinical pathways tool allows health professionals to use the visual process in different ways, for example:

- General practitioners use it as a decision making tool with patients – whether to refer directly to hospital or to local community services, or do more diagnostic tests. They can print off local patient information leaflets along with the pathway itself.
- Midwives use it to explain to pregnant mothers what will be happening in regular appointments.
- Nurses use it to prepare patients for discharge from hospital to community.
- Junior doctors and students use it to support audit and course work – if they are on call they can check next steps.
- Service planners and managers use it to design their services, moving staff and resources from secondary to community bases, or to develop new services and measuring how effective they could be.

Benefits

The tool can be customized to reflect local needs and conditions. This has been the case in Wales where the Map of Medicine was piloted by Informing Healthcare, the National IM&T (Information Management and Technology) Programme for NHS Wales in 2006, in three areas. The aim of the trial was to consider a range of benefits. These are set out in Table 3.1 on the next page, along with the corresponding rationale.

In reality, these benefits over the last few years have actually been realized by not just NHS Wales staff but universities and students who use the Map as part of their placement and case studies; voluntary sector and patient representatives; and social services and prison health staff. For example, drug agencies in Gwent have worked with health professionals, criminal justice interventions teams and the Probation Service to plot the care of people who misuse substances, from needle exchange clinics, prison, magistrates court etc. through to referral and inpatient rehabilitation.

Table 3.1 *Benefits realization of the Map of Medicine*

Benefits Realization	
Objective	**Rationale**
1. To improve the support for clinical decision making in an operational setting	To empower NHS Wales clinical staff across primary and secondary care with an easily accessible set of evidence-based clinical pathways for a wide range of conditions and across primary and secondary care so as to inform operational clinical decision making in a clinical setting at any point in the patient journey
	To increase patient safety by increasing the clinician's knowledge of the clinical pathway and assisting the clinician in the diagnosis and treatment needed, including informing the clinician of cross-referencing and patient interactions for conditions
	To provide NHS Wales clinical and other staff with the ability and functionality to empower the patient with clinically mediated patient information in relation to their condition and likely patient journey so as to improve the patient's experience, satisfaction and understanding of their pathway of care
2. To reduce the burden on the clinician	To significantly reduce the time and cost burden on NHS Wales clinical and other staff to synthesize on an ongoing basis the vast amounts of new and existing evidence, guidelines, research and knowledge needed to ensure up-to-date evidence-based clinical pathways across a wide range of conditions
3. To provide functionality for NHS Wales Service Re-configuration and Service Improvement	To provide a single national system and a clinical starting or reference point to inform the creation of new clinical pathways avoiding the need to start from scratch at any level (e.g. national, regional, local)
	To provide NHS Wales with ready-made functionality to add text based information to points in the clinical pathway and patient journey and communicate to their defined user community
	To provide NHS Wales with ready-made functionality to modify the clinical pathway/patient journey and communicate to the clinical and non-clinical user community
	To provide NHS Wales service planners and commissioners with an easily accessible and visual system setting out evidence-based clinical pathways to inform their work in understanding and redesigning services and any new com-missioning arrangements as a result of new regional commissioning models
4. To effect service improvement, cost savings, and staff development though technology	To provide opportunities for cost improvement to NHS Wales by national level procurement as opposed to local procurement
	To maximize the opportunities to link to the emerging Individual Health Record across NHS Wales
	To provide an online resource for NHS Wales staff education and professional development through a greater understanding of national and local clinical pathways

Developing the pathways

The Map of Medicine is made of up clinical pathways. Clinical pathways are known by a variety of terms, such as practice guidelines, clinical protocols, parameters and benchmarks. Clinical pathways represent a continuum of care that identifies structures (institutions, facilities, etc.), caregivers (clinical professionals) and processes (treatment paradigms) that intervene at critical points to efficiently treat the patient and achieve a defined outcome (Hoxie, 1996). This process is important to ensure patients receive the right care at the right place at the right time by the right clinician/professional, and to improve the quality of patient care using the best evidence available.

Figure 3.2 outlines the process of developing a pathway. Within Wales, UK NHS pathways that are already on the Map are adapted (by adding Welsh-specific guidance and references) to ensure their appropriateness at a local level. Each pathway is developed by a group made up of a range of professionals that may include:

- clinical lead (clinical specialist or expert in their field – first approver who accepts medicolegal responsibility for the clinical content)
- pathways co-ordinator (main contact to liaise with different groups)

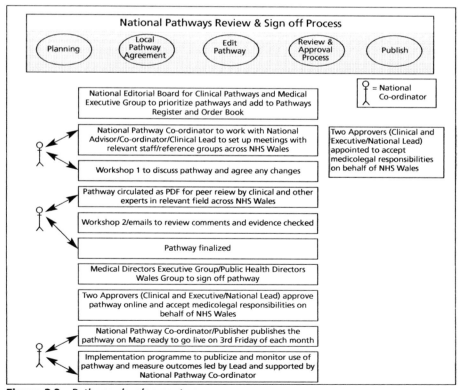

Figure 3.2 *Pathway development process*

- librarian (although clinical leads tend to check the evidence with the pathways co-ordinator)
- information specialist/IT specialist/data analyst
- finance
- clinical governance/patient safety/quality improvement
- human resources/workforce planner
- senior manager
- executive (second approver who may not be part of initial group but who accepts medicolegal responsibility on roll out across organization)
- patient representative/service user – voluntary sector
- representation from primary and secondary care:
  - consultant
  - nurse specialist/practice nurse
  - general practitioner
  - allied health professional (physiotherapist, occupational therapist, speech and language therapist, podiatrist, pharmacist, radiologist)
  - public health specialist
  - Welsh Ambulance Service paramedic.

Where do health library and information professionals fit in?

The pathway co-ordinator role provides a challenging opportunity for a health librarian to use a range of traditional library skills (as well as develop new ones – see the case study by Joanna Dundon in Chapter 7). The co-ordinator ensures that the draft pathway is circulated as widely as possible for feedback, and evidence agreed by the clinical lead is added as references and hyperlinks wherever it is required; evidence from local patient organizations is also incorporated. Once approved by two experts, the pathway can go live.

'Just-in-Time' question answering service – Jessie McGowan
Introduction

The 'Just-in-Time information' (JIT) librarian consultation service project was designed to test whether a library-related service could be used to address an information gap in primary health care by assisting clinicians in answering their questions. A randomized controlled trial (RCT) was used to test whether or not a librarian consultation service could have a positive impact for primary care physicians. The main results are published (McGowan et al., 2008) – here the focus is on the way the service was organized, and technology applied. The JIT service was implemented in an area of Ontario, Canada, and ran for two years with 88 participants. Four librarians worked in the service and participated in interviews after the service closed. The primary outcome was time to receive a response; whether time for JIT librarians to locate information to provide a response to a question, or a participant's time to search for the information. Librarians provided their responses to clinical questions in less than

15 minutes. This time was quicker than the response time of the participants. Of the responses provided to intervention questions, participants rated 63% as having a highly positive impact on their decision making. Most participants said that they would consider using a similar service, and most participants preferred this service to be delivered by a handheld wireless device or web interface.

Service delivery

The selection of a service delivery model was important for supporting the librarians so that any technical issues related to the receipt, delivery, tracking and management of information could be quickly resolved. After reviewing existing similar question and answering services, and planning our technological needs, a 'contact centre' approach to manage incoming questions was chosen. It was determined that web-based contact centre software through a web-based platform that supported the use of both handheld devices and desktop or laptop computers with internet access would allow us to have the best flexibility and ability to timestamp all the activities of the project. This was very important to the project team so that quantifiable units could be captured for evaluation of the project. A local information technology company developed the web-based contact centre software. The project team worked with the company to determine the requirements needed for the project.

Both handheld and web-based solutions were considered as service options. The librarian requirements for handheld and contact centre technology included the following:

- the ability to track all incoming requests from participants
- the ability to build and easily maintain a frequently asked questions database to allow for reuse of previous research
- a performance monitoring system to track response times and usefulness of data being provided
- a tracking system to monitor the use of the library service by clinics and individual participants.

A handheld solution

Two handheld products were considered at the outset of the project: Research in Motion (RIM) BlackBerry™ and Palm Tungsten™ Palm handhelds. The BlackBerry was chosen as the wireless e-mail solution for the clinical information service for several reasons. The BlackBerry devices did not require a wireless base station in order to send and receive e-mail. This would allow participants to submit questions from anywhere in their clinics and the full geographic region of the JIT project. Participants would not need to have internet access in their offices in order to use the BlackBerry on-site. Participants would be able to send questions to the project librarians from various locations within their clinics, including examining rooms, offices, reception desks and hallways. Because BlackBerry uses 'push' technology, it would allow primary care participants to be automatically notified when project librarians sent replies to their clinical questions by e-mail.

Each participant was then assigned a BlackBerry handheld device to submit their clinical questions. A professional medical librarian located information following an evidence-based protocol that was specifically developed for different types of clinical questions (therapy, diagnosis, etiology, prognosis, prevention and other). The response to the question was e-mailed to the participant in a structured format.

The web contact centre (Figure 3.3) developed for the JIT project logged all activity associated with each clinical question (or 'ticket'), whether sent from the primary care participant's BlackBerry or from the participant interface of the JIT web portal. Each information request, whether sent by BlackBerry or by using the participant interface on the web portal was 'time and date' stamped, recorded in the database and sent to the librarians' computers in the form of a pop-up notification. In most instances, the notification was received less than 60 seconds after the question had been sent by the participant. All answers were also recorded using the contact centre software, enabling librarians to search for and retrieve them at any time. Ensuring the privacy of both patient data and participant identity was a significant consideration during the planning and operational phases of the service. The consent form for entry into the JIT project included a statement reminding participants that they were responsible for ensuring that no data that might identify a patient be entered into the BlackBerry. Participants were also assigned coded identification numbers and told that only the project librarians and project manager would be able to link identification numbers to individual participants. Legal liability was also an important consideration.

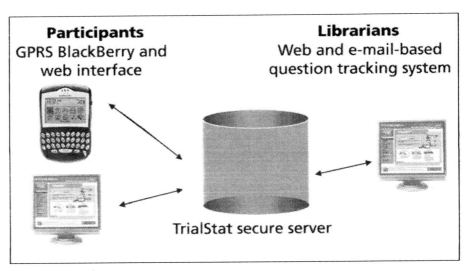

Participants
GPRS BlackBerry and web interface

Librarians
Web and e-mail-based question tracking system

TrialStat secure server

Figure 3.3 *Web contact centre*

Roles for health library and information professionals

The training and preparation that the librarians received prior to answering questions were informal and, to a degree, self-directed as all were experienced medical librarians who had worked in a teaching hospital or a university setting. In exit interviews, all noted that it was adequate for this part of the job. Once on the job, librarians continued to learn more about databases. They indicated that the preparation for meeting with participants was greatly aided by a session with a clinical nurse specialist. In addition to the information resources, colleagues provided a great deal of support. The availability of a project assistant during a busier phase was appreciated. Each librarian mentioned different additional supports: visual aids, referrals to the Canadian Library of Family Medicine (at the University of Western Ontario) service when necessary, and the information technology support from the University of Ottawa (at times problematic, but this was beyond the project team's control). All spoke very highly of their colleagues and work atmosphere. Overall, JIT fostered a highly collaborative and egalitarian space, where the support of colleagues exceeded expectations.

Conclusion

The Just-in-Time question answering service and the Map of Medicine provide examples of health librarian involvement in Clinical Information Systems (CIS). As Nick Hardiker describes, clinicians have varied information needs and a range of systems and approaches have been developed to meet them. However, Nick also notes that CIS have not yet received widespread acceptance nor overcome all the challenges associated with them. The examples clearly show that health librarians have a role to play here. In the future, librarians need to seek out these areas and challenges and look at developing their roles to help overcome them.

References

Cimino, J. J. (2007) An Integrated Approach to Computer-based Decision-support at the Point of Care, *Transactions of the American Clinical and Climatological Association*, **118**, 273–88.

Cimino, J. J. and Borovtsov, D. V. (2008) Leading a Horse to Water: using automated reminders to increase use of online decision support, *AMIA Annual Symposium Proceedings 2008*, 116–20.

Davies, K. (2007) The Information-seeking Behaviour of Doctors: a review of the evidence, *Health Information and Libraries Journal*, **24** (2), 78–94.

Dawes, M. and Sampson, U. (2003) Knowledge Management in Clinical Practice: a systematic review of information seeking behaviour in physicians, *International Journal of Medical Informatics*, **71** (1), 9–15.

Del Fiol, G., Rocha, R. A. and Clayton, P. D. (2006) Infobuttons at Intermountain Healthcare: utilization and infrastructure, *AMIA Annual Symposium Proceedings 2006*, 180–4.

Ely, J. W., Osheroff, J. A., Chambliss, M. L., Ebell, M. H. and Rosenbaum, M. E. (2005) Answering Physicians' Clinical Questions: obstacles and potential solutions, *Journal of the American Medical Informatics Association*, **12** (2), 217–24.

Ely, J. W., Osheroff, J. A., Maviglia, S. M. and Rosenbaum M. E. (2007) Patient-care Questions that Physicians are Unable to Answer, *Journal of the American Medical Informatics Association*, **14** (4), 407–14.

Hoxie, L.O. (1996) Outcomes Measurement and Clinical Pathways, *Journal of Prosthetics Orthotics*, **8** (3), 93–5.

Maviglia, S. M., Yoon, C. S., Bates, D. W. and Kuperman, G. (2006) KnowledgeLink: impact of context-sensitive information, *Journal of the American Medical Informatics Association*, **13** (1), 67–73.

McGowan, J., Hogg, W., Campbell, C. and Rowan, M. (2008) Just-in-Time Information Improved Decision-making in Primary Care: a randomized controlled trial, *PLoS One*, **3** (11), e3785.

National Health Service (England) (2010a) *Clinical Knowledge Summaries*, www.cks.nhs.uk/home.

National Health Service (England) (2010b) NHS Evidence, www.evidence.nhs.uk.

Oliver, K. B. and Roderer, N. K. (2006) Working Towards the Informationist, *Health Informatics Journal*, **12** (1), 41–8.

Osheroff, J. A., Pifer, E. A., Teich, J. M., Sittig, D. F. and Jenders, R. A. (2005) *Improving Outcomes with Clinical Decision Support: an implementer's guide*, Chicago, Health Information Management Systems Society.

Rocha, R. A., Bradshaw, R. L., Bigelow, S. M., Hanna, T. P., Del Fiol, G., Hulse, N. C., Roemer, L. K. and Wilkinson, S. G. (2006) Towards Ubiquitous Peer Review Strategies to Sustain and Enhance a Clinical Knowledge Management Framework, *AMIA Annual Symposium Proceedings 2006*, 654–8.

Sittig, D. F., Wright, A., Simonaitis, L., Carpenter, J. D., Allen, G. O., Doebbeling, B. D., Sirajuddin, A. M., Ash, J. S. and Middleton, B. (2010) The State of the Art in Clinical Knowledge Management: an inventory of tools and techniques, *International Journal of Medical Informatics*, **79** (1), 44–57.

Smith, R. (1996) What Clinical Information do Doctors Need?, *British Medical Journal*, **313** (7064), 1062–8.

4

The influences of governance, consumers and evidence-based practice

Gareth Lawrence, Alison Yeoman, Alison Brettle and Prudence Dalrymple

Introduction

UK Government policy over the last 15 years has increasingly focused on the need for improved quality, improved accountability and improved choice and involvement for patients (e.g. NHS Executive, 1996, 1999a, 1999b; Secretary of State for Health, 1997, 2002; Department of Health, 2010a). Alongside this, there has been an increasing recognition of the importance of the role of information in the NHS (e.g. NHS Executive, 1998; Department of Health, 2001, 2010b) and the spread of evidence-based practice across health care and policy-making as a whole (Cabinet Office, 1999). This increased recognition of the role of information and evidence has resulted in implications and opportunities for health library and information professionals. This chapter explores these concepts, their corresponding information requirements and implications for health librarians in more detail. Firstly Gareth Lawrence describes information management requirements for clinical governance and how this is used to improve clinical performance. Alison Yeoman explores consumer health information using a study of women's information practices to describe the information needs and choices that consumers face when considering information about their health. Alison Brettle describes the concept of evidence-based practice and its implications for health library and information professionals and Prudence Dalrymple examines how the concept of 'evidence' is perceived by clinicians in practice.

WHAT DOES INFORMATION MANAGEMENT FOR CLINICAL GOVERNANCE INVOLVE?
Gareth Lawrence

What is clinical governance?

Clinical governance is 'a framework through which NHS organizations are accountable for continuously improving the quality of their services and safeguarding high standards of care by creating an environment in which excellence in clinical care will flourish' (Department of Health, 1999a). It requires high quality information and knowledge both for clinical decision making and performance management, alongside a supportive infrastructure. In discussing information requirements of clinical governance, Booth (2004) suggests that clinical governance requires 'evidence based practice which puts library-derived research literature at the centre, patient information which requires a hybrid informatics response and risk management and clinical computing which exists almost entirely outside libraries'.

This section examines information for clinical governance but begins by defining terms to help understand the boundaries within which the terms apply. The remaining sections in this chapter cover consumer health information and evidence-based practice. This discussion of information governance covers the UK, and particularly the implementation of clinical governance structures within England. Although not traditionally the role of libraries and librarians, as can be seen from the case studies in part 2, librarians are becoming increasingly involved in information management issues outside the traditional library.

Information management for clinical governance

Information management is 'the management of an organization's information resources in order to improve the performance of the organization. Information management underpins knowledge management, as people derive knowledge from information' (NHS Evidence, undated).

Information governance is 'the structures, policies and practice of the Department of Health, the National Health Service (NHS) and its suppliers to ensure the confidentiality and security of all records, and especially patient records, and to enable the ethical use of them for the benefit of individual patients and the public good' (Cayton, 2006).

Information management is constrained by the rules of information governance. Information that has been gathered for clinical care is then used to support clinical governance, as depicted in Figure 4.1.

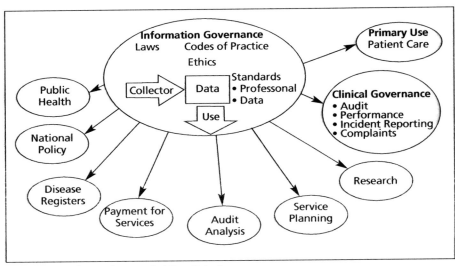

Figure 4.1 *Information needed for clinical governance*

The key elements in managing information to deliver patient care and support clinical governance are data standards and data quality, and consent and confidentiality.

Data standards and data quality

Data that is collected during patient care is used locally, nationally and internationally to develop services, support research and to improve clinical performance. To be meaningful across geographic boundaries, data has to be recorded to a defined standard.

Standards

The NHS Data Model (NHS Connecting for Health, 2010a) defines the structure of the data sets that trusts build to pass information outside the organization. The data sets contain information such as the patient reference and treatment data.

Crucially the data sets contain the patient's condition, diagnosis and treatment, held in a coded format, which is internationally recognized. Within primary care, the coding will be Read Codes or Systematized Nomenclature of Medicine Clinical Terms (SNOMED-CT) (NHS Connecting for Health, 2010b). These codes are allocated when the primary care clinician updates their computer systems, since all GPs use electronic health record systems.

Within secondary care the code will be SNOMED-CT, International Classification of Diseases and Health Related Problems (ICD10) or National Classification of Operations and Interventions (OPCS4) (NHS Connecting for Health, 2010c). Where health records are held on paper the codes will be assigned to a computer record by specialist staff (clinical coders) who analyse the clinician's notation.

In NHS organizations, in England and Wales, patients are allocated a single unique identifier, the NHS Number (NHS Connecting for Health, 2010d), to support continuing patient care by giving the ability to link patient data in disparate systems and to support care across the NHS. Where a variety of disparate systems are used within an organization it is common to link the data through a data warehouse, which becomes the central point for information production.

For secondary care, the Royal College of Physicians (undated) have developed standards for clinical documentation such as medication records and care events. Standards are necessary to ensure safe patient care and to support clinical practice, as explained on the Health Informatics Unit web pages (http://hiu.rcplondon.ac.uk/).

Assuring data quality

For information to be considered as having quality, it must be:

- accurate
- up to date
- free from duplication, (for example, where two or more different records exist for the same patient)

- free from confusion, (where different parts of a patient's records are held in different places, possibly in different formats) (NHS Connecting for Health, 2010e).

There are a number of ways the NHS ensures data quality:

1 Organizations will have internal policies and procedures for capturing data in accordance with data standards.
2 Training programmes on how to use systems will be in place and there will be audit and verification programmes (NHS Connecting for Health, 2010f) to ensure that recorded data is accurate.
3 Audits will be conducted internally by an organization and externally where the standards of data quality across the NHS can be assessed, for example, the Payment by Results programme (Audit Commission, 2010).

Improving clinical performance

In England and Wales data is submitted to the NHS Information Centre, which is 'England's central, authoritative source of health and social care information for frontline decision makers' (NHS Information Centre, 2010). The Information Centre analyses collected data to produce a wide range of information on, for example, health and lifestyles, clinical audits, hospital care and specialist mental health service, with the aim of improving decision making, delivering better care and increasing productivity. In Scotland, the Public Health Observatory fulfils a similar function in providing health information with standards defined by Information Services Division (ISD) Scotland and NHS Health Scotland (Scottish Public Health Observatory, 2010).

A market has also developed for companies such as CHKS (2010) and Dr Foster Intelligence (2010) who, on a subscription basis, offer a range of services including benchmarking data and clinical performance indicators. These facilities can be used by organizations or individual clinicians who can compare their clinical outcomes (i.e. results of treatment) with those of other organizations or, nationally, to improve clinical performance.

Users can place reliance on the information provided by organizations that have demonstrably robust data quality practices in place.

The benefit of benchmarking and the importance of accurate data to clinical governance are highlighted in the case of Mid Staffordshire General Hospital (Whitfield, 2010). In 2007, Dr Foster Intelligence highlighted a high mortality rate of patients that was attributed by the Trust Board to poor data quality. Subsequent investigation revealed a number of failings in the quality of care that the data had accurately reflected.

Consent and confidentiality

The information passing between a patient and health care professional is always confidential. Confidentiality is a responsibility of health care professionals worldwide and is confirmed as such in the UK under the Common Law Duty of Confidentiality and the NHS Code of Confidentiality (Department of Health, 2003), whilst personal data is protected under the Data Protection Act of 1998 and Article 8 of the European Convention of Human Rights (see Information Commissioner's Office (undated) for more details).

As noted above, data that is collected is used in many ways and there can be tension between the desire to use medical data and the need to maintain medical confidentiality. As health care organizations have moved away from paper records, and the ability to easily transmit data electronically and build databases now exists, the concerns of data security and the legitimacy of the use to which data is put has grown. This has resulted in the growth of information governance as a discipline.

To maintain confidentiality, the only people who should have access to medical information are the health care team involved in treating the patient, although conducting clinical audit internally to improve health care is recognized as an ethical use of medical information.

All other uses of patient data, including research, require patient consent or a statutory instrument to permit the use of data (e.g. the collection of data in cancer registries).

Consent is only valid when the patient has been fully informed of the how the data will be used and who will have access to it.

There is an opportunity in England and Wales to use patient data for research without consent by gaining approval from the Ethics Committee of the National Information Governance Board, who have the power to approve research under S251 of the Health and Social Care Act.

To support medical research, the goal of the Information Centre is to be able to provide a comprehensive source of anonymized data. Research provides much of the 'evidence' for evidence-based practice, described below, and the librarian's role within research is described in more detail in Chapter 8.

CONSUMER HEALTH INFORMATION
Alison Yeoman

In line with the increasing policy focus on choice for health consumers, this section explores consumer health information and their information practices, taking as an example a study of women's information practices relating to the menopause (Yeoman, 2009) to illustrate how consumers perceive health information, how they obtain it and the choices they make in relation to their care.

The information practices of consumers
In 2001 Meadows et al. interviewed 24 women from rural areas in Canada as part of

a project on midlife women's health. As a result of their study, they confirmed that women moved literally and figuratively back and forth between the popular and professional health care sectors and had to take decisions about whether a specific health need was important enough to warrant accessing the professional sector. They also had to second-guess the perception of the professional sector as to the legitimacy and potential urgency of the problem. The authors found that both the popular and professional sectors have their own fundamental assumptions about health and illness and their own language through which knowledge is expressed. The transfer of knowledge between the two sectors was often inhibited by a clash of messages and women often found themselves 'silenced' by dismissive statements as they tried to bring their knowledge from the popular sector into the professional encounter.

These findings were echoed in a more recent study of the information practices of midlife women (Yeoman, 2009). In this study 35 interviews were conducted with midlife women, the majority of whom (26) were or had been patients at a community menopause clinic in England. Participants revealed a mesh of interwoven encounters that could take place over many years as menopause-related symptoms and personal situations changed, and as they sought to compare and confirm information (especially in the light of frequent and widely reported developments in the debate about the relative risks/benefits of hormone replacement therapy (HRT)). Women would use active and passive information practices to monitor their environment for relevant information (e.g. browsing in bookshops and libraries, spotting useful information in newspapers/magazines, or talking to friends and colleagues) and would then venture into the world of health or complementary and alternative medicine (CAM) professionals for specific advice as needed.

Where do women find information?

One participant in the menopause study claimed that many women find more information about menopause symptoms and possible treatments from magazines than they do from consumer health leaflets. Results certainly suggested that women placed a high value on informal sources of support and information, particularly sources that provided an insight into other women's experiences. The menopause stories of friends, colleagues and family members were welcomed, as well as anecdotal stories passed on either orally or in magazines. Women used these stories to inform their own decisions about the management of their menopause but also used them to contextualize their own experiences and to find solidarity – making them feel less isolated. There is an established literature supporting women's preference for obtaining information and support from informal sources and for the importance of social networks (e.g. Harris et al., 2001; Davies and Bath, 2002; Dunne, 2002; Raupach and Hiller, 2002; McKenzie, 2003; Warner and Procaccino, 2004). Along with friends and family, such social support can come from networking with others in a similar situation. Avery and Braunack-Mayer (2007) found that women suffering from polycystic ovarian syndrome had benefited from participation in a clinical trial that had brought them into contact with other sufferers and gave them the opportunity to share experiences and exchange information. Examples from Yeoman's (2009) menopause study included membership of an online support group for women who had gone through an early menopause, or talking to other women on the gynaecology ward when in hospital for a hysterectomy.

The desire to hear other people's stories was a theme that emerged strongly from the study. Women empathized with others and saw the menopause as a common experience that only another woman could truly understand. In recent years, providers of consumer health information have recognized the value of 'real stories' as a way of engaging with consumers. National government organizations, such as the NHS in the UK and the National Institute of Mental Health in the USA, and health charities (e.g. healthtalkonline.org and Macmillan Cancer Support) include videos of patients talking about conditions and treatments/services on their websites. These websites not only provide videos but encourage membership of online communities, enabling members to share experiences and exchange support and information. Such communities may also provide support to family members of those affected by health issues. For example, the Macmillan Cancer Support website has a section called 'Why bother?' that aims to provide information, support and resources for young people affected by cancer and which again includes the real life stories of young people whose family members have been diagnosed with cancer. The growing influence of social media allows consumers to extend their networks even further, providing 'an instant stream of information between people around the world' and allowing health professionals 'to engage in a conversation, not only to "pass down" information' (McNab, 2009).

According to McNab (2009), Twitter and other social media tools might not bring health to all but may help to bring accurate health information to a great many more people than ever before. McNab acknowledges that along with the potential advantages for the dissemination and exchange of information come the challenges of establishing how to best use social media to achieve public health outcomes and how to ensure that information is credible and accurate.

Use of technology

In a review of consumer health information in the UK, Smith and Duman (2009) point out that the 'incredible changes in new technology have fundamentally changed the way we all access information and in future they will have a significant impact on how patients and the public communicate about health and how they feedback their opinions and needs into a more patient-centred health service'. They claim that the move towards user-led, audience-specific and multi-format information resources is genuinely starting to improve the patient experience. Along with initiatives, such as those mentioned above, which allow consumers to hear about other patients' experiences, Smith and Duman point to the development of the 'Information Prescription' programme (Department of Health, 2007) that aims to embed the provision of information into the clinical encounter; to the popularity of the NHS

Choices website (www.nhs.uk – accessed by 5.2 million unique visitors in May 2009); and to Patient Opinion (www.patientopinion.org.uk/) that gives patients and carers the opportunity to post their experiences of services online. Through Patient Opinion, consumers' views of services, whether good or bad, are fed back to the relevant organization that then has the 'right to reply'.

Information overload

Although participants in the menopause study appreciated advice from family, friends and other members of the lay community, it added to the often overwhelming amount of information that women were required to sift through in order to make sense of their situation and take informed decisions about managing their health. Participants complained of having to extract information that was relevant to them amidst the plethora of resources that deal with 'the average woman' whilst being bombarded by 'all other people's opinions' about HRT. They struggled to locate sources of support that offered advice tailored to their own individual mix of circumstances and, for this reason, valued access to specialized services such as the community menopause clinic. They viewed the clinic as somewhere they were treated as individuals, were taken seriously, were able to access trustworthy advice from an expert and where they were given time to explore all the factors that impacted on their menopause experiences, which helped them come to an informed decision about treatment options.

Making judgements about trust and authority can be a challenge. Huston, Jackowski and Kirking (2009) found that physicians were the most important source of information for all groups of participants although women who had never used HRT rated health care professionals as significantly less trustworthy than did HRT users. Perceptions of lack of interest on the part of health professionals or of bias can influence levels of trust. Salkovskis, Wroe and Rees (2004) suggest that taking account of patients' values and beliefs should be an integral part of the decision making process. In the context of the menopause this becomes particularly salient in decisions about the use of HRT or CAMs.

Alternative viewpoints

Debates and information about CAM products is an area that highlights an incompatibility between the popular and professional sectors. The clash that sometimes results from efforts to transfer knowledge between the two communities can result in women feeling that their values are being dismissed and that they are not true participants in the decision making process. This can, in turn, impact negatively on the trust they place in health professionals' advice as shown in a study of patient-doctor primary care encounters in New Zealand (Dew et al., 2008). Huston, Jackowski and Kirking (2009) recommend the presentation of balanced information and acknowledgement of the validity of alternative viewpoints as a way of reducing perceptions of bias. Skea et al. (2004) who studied decision making about hysterectomy also found that perceptions of lack of balance in information provided in the patient-doctor encounter can have a negative impact on satisfaction levels. Participants also felt that effective, shared decision making was inhibited by the uncaring attitude of doctors, by feeling under pressure to make up their minds quickly or by conditions in the consultation room.

Making sense of health information

Like McNab (2009) cited above, Huston, Jackowski and Kirking have concerns about the reliability and validity of information gleaned from sources in the lay sector. They recommend that health care professionals should consider discussing these issues with their patients. Menopause study participants were wary of media reports about the risks/benefits of HRT use and were concerned that authors of books or magazine articles 'tend to come down on one side or the other' without presenting a balanced argument. They had to contend with a range of competing and often conflicting information, even from within the medical profession, and could be left feeling that they were 'running round in circles' not knowing what to trust.

Other studies have confirmed that users often struggle with evaluating resources and judging the quality and objectivity of the information provided. This is particularly the case with online health information, and concerns have been expressed (e.g. by Woloshin et al., 2003; Childs, 2004; Ellins and Coulter, 2005; McCray, 2005) that many consumers do not have the skills to access online information or to judge the relevance and the quality of internet resources in the same way that they would be able to judge information provided through traditional media (i.e. by assessing the nature of the outlet, the look and feel of the publication and by knowing who to contact for further information) (Wilson, 2002).

Quality of information

In a series of focus groups held for consumers of health information, Childs (2004) found that users tended to struggle with judging the quality of websites and attempting to validate the medical information presented on them. Concerns identified during the sessions included:

1 Do sites contain unbiased information – who is writing or sponsoring them?
2 Users can sometimes be unaware that they are accessing non-British sites.
3 Interactive features such as e-mail lists and chat rooms can be misused.
4 It can be difficult to put the information into context – information can disempower people if not clearly explained/discussed.

The participants also felt they would benefit from guidance to cover searching skills, judging information quality and managing information in partnership with health professionals. Of course some of the concerns listed above are not exclusive to online sources. Hard copy resources can also be disempowering if they are not easily comprehensible and may be seen as value laden (Payne, 2002). For example, patient information leaflets supplied in GP surgeries and pharmacies are frequently sponsored by pharmaceutical companies and consumers may be wary that they are intended to persuade and influence the reader (Rogers, 1997; Coupland and Williams, 2002).

Consumers' concerns about their ability to make the necessary judgements about the reliability and value of health information link to the concept of 'health literacy'. According to Smith and Duman (2009), the meaning of the term has evolved from the simple ability to read and understand written information to become 'an essential requirement of achieving and maintaining good health because it enables the individual to make informed choices about their health, to self-care, to access services and to navigate their way through an increasingly complex healthcare system'. The Department of Health (2010c) suggests that low levels of health literacy impact negatively on an individual's ability to take action to improve their health. Initiatives hoping to redress this include the 'Skilled for Health' programme and the development of quality assurance schemes for consumer health information. The Skilled for Health programme is run by the Department of Health, the Department for Business, Innovation and Skills, and the charity ContinYou. It embeds Skills for Life learning into health improvement topics with the intention of addressing both the low skills and health inequalities prevalent within traditionally disadvantaged communities (Smith and Duman, 2009; ContinYou, 2011). An example of a quality assurance scheme is the DISCERN instrument (www.discern.org.uk/discern_instrument.php), designed to help users of consumer health information judge the quality of written information about treatment choices and act as a quality checklist for authors and producers of information.

Consumers' conclusion

Consumers now have a wide range of information sources available to them in both the lay and professional sectors. Contact with professionals is no longer limited to the medical consultation itself. Consumers can access medical advice through online services such as MEDLINEPlus in the USA or NHS Direct in the UK, which also provides a telephone helpline. Consumers may move between the sectors, dipping into different sources as their needs and circumstances change. A preliminary information behaviour model developed by Ankem (2007) showed that women's needs and sources of information changed over time, sometimes relying on personal networks or self-education and then on health professionals.

The menopause study demonstrates that lack of information or lack of access to information is not necessarily the main barrier to successful information seeking. Finding the information is only the first step. Understanding and evaluating it and then being able to apply it to the individual set of circumstances may be just as crucial to the success of the process. With skills in all these areas, health information professionals undoubtedly have a role to play in improving access to health information for consumers.

❖❖❖

EVIDENCE-BASED PRACTICE AND WHAT IT MEANS FOR HEALTH LIBRARY AND INFORMATION PROFESSIONALS
Alison Brettle

Introduction

Originating in medicine, evidence-based practice (EBP) is a method of applying research evidence to clinical decision making. It has been defined as 'The process of systematically finding, appraising, and using contemporaneous research findings as the basis for clinical decisions' (Rosenberg and Donald, 1995, 1122).

Advocates argue that EBP is a method of keeping up to date with an exponentially growing body of research, thus ensuring decisions are based on current research. This is particularly important in health care with the continuous development of new pharmaceuticals, treatments and procedures. Furthermore EBP can create a bridge between research and practice (Rosenberg and Donald, 1995). In contrast critics have argued that it seeks to reduce costs and remove clinical freedom. A further definition aims to mitigate these issues by describing it as 'The conscientious, explicit, and judicious use of current best evidence in making decisions about the care of individual patients. The practice of evidence-based medicine means integrating individual clinical expertise with the best available external clinical evidence from systematic research' (Sackett et al., 1996, 71).

It is often noted, for example by Rosenberg and Donald (1995) and McKibbon, Eady and Marks (1999), that there are four or five steps to the evidence-based process (see Figure 4.2), which include:

1. Defining the question (recognizing there is a need for evidence).
2. Finding the evidence (to answer the question).
3. Critically appraising the evidence (evaluating evidence for its relevance and validity).
4. Implementing the evidence (applying the evidence to practice).
5. Evaluation of the process.-

Figure 4.2 *Five stages of the evidence-based process*

Expansion of the evidence-based paradigm

The evidence-based paradigm has been adopted in a range of other disciplines and professions to varying degrees, often according to the level of enthusiasm or scepticism within the discipline (Trinder and Reynolds, 2000). It is advocated by the Department of Health to enhance the quality of patient care (Department of Health, 1999b) and by the government as a whole to inform policy making (Cabinet Office, 1999). Health care disciplines that have adopted the evidence-based approach include nursing, public health, dentistry and allied health professionals, and more widely EBP has been adopted in social care, education and library and information practice. Most have developed their own profession-specific definitions, but the principles of using best evidence combined with professional judgement remain common themes (Trinder and Reynolds, 2000). One such expansion has been into the field of 'evidence-based library and information practice' (EBLIP) that was initially driven by health information professionals, from their background and experience in evidence-based health care, but has seen a gradual uptake by other areas of the profession (Booth and Brice, 2007).

> EBLIP seeks to improve library and information services and practice by bringing together the best available evidence and insights derived from working experience, moderated by user needs and preferences. EBLIP involves asking answerable questions, finding, critically appraising and then utilizing research evidence from relevant disciplines in daily practice. It thus attempts to integrate user-reported, practitioner-observed and research-derived evidence as an explicit basis for decision-making.
>
> (Booth, 2006, 65)

Increasingly, evidence-based practice has been cited as a model for closing the research–practice gap in librarianship in general. The first international conference on evidence-based librarianship was held in 2001 at the University of Sheffield and the open access online journal *Evidence Based Library and Information Practice* began publication in 2006 (ejournals.library.ualberta.ca). An article on evidence-based practice was included in the latest edition of the *Encyclopedia of the Library and Information Professions,* published in 2010. Indeed, EBLIP has been hailed as one of the most viable ways of addressing the much decried lack of research-based practice within librarianship (Haddow and Klobas, 2004).

What is best evidence?

One of the questions arising in the implementation of EBP, and one of the issues that has caused debate amongst supporters and sceptics alike, is what constitutes 'best evidence'? Proponents of evidence-based medicine advocate a 'hierarchy of evidence' that places research designs in descending order of quality according to their ability to limit bias. Other disciplines, some within health care, have rejected this hierarchy arguing that RCTs (the study design at the top of the hierarchy) are not always appropriate (especially in the case of complex interventions), when the question of interest is not to determine cause and effect (Pawson et al., 2005), when an RCT would be unethical or unfeasible (Hill et al., 2008) or when there is a lack of skills and research evidence within the discipline (Crumley and Koufogiannakis, 2002). A further issue in this debate is often a lack of 'high' quality evidence for a range of interventions and conditions. Organizations such as the Cochrane Collaboration and the NHS

Centre for Reviews and Dissemination produce high quality systematic reviews that bring together, summarize and analyse the available research evidence for a wide range of areas. However, systematic reviews are often inconclusive and call for more research to be undertaken due to a lack of high quality studies and practitioners complain that the research evidence available is not always relevant to their practice. NICE provides guidance and sets quality standards to improve people's health and prevent and treat ill health, based on 'best available evidence', which is graded according to its quality. Their recommendations, standards and services follow a standard procedure (see Mike Raynor's case study in Chapter 7) and are developed in consultation with industry and health experts, academics, patients and other members of the public.

Libraries and evidence-based practice

As well as the academic debate over what constitutes best evidence, health professionals who are required to use best evidence in their practice face practical difficulties including a lack of skills to find and appraise the evidence, time and access to resources (Pyne et al., 1999; Brettle, Hulme and Ormandy, 2006, 2007). With its emphasis on 'finding evidence', EBP has offered health information professionals a wide range of opportunities for using and promoting their skills and expertise. Health librarians have adopted roles in these areas, training health professionals to use resources and providing access to resources and becoming involved in the development of resources such as NHS Evidence (formerly the National Library for Health). Furthermore health librarians have begun to practise what they preach and become involved in evidence-based library and information practice. These issues and examples of practitioners who have adopted these roles will be explored further in Chapter 8, 'The librarian within research and evidence-based practice'. As may be imagined, EBP has implications for clinicians who need to find and apply that evidence in practice and librarians need to be mindful of these in establishing services that support EBP. Prudence Dalrymple below describes a research study that highlights these implications in everyday clinical practice.

NOT AS EASY AS IT SEEMS: WHAT HEALTH PROFESSIONALS CAN TELL US ABOUT APPLYING EVIDENCE IN PRACTICE
Prudence Dalrymple

While evidence-based practice may represent a desirable goal, the challenge of applying evidence to practice is substantial. This section presents a study that reports on the role of evidence (professional guidelines) in the clinical decisions made by internal medicine residents.

Evidence in practice

The Institute of Medicine (IOM) recommended developing and disseminating clinical guidelines and providing tools and systems to support their implementation (2001). In that report, the average time period required for research to be implemented in practice was estimated at 17 years. The development and publication of evidence-based guidelines was expected to reduce the gap, but many authors have also noted that other factors such as environmental, organizational and individual level (practitioner) factors also affect the implementation of evidence into practice. It was against this backdrop that the research study presented here was conducted at a major academic medical centre in the US in an effort to understand the factors that determine whether and how clinicians adapt their practice to incorporate evidence-based guidelines.

How do clinicians adapt practice to incorporate evidence-based guidelines?

The example of heparin

The problem chosen was the use of management of unfractionated heparin, a high risk anticoagulant (blood thinning) drug used both to treat and prevent blood clots. Heparin must be managed very carefully because it has a narrow therapeutic window: too much heparin and the patient may haemorrhage causing a stroke; too little heparin and a blood clot may form, increasing the potential for sudden death. Guidelines developed by the American College of Chest Physicians have been published in top tier journals such as *Chest*, and residents at the institution where the study took place are advised of the clinical challenges associated with heparin management (Hirsh et al., 2008; Schulman et al., 2008). They are also provided with a pocket manual containing dosage guidelines to achieve and maintain what is known as a therapeutic level. The level is determined by means of a blood test known as the activated partial thromboplastin time (aPTT). Heparin administration is almost always limited to the inpatient setting where access to laboratory testing is readily available, and patients are monitored closely for deviations from the therapeutic level. At the time of the study, it was being reported that patients undergoing heparin therapy were experiencing variances in aPTT tests that were characterized as 'panic levels'. In other words, patients were slipping in and out of the therapeutic range, putting them at risk for either haemorrhage or clot. Because of the clinical importance of optimal heparin management, an exploratory study was undertaken to identify the barriers to optimal management of therapeutic heparin despite the presence of readily accessible evidence-based guidelines. Using qualitative methods triangulated with clinical data, interviews with a group of internal medicine residents were conducted to learn first-hand their experiences with dosing therapeutic heparin, their knowledge and use of clinical evidence and any barriers or incentives for adopting the guidelines presented to them. Rogers' diffusion of innovation theory was used as a theoretical framework in designing the questions and in analysing the data (Rogers, 2003). What follows are selected insights gleaned from the study.

Data collection

The interviews were conducted on the clinical units in a naturalistic setting and the study protocol was approved by the institution's human subjects review board. To open the interview, the resident was first asked to recall a specific situation or 'critical incident' (Flanagan, 1954; Arora et al., 2005), in which they had ordered therapeutic heparin for an inpatient on the medicine service. This approach yielded stories that provided a rich context for understanding the residents' experiences and attitudes and revealed how the residents grappled with the challenges of medical practice. As might be expected, the critical incidents the residents described were frequently complex clinical situations (see Figure 4.3). In order to gain greater understanding of the ways in which the residents referred to information sources, each resident was also asked to identify wherever possible the source(s) of information consulted when they had questions about heparin management; describe any problems encountered in applying the heparin guideline and comment on what features they thought would be desirable to incorporate in an electronic clinical decision support system (CDSS).

Example: patient with pulmonary embolism described by an intern
Yeah, a pulmonary embolism . . . I'll usually start with a bolus or a half bolus, in a patient who's smaller . . . , so this was a kind of a bigger guy, so I started with a bolus, and I got it therapeutic pretty quickly and . . . right at the beginning I think I was checking PTT ratios every 4 hours with every scheduled lab draw and adjusting the rate based on that. In the Guide, there's a little chart, I'm not sure it's the best way to do it, I'm not sure it's the worst way to do it. But it usually seems to help me get therapeutic pretty quickly and it suggests when you should next check the PTT ratio (R109).

Example: patient with two pulmonary emboli being evaluated for cancer in the thigh, described by a senior resident
A lot of the interns use a kind of standard approach. When you use this though, and you do a bolus, and if you do exactly what they say to do here, I think at least half of time, it's over shot and the levels are usually super therapeutic . . . I usually down play it a little bit. So whatever this came out to be, say, it came out to be a 5000 unit bolus, I would tend to do like a 3000 unit bolus. And then if it said to start the drip at 1000, I would usually start the drip at 800 . . . if they needed to be therapeutic quickly with a PE or something, I'd bolus . . . to do the trick. But I usually underplay it a little bit based on the gold standard calculation (R308).

Figure 4.3   *Selected critical incidents*

Sources of evidence

The information source the residents referred to most often was the pocket manual distributed during orientation to the service, but several consulted other sources – some from the literature and others from other institutions. Most described the guideline as based on evidence, and although most tried initially to use it, they abandoned it as they encountered difficulty in implementing it. Any authority that may have been attributed to the guideline because it was in the 'official manual' did not take precedence over the residents' pragmatic approach to anticoagulation. Most residents used quick reference tools such as MICROMEDEX (Thomson Reuters) and UptoDate

(Wolters Kluwer). One resident reported finding a new guideline in the *Annals of Internal Medicine* (Snow et al., 2007) that he adopted in preference to the guideline in the residents' manual.

Modifying the evidence

The interviews were transcribed and analysed using diffusion theory as an explanatory framework. According to this theory, adaptability is an important factor in predicting behaviour change. Ideas or practices that can be adapted or modified to fit local conditions easily are more likely to be adopted, and the residents' interviews revealed that the residents modified their evidence-based guideline to fit their experience. The following are typical comments:

'In the beginning, when I used the protocol, it never worked and then I found my own.'

(R103)

'Everyone develops their own system; you have the template and develop from there.'

(R106)

Adoption is also affected by relative advantage over existing patterns of behaviour. In this study, the guideline was available, convenient and in a portable format, but, as residents found that when they followed it, patients could exceed the target range for the blood test, they adopted new approaches. One of the key factors in their decision was the lack of predictability in obtaining a blood draw from the phlebotomy team in a timely manner. This problem often led them to resort to workarounds, as illustrated in these comments:

'. . . you kind of have to time it . . . But I've learned a little trick, to order it STAT, and then they'll get it within a reasonable time. Sometimes it's hard to time it perfectly.'

(R104)

'It can be really hard to get it every, even eight hours, it can be a challenge. It's possible, but it can be very hard to get it . . . Too, we're not as good as the phlebotomists and so we often need to stick people multiple times, and it's very unpleasant for the patient.'

(R107)

Communicating evidence

The communication channels most used by residents were the senior residents and each other, relying more on their own judgement as they gained experience. While peer communication and experience greatly influenced the residents' practice patterns, the literature was also a factor in changing behaviour. For example, late in the study, one resident cited an American College of Physicians guideline published two months earlier that supported the use of low molecular weight heparin (LMWH enoxaparin Lovenox® sanofi-aventis) (Snow et al., 2007) rather than unfractionated heparin. Adopting this guideline eliminates the need for frequent blood draws, a feature that provided a distinct advantage to a busy resident. As word about Lovenox spread, several other residents began to use it as well. The comments here reflect its perceived relative advantage over unfractionated heparin:

'I would try to find a reason to use Lovenox because we don't have to titrate that.' (R113)

'I would much rather use Lovenox over heparin any day so I try to use Lovenox as much as possible.' (R112)

Barriers to using evidence

Observers of clinician behaviour acknowledge that adoption of guidelines is a complex process complicated by many barriers. In this study, the problems the residents faced and their ways of coping with them in the messy, real world of clinical practice suggest that environmental and organizational factors may need to be considered when introducing guidelines that require behavioural changes, particularly those that are enhanced or supported by technology (Lorenzi et al., 2008). Acquiring this level of understanding is especially important for non-clinicians such as information professionals and systems designers who are called upon to design systems to facilitate the application of evidence to practice.

Changing practice

In this study, it was clear that simply making the guideline available was not sufficient to change practice. The residents did not ignore the guideline because they did not appreciate the value of evidence-based practice; rather, most found that following the guideline did not fit into their workflow and any authoritative advantage of the guideline was outweighed by the 'cost' of using it. Once the residents learned of an evidence-based approach that was compatible with their responsibilities and workflow – eliminating their dependence on the phlebotomists – they adopted it with enthusiasm. This suggests that understanding how organizational context, particularly interdependencies among organizational units, affects clinical behaviour is essential to applying evidence in practice (Fitzgerald et al., 2002; Grimshaw et al., 2004). Since the attitudes and behaviours learned during residency are likely to remain for many years afterward, the responses that these residents had to this guideline may be informative to those seeking to introduce guidelines in other comparable environments.

Relevance to the role of the health information professional

Alison Brettle (above and in Chapter 8) notes the ways in which evidence-based practice has introduced new roles for the health information professional. The ideals espoused by the evidence-based movement imply that bringing evidence to practice will result in changed behaviour and better outcomes. In such a scenario, potential roles for the information professional are easily recognized. The appropriately prepared information professional may conduct the systematic review in response to a query that is negotiated with the user in response to a problem. The retrieved evidence is appraised and presented to the user community – sometimes that is a professional group, sometimes a research team, or occasionally to an individual user such as a researcher or clinician. When the ultimate goal for the systematic review is incorporating it into a clinical guideline, or to provide a basis for practice, the expectation is that the evidence will be adopted. After all, evidence-based decision making is a fundamental tenet of professional practice and quality improvement.

It is here, in the application of the evidence to practice, that complications may arise and context must be considered. Whether that context is a clinical environment of a hospital, or a library or information agency, the process of adoption is deeply affected by the institutional and organizational culture and workflow. As was learned in the study of residents' adoption of an evidence-based guideline, the contingencies faced by an individual practitioner – whether clinician or library professional – when attempting to apply evidence to practice will have an impact on the decision to adopt.

The study highlights that the difficulty with applying evidence-based practice is in human behavioural change and this is another area where information professionals can play a part in evidence-based practice. By investigating the various contingencies that affect the application of evidence to practice in a given domain, information professionals are better able to design ways of presenting evidence effectively. They can harness this knowledge to partner with their user community to facilitate the evidence adoption by understanding the patterns of information flow within that community. They can use their understanding of the user's information need and the ways in which context affects those needs to set realistic expectations about adoption of evidence and to advocate for evidence-based practice without becoming doctrinaire about its application.

Conclusion

This chapter examines the way in which information is being used to improve quality and accountability within the UK health service and the challenges this poses. There is an increasing focus on the need to give patients more choice and say in their health care yet, as can be seen by Alison Yeoman's study on women's health, this is fraught with difficulties. Integrating patient choice is one aspect of evidence-based practice along with professional judgement and research-derived evidence. As can be seen in Alison Brettle's section above and in Chapter 8, evidence-based practice has provided a wealth of opportunities for health library and information professionals to demonstrate their skills and contribute to high quality patient care. Yet issues remain in deciding what is best evidence and ensuring that this is made readily available to the clinicians who need it. Prudence Dalrymple's study highlights the difficulties involved in applying evidence, even when best evidence exists. Information management is also crucial to the quality and performance agenda within health care. Health is a knowledge-based industry and systems and standards governing its use such as those described by Gareth Lawrence are crucial to evidence-based decision making throughout the health service. Finding ways of overcoming these challenges within the health sector will offer health library and information professionals a wide range of opportunities.

References

Ankem, K. (2007) Information-seeking Behavior of Women in their Path to an Innovative Alternative Treatment for Symptomatic Uterine Fibroids, *Journal of the Medical Library Association*, **9** (2), 164–72.

Arora, V., Johnson J., Lovinger, D., Humphrey, H. J. and Meltzer, D.O. (2005) Communication Failures in Patient Sign-out and Suggestions for Improvement: a critical incident analysis, *Quality & Safety in Health Care*, **14** (6), 401–7.

Audit Commission (2010) *Improving Data Quality in the NHS. Annual report on the PbR assurance programme 2010*, www.audit-commission.gov.uk/nationalstudies/health/pbr/pbr2010/Pages/default.aspx.

Avery, J. C. and Braunack-Mayer, A. J. (2007) The Information Needs of Women Diagnosed with Polycystic Ovarian Syndrome – implications for treatment and health outcomes, *BMC Women's Health*, **7** (9), www.biomedcentral.com/1472-6874/7/9.

Booth, A. (2004) Clinical Governance and National Service Frameworks. In Walton, G. and Booth, A. (eds), *Exploiting Knowledge in Health Services*, Facet Publishing.

Booth, A. (2006) Counting what Counts: performance measurement and evidence-based practice, *Performance Measurement and Metrics*, **7** (2), 63–74.

Booth, A. and Brice, A. (2007) Prediction is Difficult, Especially the Future: a progress report, *Evidence Based Library & Information Practice*, **2** (1), 89–106.

Brettle, A., Hulme, C., and Ormandy, P. (2006) The Costs and Effectiveness of Information Skills Training and Mediated Searching: quantitative results from the EMPIRIC project, *Health Information and Libraries Journal*, **23** (4), 239-47.

Brettle, A., Hulme, C., and Ormandy, P. (2007) Effectiveness of Information Skills Training and Mediated Searching: qualitative results from the EMPIRIC project, *Health Information and Libraries Journal*, **24** (1), 24-33.

Cabinet Office (1999) *Modernising Government*, www.archive.official-documents.co.uk/document/cm43/4310/4310.htm.

Cayton, H. (2006) *Information Governance in the Department of Health and the NHS*, www.connectingforhealth.nhs.uk/crdb/boardpapers/igreview/igreview.pdf.

Childs, S. (2004) Developing Health Website Quality Assessment Guidelines for the Voluntary Sector: outcomes from the Judge Project, *Health Information and Libraries Journal*, **21** (suppl. 2), 14–26.

CHKS (2010) *Products and Services*, www.chks.co.uk/index.php?id=31.

ContinYou (2011) *Skilled for Health*,
www.continyou.org.uk/health_and_well_being/skilled_health/.

Coupland, J. and Williams, A. (2002) Conflicting Discourses, Shifting Ideologies: pharmaceutical, 'alternative' and feminist emancipatory texts on the menopause, *Discourse and Society*, **13** (4), 419-45.

Crumley, E. and Koufogiannakis, D. (2002) Developing Evidence-based Librarianship: practical steps for implementation, *Health Information & Libraries Journal*, **19** (2), 61-70.

Davies, M. M. and Bath, P. A. (2002) Interpersonal Sources of Health and Maternity Information for Somali Women Living in the UK: information seeking and evaluation, *Journal of Documentation*, **58** (3), 302-18.

Department of Health (1999a) *Clinical Governance: in the new NHS*,
www.dh.gov.uk/en/Publicationsandstatistics/Lettersandcirculars/Healthservicecirculars/ DH_4004883.

Department of Health (1999b) *Making a Difference: strengthening the nursing, midwifery and health visiting contribution to health and healthcare*,
www.dh.gov.uk/en/Publicationsandstatistics/Lettersandcirculars/Healthservicecirculars/ DH_4004153.

Department of Health (2001) *Building the Information Core Implementing the NHS Plan*,
www.dh.gov.uk/en/Publicationsandstatistics/Publications/PublicationsPolicyandGuidance/ DH_4005249.

Department of Health (2003) *Confidentiality: NHS Code of Practice*,
www.dh.gov.uk/en/Publicationsandstatistics/Publications/PublicationsPolicyandGuidance/ DH_4069253.

Department of Health (2007) *About the Information Prescription Project,*.
www.informationprescription.info/.

Department of Health (2010a) *Equity and Excellence: liberating the NHS*,
www.dh.gov.uk/en/Publicationsandstatistics/Publications/PublicationsPolicyandGuidance/ DH_117353

Department of Health (2010b) *An Information Revolution: a consultation on proposals*,
www.dh.gov.uk/en/Consultations/Closedconsultations/DH_120080.

Department of Health (2010c) *Health Literacy*,
http://webarchive.nationalarchives.gov.uk/+/www.dh.gov.uk/en/Publichealth/ Healthimprovement/Healthliteracy/index.htm.

Dew, K., Plumridge, E., Stubbe, M., Dowell, T., Macdonald, L. and Major, G. (2008) 'You Just Got to Eat Healthy': the topic of CAM in the general consultation, *Health Sociology Review*, **17** (4), 396-409.

Donaldson, C. (2004) Effectiveness and Efficiency of Guideline Dissemination and Implementation Strategies, *Health Technology & Assessment*, **8** (6), iii-iv, 1-72.

Dr Foster Intelligence (2010) *Dr Foster Intelligence Aims to Improve the Quality and Efficiency of Health and Social Care Through Better Use of Information*, www.drfosterintelligence.co.uk.

Dunne, J. E. (2002) Information Seeking and Use by Battered Women: a 'person-in-progressive-situations' approach, *Library & Information Science Research*, **24** (4), 343-55.

Ellins, J. and Coulter, A. (2005) *How Engaged are People in their Health Care? Findings of a national telephone survey*, The Health Foundation, www.pickereurope.org/item/document/36.

Fitzgerald, L., Ferlie, E., Wood, M. and Hawkins, E. (2002) Interlocking Interactions: the diffusion of innovations in health care, *Human Relations*, **55** (12), 1429–49.

Flanagan, J. C. (1954) The Critical Incident Technique, *Psychological Bulletin*, **51** (4), 327–58.

Grimshaw, J. M., Thomas, R. E., MacLennan, G., Fraser, C., Ramsay, C. R., Vale, L., Whitty, P., Eccles, M. P., Matowe, L., Shirran, L., Wensing, M., Dijkstra, R. and Donaldson, C. (2004) Effectiveness and Efficiency of Guideline Dissemination and Implementation Strategies, *Health Technology Assessment*, **8** (6), iii–iv, 1–72.

Haddow, G. and Klobas, J. E. (2004) Communication of Research to Practice in Library and Information Science: closing the gap, *Library & Information Science Research*, **26** (1), 29–43.

Harris, R., Stickney, J., Grasley, C., Hutchinson G., Greaves L. and Boyd T. (2001) Searching for Help and Information: abused women speak out, *Library & Information Science Research*, **23** (2), 123–41.

Hill, A., Brettle, A., Jenkins, P. and Hulme, C. (2008) *Counselling in Primary Care: a systematic review of the evidence*, British Association of Counselling and Psychotherapy.

Hirsh, J., Bauer, K. A., Donati, M. B., Gould, M., Samama, M. M. and Weitz, J. I. (2008) Parenteral Anticoagulants. American College of Chest Physicians Evidence-Based Clinical Practice Guidelines, 8th edn, *Chest*, **133** (suppl. 6), 141S–59S.

Huston, S. A., Jackowski, R. M. and Kirking, D. M. (2009) Women's Trust in and Use of Information Sources in the Treatment of Menopausal Symptoms, *Women's Health Issues*, **19**, 144–53.

Information Commissioner's Office (undated) *Data Protection Act*, www.ico.gov.uk/for_organisations/data_protection.aspx.

Institute of Medicine (2001) *Crossing the Quality Chasm: a new health system for the 21st century*, National Academy Press. 2–4.

Lorenzi, N. M., Novak, L. L., Weiss, J. B., Gadd, C. S. and Unertl, K. M. (2008) Crossing the Implementation Chasm: a proposal for bold action, *Journal of the American Medical Informatics Association*, **15** (3), 290–6.

McCray, A. T. (2005) Promoting Health Literacy, *Journal of the American Medical Informatics Association*, **12** (2), 152-63.

McKenzie, P. J. (2003) A Model of Information Practices in Accounts of Everyday-life Information Seeking, *Journal of Documentation*, **59** (1), 19–40.

McKibbon, K., Eady, A. and Marks, S. (1999) *PDQ: evidence based principles and practice*, BC Decker.

McNab, C. (2009) What Social Media Offers to Health Professionals and Citizens, *Bulletin of the World Health Organization*, **87** (8), 566.

Meadows, L. M., Thurston, W. E. and Berenson, C. A. (2001) Health Promotion and Preventive Measures: interpreting messages at midlife, *Qualitative Health Research*, **11** (4), 450–63.

NHS Connecting for Health (2010a) *NHS Data Model and Dictionary Service*, www.connectingforhealth.nhs.uk/systemsandservices/data/nhsdmds.

NHS Connecting for Health (2010b) *UK Terminology Centre*,
www.connectingforhealth.nhs.uk/systemsandservices/data/uktc.

NHS Connecting for Health (2010c) *Classifications Service*,
www.connectingforhealth.nhs.uk/systemsandservices/data/clinicalcoding.

NHS Connecting for Health (2010d) *NHS Number: information for staff*,
www.connectingforhealth.nhs.uk/systemsandservices/nhsnumber/staff.

NHS Connecting for Health (2010e) *What is Data Quality?*,
www.connectingforhealth.nhs.uk/systemsandservices/data/dataquality/whatisdq/
index_html#1.

NHS Connecting for Health (2010f) *NHS Information Governance Toolkit*,
www.igt.connectingforhealth.nhs.uk/requirementsorganisation.aspx?tk=
404657460467335&cb=18%3a00%3a10&lnv=4&clnav=YES.

NHS Evidence – knowledge management (undated) *Glossary of Health Knowledge Management Terms*, www.evidence.nhs.uk/search?q=knowledge+management+glossary.

NHS Executive (1996) *Promoting Clinical Excellence: a framework for action in and through the NHS*, NHS Executive.

NHS Executive (1998) *Information for Health: an information strategy for implementation*, Department of Health.

NHS Executive (1999a) *Clinical Governance: quality in the new NHS*, NHS Executive.

NHS Executive (1999b) *Patient and Public Involvement in the New NHS*, Department of Health.

NHS Information Centre (2010) *NHS Information Centre - about us*,
www.ic.nhs.uk/about-us.

Pawson, R., Greenhalgh, T., Harvey, G. and Walshe, K. (2005) Realist Review: a new method of systematic review designed for complex policy interventions, *Journal of Health Services Research and Policy*, **10** (suppl. 1), 21-34.

Payne, S. A. (2002) Balancing Information Needs: dilemmas in producing patient information, *Health Informatics Journal*, **8** (4), 174-9.

Pyne, T., Newman, K., Leigh, S., Cowling, A. and Rounce, K. (1999) Meeting the Information Needs of Clinicians for the Practice of Evidence-based Healthcare, *Health Libraries Review*, **16** (1), 3-14.

Raupach, J. C. A. and Hiller, J. E. (2002) Information and Support for Women Following the Primary Treatment of Breast Cancer, *Health Expectations*, **5** (4), 289-301.

Rogers, E. M. (2003) *Diffusion of Innovations*, 5th edn, Free Press.

Rogers, W. (1997) Sources of Abjection in Western Responses to Menopause. In Komesaroff, P. A., Rothfield, P. and Daly, J. (eds) *Reinventing Menopause: cultural and philosophical issues*, Routledge, 225-38.

Rosenberg, W. and Donald, A. (1995) Evidence Based Medicine: an approach to clinical problem-solving, *BMJ*, **310** (6987), 1122-6.

Royal College of Physicians (undated) *Health Informatics Unit*,
www.rcplondon.ac.uk/resources/clinical-resources/standards-medical-record-keeping.

Sackett, D. L., Haynes, R. B. and Tugwell, P. (1985) *Clinical Epidemiology: a basic science for clinical medicine*, 1st edn, Little, Brown.

Sackett, D. L., Rosenberg, W. M., Gray, J. A., Haynes, R. B. and Richardson, W. S. (1996) Evidence Based Medicine: what it is and what it isn't, *BMJ*, **312** (7023), 71–2.

Salkovskis, P. M., Wroe, A. L. and Rees, M. C. P. (2004) Shared Decision-making, Health Choices and the Menopause, *Journal of the British Menopause Society*, **10** (suppl. 1), 13–17.

Schulman, S., Beyth, R. J., Kearon, C. and Levine, M. N. (2008) Hemorrhagic Complications of Anticoagulant and Thrombolytic Treatment: American College of Chest Physicians Evidence-Based Clinical Practice Guidelines, 8th edn, *Chest*, **133** (suppl. 6), 257S–98S.

Scottish Public Health Observatory (2010) *Scottish Public Health Observatory*, www.scotpho.org.uk/home/home.asp.

Secretary of State for Health (1997) *A First Class Service: quality in the new NHS*, Department of Health, www.dh.gov.uk/en/Publicationsandstatistics/Publications/PublicationsPolicyAndGuidance/DH_4006902.

Secretary of State for Health (2002) *National Health Service Reform and Health Care Professions Act*, www.legislation.gov.uk/ukpga/2002/17/contents.

Skea, Z., Harry, V., Bhattacharya, S., Entwistle, V., Williams, B., MacLennan, G. and Templeton, A. (2004) Women's Perceptions of Decision-making About Hysterectomy, *British Journal of Obstetrics and Gynaecology*, **111** (2), 133–42.

Smith, S. and Duman, M. (2009) The State of Consumer Health Information: an overview, *Health Information and Libraries Journal*, **26** (4), 260–78.

Snow, V., Qaseem, A., Barry, P., Hornbake, E. D., Rodnick, J. E., Tobolic, T., Ireland, B., Segal, J. B., Bass, E. B., Weiss, K. B., Green, L., Owens, D. K. and the Joint American Academy of Family Physicians/American College of Physicians Panel on Deep Venous Thrombosis/Pulmonary Embolism (2007) Management of Venous Thromboembolism: a clinical practice guideline from the American College of Physicians and the American Academy of Family Physicians, *Annals of Internal Medicine*, **146** (3), 204–10.

Trinder, L. and Reynolds, S. (2000) *Evidence-based Practice: a critical appraisal*, Blackwell Science.

Warner, D. and Procaccino, J. D. (2004) Toward Wellness: women seeking health information, *Journal of the American Society for Information Science and Technology*, **55** (8), 709–30.

Whitfield, L. (2010) Mid Staffs Report Demands Stats Overhaul, *E Health Insider Primary Care*, 24 February, www.ehiprimarycare.com/news/5672/mid_staffs_report_demands_stats_overhaul.

Wilson, P. (2002) How to Find the Good and Avoid the Bad or Ugly: a short guide to tools for rating quality of health information on the internet, *British Medical Journal*, **324**, www.bmj.com/content/324/7337/598.

Woloshin, S., Schwartz, L. M. and Ellner, A. (2003). Making Sense of Risk Information on the Web, *British Medical Journal*, **327**, 695–96.

Yeoman, A. (2009) *Information Behaviour in Accounts of the Menopause Transition*, PhD thesis, Aberystwyth University.

Acknowledgements

Prudence Dalrymple's study reported here was funded by NLM Grant T15LM007452. Prudence wishes to thank the residents, physicians and nurses at Johns Hopkins Hospital as well as Nancy K. Roderer, MS, Harold P. Lehmann, MD, PhD and Michael B. Streiff, MD, for their guidance and support. Portions of this research were presented at the 5th International Evidence-Based Library and Information Practice conference in Stockholm, Sweden, 29 June–3 July 2009.

Part 2
Roles

5
Skills, competencies and knowledge

Christine Urquhart

Introduction

This chapter sets the scene for this second part, which focuses on roles. Later chapters discuss some case study examples of the ways in which some health library and information professionals have developed their roles in all sorts of working environments. First of all, we need to remember what is meant by role, as discussed earlier in the overview. Sociologists can help us unpick some of the assumptions we make about roles in a working environment, and why roles can be seen as a problem or an opportunity. Second, we need to think about the distinguishing features of roles – what are the expectations of this role or that role? What should some professionals be expected to be able to do, and what skills do they need in order to be able to perform in their roles? Third, what does interprofessional working really mean, and how do we learn from reflection on our own practice, and from observing others? How do our information professional colleagues and other colleagues help us develop professionally?

The Chartered Institute of Personnel Development (CIPD) points out that there is a distinction between competencies and competences, although many people do not now distinguish between the terms. Strictly speaking, competency is precisely defined as 'the behaviours that employees must have, or must acquire, to input into a situation in order to achieve high levels of performance' (CIPD, 2010). The focus is on the person, and behaviour and performance. The CIPD (2010) define competence in terms of a system of minimum standards or a demonstration of performance and outputs, and the focus here is on the job. Occupational standards, which are concerned with expectations of particular job roles, deal with competences. This chapter will be focusing on competencies, and some of the competency frameworks that have been developed and used to analyse and assess health information and library workers and the work they do. Some frameworks mix competencies and competences, but sometimes the purpose of the framework helps to identify whether the focus is on the individual or the job. We need to think about expertise, the definitions of professional expertise and knowledge, and how that knowledge is acquired and developed to make a professional perform well in practice. Sometimes competencies may be identified and formal courses devised (e.g. Oliver et al. (2008) describe a special course for searching for informationists devised by an interprofessional team). In other cases learning happens as social learning, informal learning within the workplace.

This chapter should provide you with some ideas on how to appraise those case studies in the following chapters, beyond a feeling of 'didn't she do well!' Ideally, you should be able to analyse the set of competencies involved – the combination of technical and softer skills, together with personal attributes, required. You should be able to assess how the roles described might fit into some of the occupational standards, what competences or skills are necessary, and you should be able to consider how that person developed their role, or was supported to do so. So, it is not only admiration of the career pathway in 'didn't she do well' but 'how did she do well?' and 'what would I need to move from here to there?'

Social learning theory

Various psychologists have studied social learning, but one of the most relevant to this chapter is probably Albert Bandura. His theory of social learning (Bandura, 1977) describes and explains in terms of attention (choosing what we want to learn about and how we value it), retention (memorizing what is happening and mentally rehearsing), motor reproduction (actually practising the actions and behaviour involved) and motivation (intrinsic and the effect of encouragement from others). Reflecting on these four components (attention, retention, motor reproduction, motivation) should help you realize why 'sitting with Nellie' can be an effective way of on the job training, but only if all these components are in place. It is not going to work if Nellie does not help with attention, ensuring that the trainee is watching carefully at appropriate moments, or if Nellie cannot help with the mental rehearsal, or is unwilling to let the trainee have a practice attempt. And both the trainee and Nellie need to be motivated and prepared to offer encouragement to the other.

Another of Bandura's contributions to work on competencies in the workplace is the idea of self-efficacy: 'the belief in one's capabilities to organize and execute the courses of action required to manage prospective situations' (Bandura, 1995, 2). In other words, self-efficacy is a person's belief that they are capable of succeeding in a particular situation.

Communities of practice

Social learning is also seen in communities of practice, a term coined by Jean Lave and Etienne Wenger (Lave and Wenger, 1991; Wenger, 1998), to describe the type of learning that occurs among groups of people who share an interest in something and learn to do it better as they interact. The research on communities of practice examined social learning in many different situations, and a key idea is legitimate peripheral participation, the idea that you can be an observer at the start of your learning trajectory, and later become more expert (if that is how events develop). But you are still a legitimate member of the community of practice as an interested observer. Usually you will be motivated to learn more, and become a more active participant in the community, but you may be involved in many different communities of practice. You may remain a legitimate peripheral participant in some of these – and become a more active participant in others. Lave and Wenger also discussed situated learning, the idea that experiential learning is more than learning by doing, but that knowledge and learning and the context are hard to disentangle. Learning institutions were fond of the notion of 'transferable' skills, the idea that students might learn skills or knowledge in an assignment that they could then transfer to other assignments or in later years to their workplace. There was never a huge amount of evidence that skills could be decontextualized and transferred, and in the words of one year eight I was teaching, when encouraging him to think back to what he learnt the previous year and how he could use that to help solve the problem, 'But that was last year, Miss', as if last year's learning was a whole world apart.

The theory behind communities of practice has been used to guide the development of knowledge management initiatives in the health sector, in particular the Specialist Collections in NHS Evidence (Yeoman, Urquhart and Sharp, 2003; Cooper et al., 2005; Urquhart et al., 2010). The Specialist Collections are mostly virtual communities of practice, with some face to face meetings. The content and the organization of their websites reflect the principles of working of effective communities of practice. A synthesis review of communities of practice in the health sector (Li et al., 2009a, 2009b) found that meanings associated with communities of practice had changed in emphasis over time. The review (covering literature to 2005) found that it was difficult to judge whether communities of practice were truly effective, and there can be power imbalances in a community of practice if one or two individuals dominate so much that others are deterred from participating. One longitudinal study (not retrieved in the synthesis review by Li et al.) formed the basis of the framework used in the NHS research, and subsequent evidence on communities of practice is considered in a later paper (Urquhart et al., 2010). The evidence is mainly qualitative, but the theory of communities of practice and the framework developed in Yeoman, Urquhart and Sharp (2003) was effective in identifying what components of a virtual community of practice should be in place, and the type of supporting structures that are desirable. The second evaluation of the Specialist Collections (or Specialist Libraries as they were at the time) (Urquhart et al., 2010) found that the information scientists who were co-ordinating the Specialist Libraries (Collections) were in fact acting in a community of practice of their own. Their role development depended on sharing experience with others working in similar situations.

Interprofessional collaboration

Interprofessional collaboration is a necessary part of health care, but just what does collaboration mean? A collaborator also means someone who works with the enemy, and some researchers have devised the idea of the collaborative continuum (Hudson et al., 1997a, 1997b) to describe how increasing co-operation, information exchange and trust develops, from a beginning where it may seem like working with the enemy. D'Amour et al. (2005) reviewed the theories around interprofessional collaboration and found that collaboration was usually defined through the five concepts of sharing, partnership, power, interdependency and process. Frameworks that have been used in the health sector include work on health team effectiveness in the UK (West, Borril and Unsworth, 1998; Haward et al., 2003) and a structuration model of interprofessional collaboration (D'Amour et al., 2004). The review by D'Amour et al. (2005) identified that a potential weakness of all the models of interprofessional collaboration was that fact that the role of the patient was neglected, despite the fact that most of the collaboration was intended to benefit the patient. This is an interesting observation when reflecting on the ways in which health information services previously aimed only at health care students, and staff might broaden their scope to providing information for patients and the public. We may place too much emphasis on how to organize intersectoral library working and forget to involve the main person involved – the member of the public with a health information problem.

Competency and frameworks of competences

Competence and competency confusion is common in many professional fields. In postgraduate medical education, Ten Cate and Scheele (2007) reflect on some of the confusion produced when trying to define competency (the ability to do something successfully) in terms of a list of competences, or skills, to do certain activities. They propose that competencies should be defined as general attributes, and that entrustable professional activities be defined as well. One of their examples of a general competency is 'the ability to learn from clinical practice and to improve it', and an 'entrustable professional activity' for obstetrics would include 'care of uncomplicated pregnancies' and 'the high risk complicated delivery'. Their main argument is that there is no point in reducing all the activities to a set of skills 'can do x', 'can do y', when professional competency requires someone to be able to put all the necessary activities together – to deal with the high risk complicated delivery, for example. Their framework allows for the degree of responsibility that could be entrusted to the trainee – they may simply have some knowledge (level one), they may be able to act under moderate supervision (level three) or they may have reached the stage of being able to instruct others (top level five). Other writers on continuing education talk about performance, and stress the importance of the communities and culture within which professionals are working. Nowlen (1988), for example, emphasizes that a larger frame of reference is required to take into account all the factors that affect performance – 'developmental stages are fragile partnerships of environment, and self, past and future' (67).

The Knowledge and Skills Framework (KSF) for the NHS (UK) has a different purpose to the type of frameworks that are established to assess whether professionals are competent to practise. The KSF was established as part of the Agenda for Change initiative, to be applied to pay and career progression for most staff working in the NHS. Under the Health Informatics Career Framework (NHS Connecting for Health, 2009) there are role descriptions for many common roles within health informatics. Each description refers to relevant national occupational standards (competences), and the appropriate KSF level (1 through to 4) applicable to that role. The KSF itself has six core dimensions (e.g. communication, health, safety and security) that apply to all staff in the NHS. The other 24 specific dimensions apply to some, but not all, jobs in the NHS (medical staff have their own scheme). One set of specific dimensions is the Information and Knowledge Processing (IK) set, obviously relevant to information professionals. Level four of IK1: Information processing requires an individual to 'Develop and modify data and information management models and processes'. A principal information analyst, dealing with the manipulation of data around patient activity, for monitoring and forecasting, is expected to be performing at this level, and the role description gives a more specific description under the relevant national occupational standard. For IK2: Information collection and analysis, the principal analyst should be expected to 'analyse data and information and present outputs of analysis' (national occupational standard), which relates to the KSF: 'Gather, analyse, interpret and present extensive and/or complex data and information' (level 3). The library services manager needs to 'search for clinical information and evidence according to an accepted methodology' (national occupational standard), which relates to the KSF IK2: 'Gather, analyse and report a limited range of data and information' (level 2). For IK3: Information and knowledge resources, the library services manager should be able to 'appraise information and knowledge resources' (national occupational standard) relating to the KSF for IK3: 'Develop the acquisition, organization, provision and use of knowledge and information' (level 4), whereas the principal information analyst should 'promote and facilitate use of information and knowledge' for the same level of KSF IK3. The KSF framework has avoided the use of the term competence and competencies, preferring to use the term dimension, which might loosely be interpreted as a competency. The national occupational standards are concerned with activities, and the skills and knowledge (more akin to the competences) required to carry these out.

The Medical Library Association (MLA) outlines a set of professional competencies (MLA, 2007), which could be understood as general attributes of the health information professional. Unlike the KSF framework, which is a general framework for health care staff, the MLA competencies apply only to health information professionals. However, the MLA competencies include some general organizational and managerial competencies that might be applicable to many other professional staff in a health care organization, such as those grouped under:

- health sciences and health care environment and information policies (understanding the issues, trends, cultural, legal and ethical issues)
- leadership and management theory and techniques (understanding the application of leadership, finance, communication and management theory).

These are similar to the general dimensions of the KSF, without the information about performance expectations – the minimum standards at different levels. The more specialized health information competencies within the MLA list are:

1 Health sciences information services: understand the principles and practices related to providing information services to meet users' needs (differentiating needs of different groups, including patients and the public, and how to design and manage services accordingly, in line with institutional information policies).

2 Health sciences resource management: have the ability to manage health information resources in a broad range of formats (covering selection, acquisition, licensing, intellectual property considerations, conservation, preservation, archiving, cataloguing, classification, national standards for collection management and trends in information formatting and dissemination).

3 Information systems and technology: understand and use technology and systems to manage all forms of information (systems analysis principles, evaluation of technologies, integration techniques, solutions for permanent access to electronic information, applications in emerging areas of biomedicine, computational biology and health information, including electronic health care systems and records, communications infrastructure such as the internet and web).

4 Curricula design and instruction: understand curricular design and instruction and have the ability to teach ways to access, organize and use information (adult learning theory, cognitive psychology, educational needs assessment, evaluations, instructional methodologies and technologies, management of education services).

5 Research, analysis and interpretation: understand scientific research methods and have the ability to critically examine and filter research literature from many related disciplines (quantitative and qualitative methodologies, techniques, and interpretation, location and critical evaluation of research literatures, using principles of evidence-based practice to support decision making, conducting research and dissemination of findings).

This is a very comprehensive list of competencies, and individuals would usually be more capable in some areas than others. For example, librarians involved in outreach training would be expected to be performing at a high level on curricula design and instruction, whereas a librarian responsible for a special historical collection would be aware of ways of helping users access the collection but would only need to be aware of methods for educational assessment. With the MLA scheme, it may be possible to engineer more creative combinations of some competencies for particular new or developing roles.

Competencies, new roles and continuing professional development

Health information professionals need to work with the competency frameworks that are used in their own environments, for the very obvious reason that such frameworks often determine their level of salary and immediate career progression. Local frameworks should not become a straightjacket to thinking about new prospects and opportunities. The KSF and the national occupational standards for health informatics for the NHS are a mixture of roles, with minimum levels of performance and competences defined for roles (which may have different job titles). The NHS scheme is very detailed and expresses what certain roles should do, unlike the MLA competencies, which are less detailed and express what health information professionals could do.

To take on a new role as a health information professional the first concern may be how to bridge the gap in knowledge and skills that may be required to go from the current role to a new role. There have been several training needs analyses of health library staff in the UK, but many of these have not used the same competency frameworks and comparisons may be difficult. A systematic review of these studies (Urquhart et al., 2005) together with workshops with health library staff, helped to identify some of the common themes. The frequently identified skills gaps were in:

- technical and ICT skills (from web page design in 1999 to knowledge management skills to support intranets in 2003)
- teaching skills (with indications that the needs of the emerging specialist trainer role will differ from the needs of the generalist, informal support role)
- research and analytic skills (quantitative and qualitative data analysis skills, critical appraisal and statistics)
- customer care skills (increasingly the need to cater for the virtual customer)
- leadership and strategic planning skills (influencing and persuading skills, political awareness).

This is perhaps a cause for concern, as a 'Guide to Working in Health Information' (England and Ortega, 2010) suggests you may gain these skills and experience when working as a health information professional. Many of the studies reviewed by Urquhart et al. (2005) were based on the subjective estimations of library staff themselves, and only a few studies attempted to identify some training needs that were unrecognized, but present. Personal development plans, and some approaches to self-directed adult learning, often assume that individuals are the best judges of their own training needs, but this ignores the human predilection for avoiding things that we do not really want to do. Therefore our own assessment of our training needs may downplay the importance of the stuff that really scares us. A review and evaluation of studies on personal development plans and self-directed learning for health care professionals (Jennings, 2007) examines why some learners may be more self-directed than others, and also notes that several studies have found that doctors are incapable of assessing their learning needs accurately. It is not surprising, therefore, that the review and evaluation of training needs analyses for health library staff (Urquhart et al., 2005) noted that few of the published studies and workshop participants or interviewees mentioned numeracy directly (or competencies for dealing with information for patients and consumers). There was an iceberg called numeracy – the studies showed that librarians wanted to be able to write successful bids, evaluate their services and support critical appraisal training, but their lack of skills in handling quantitative data was a major hurdle. The LISU report (Maynard et al., 2000; see also Maynard, 2002) noted that librarians did not themselves recognize that they lacked these skills. Having a scientific background provides a good confidence boost at the start of a career in the health library sector (Petrinic and Urquhart, 2007). This indicates that the sense of self-efficacy for those with a scientific background at the start of their career was better. Others required time to practise to gain confidence, and that implies that the environment will permit and encourage that. The training needs analysis for South Yorkshire (Urquhart, Durbin and Spink, 2004) indicated that library managers spent very little time on tasks that might be considered practice of leadership skills. As Abbott (2003) suggested, the problem is not the lack of opportunities for formal training in such skills. Managers need support through coaching to develop leadership skills after the initial training. Similarly, the critical appraisal and research skills may need practice to build not just competence but the necessary confidence in quantitative data analysis. Self-efficacy matters in these circumstances. But Jennings (2007) also concludes that much depends on the learning style, cognitive style and learning experiences of the individual. A detailed, stepwise plan to get from one level to the next higher level on the KSF might suit some individuals but would dampen the enthusiasm of others, who might in fact benefit from some structure but require some personal support from a mentor to help them along.

Much of the literature on personal development plans and self-directed learning focuses on the individual, and ignores the influences of colleagues and the social learning that occurs within communities of practice. Individuals certainly differ in their needs and two people may react differently to the same situation – one may 'reflect in action' and modify practice immediately, and the other may 'reflect on action' and modify practice later (Schön, 1987). However, the communities of practice in which we operate will influence us, and hopefully support us in our own professional development.

Knowledge, expertise and evidence-based practice

Evidence-based practice is an accepted norm for work in the health sector, and the changes that evidence-based practice requires have opened up opportunities for health library and information professionals. New roles have developed to support health care staff – professionals and managers – in their practice, but it is sometimes difficult to discern where future developments might emerge. A useful guide to mapping the literature on research utilization and evidence into practice is provided by Nutley, Walter and Davies (2003) who summarize the debates about types of knowledge (know about, know what, know how, know who and know why) and the type of frameworks that may be used to illuminate the implementation and integration of research into practice. Evidence-based practice may focus on the individual clinician and change in individual practice but the focus may also be on organizational interventions or complete systems redesign. The appropriate theories need to change according to the scale or complexity of the changes involved.

Conclusions: reflecting on the case studies

When reading the case studies, some of the questions you might need to ask are:

1 Why might that individual have wanted, or been encouraged, to make that change?
2 How did individual aspirations and the environment interact? How were barriers overcome and opportunities acted on?
3 Who else was involved, and what type of interprofessional collaboration was involved, if any?
4 What sort of teamwork, what sort of roles were involved? What worked and what did not work – and why?
5 How was a sense of personal mastery (self-efficacy) achieved?
6 How did this role fit into evidence-based practice, and at what level – individual, organizational or wider systems of health care delivery?

References

Abbott, C. (2003) *HIMSS (Hybrid Information Management: Skills for Senior Staff) Final project report. HEFCE 99/54: Good Management Practice GMP 128*, University of Birmingham.

Bandura, A. (1977) *Social Learning Theory*, General Learning Press.

Bandura, A. (1995) *Self-Efficacy in Changing Societies*, Cambridge University Press.

Chartered Institute of Personnel Development (CIPD) (2010) Competency and Competency Frameworks, www.cipd.co.uk/subjects/perfmangmt/competnces/comptfrmwk.htm.

Cooper, J., Spink, S., Thomas, R. and Urquhart, C. (2005) *Evaluation of the Specialist Libraries/Communities of Practice. Report for National Library for Health*, Department of Information Studies, University of Wales Aberystwyth, http://hdl.handle.net/2160/221.

D'Amour, D., Goulet, L., Pineault, R. and Labadie, J. F. (2004) Comparative Study of Inter-organizational Collaboration and its Effects in Four Quebec Socio-sanitary Regions: the case of perinatal care, Groupe de recherche interdisciplinaire en santé , Université de Montréal, www.ferasi.umontreal.ca/eng/07_info/IECPCP_Final_Report.pdf.

D'Amour, D., Ferrada-Videla, M., San-Martin-Rodriquez, L. and Beaulieu, M.-D. (2005) The Conceptual Basis for Interprofessional Collaboration: core concepts and theoretical frameworks, *Journal of Interprofessional Care*, (suppl. 1), 116–31, DOI: 10.1080/13561820500082529.

Department of Health (2004) *The NHS Knowledge and Skills Framework (NHS KSF) and the Development Review Process*, www.dh.gov.uk/en/Publicationsandstatistics/Publications/PublicationsPolicyAndGuidance/DH_4090843.

England, P. and Ortega, M. (2010) *Guide to Working in Health Information*, Health Libraries Group, www.cilip.org.uk/get-involved/special-interest-groups/health/Documents/Guide%20to%20Working%20in%20Health%20Inforrmation.pdf.

Haward, R., Amir, Z., Borril, C., Dawson, J., Scully, J., West, M. A. et al. (2003) Breast Cancer Teams: the impact of constitution, new cancer workload, and methods of operation on their effectiveness, *British Journal of Cancer*, **89**, 15–22.

Hudson, B., Hardy, B., Henwood, M. and Wistow, G. (1997a) Strategic Alliances: working across professional boundaries: primary health care and social care, *Public Money and Management*, **17** (4), 25–30.

Hudson, B., Hardy, B., Henwood, M. and Wistow, G. (1997b) *Inter-agency Collaboration: primary health care sub-study. Final report*, Nuffield Institute for Health.

Jennings, S. F. (2007) Personal Development Plans and Self-directed Learning for Healthcare Professionals: are they evidence-based?, *Postgraduate Medical Journal*, **83** (892), 518–24, DOI: 10.1136/pgmj.2006.053066.

Lave, J. and Wenger, E. (1991) *Situated Learning. Legitimate peripheral participation*, University of Cambridge Press.

Li, L., Grimshaw, J. M., Nielsen, C., Judd, M., Coyte, P. C. and Graham, I. D. (2009a) Evolution of Wenger's Concept of Community of Practice, *Implementation Science*, **4** (1), 11, DOI:10.1186/1748-5908-4-11.

Li, L., Grimshaw, J. M., Nielsen, C., Judd, M., Coyte, P. C. and Graham, I. D. (2009b) Use of Communities of Practice in Business and Health Care Sectors: a systematic review, *Implementation Science*, **4** (1), 27, DOI:10.1186/1748-5908-4-27.

Maynard, S. (2002) The Knowledge Workout for Health: a report of a training needs census of NHS library staff, *Journal of Librarianship and Information Science*, **34** (1), 17–32.

Maynard, S., Kinnell, M., White, S. and Yu, L. (2000) *Training Needs Census of NHS Library Staff*, University of Loughborough, Library & Information Statistics Unit.

Medical Library Association (MLA) (2007) *Competencies for Lifelong Learning and Professional Success: the educational policy statement of the Medical Library Association*, www.mlanet.org/education/policy/executive_summary.html#B.

NHS Connecting for Health (2009) *Health Informatics Career Framework*, www.hicf.org.uk/.

Nowlen, P. M. (1988) *A New Approach to Continuing Education for Business and the Professions: the performance model*, Macmillan.

Nutley, S., Walter, I. and Davies, H. T. O. (2003) From Knowing to Doing: a framework for understanding the evidence into practice agenda, *Evaluation*, **9** (2), 125–48.

Oliver, K. B., Dalrymple, P., Lehmann, H. P., McClellan, D. A., Robinson, K. A. and Twose, C. (2008) Bringing Evidence to Practice: a team approach to teaching skills required for an informationist role in evidence-based clinical and public health practice, *Journal of the Medical Library Association*, **96** (1), 50–7.

Petrinic, T. and Urquhart, C. (2007) The Education and Training Needs of Health Librarians – the generalist versus specialist dilemma, *Health Information and Libraries Journal*, **24** (3), 167–76, DOI:10.1111/j.1471-1842.2007.00717.x.

Schön, D. (1987) *Educating the Reflective Practitioner: a new design for teaching and learning in the professions*, Jossey-Bass.

Ten Cate, O. and Scheele, F. (2007) Competency-based Postgraduate Training: can we bridge the gap between theory and practice?, *Academic Medicine*, **82** (6), 542–7.

Urquhart, C., Durbin, J. and Spink, S. (2004) *Training Needs Analysis of Healthcare Library Staff. Undertaken for South Yorkshire Workforce Development Confederation*, http://hdl.handle.net/2160/212.

Urquhart, C., Spink, S., Thomas, R. and Durbin, J. (2005) Systematic Assessment of the Training Needs of Health Library Staff, *Library and Information Research*, **29** (93), 35–42.

Urquhart, C., Brice, A., Cooper, J., Spink, S. and Thomas, R. (2010) Evaluating the Development of Communities of Practice that Support Evidence-based Practice, *Evidence Based Library and Information Practice*, **5** (1), 64–81.

Wenger, E. (1998) *Communities of Practice: learning, meaning and identity*, University of Cambridge Press.

West, M. A., Borril, C. S. and Unsworth, K. L. (1998) Team Effectiveness in Organizations, *International Review of Industrial and Organizational Psychology*, **13**, 1–48.

Yeoman, A., Urquhart, C. and Sharp, S. (2003) Moving Communities of Practice Forward: the challenge for the National electronic Library for Health and its Virtual Branch Libraries, *Health Informatics Journal*, **9** (4), 241–52.

6
The librarian as information provider and educator

Pat Spoor and Debra Thornton

Introduction
This chapter describes the health librarian in the role of information provider and educator. By way of introduction, Pat Spoor and Debra Thornton describe this role from both higher education and NHS library perspectives. Four case studies in four different contexts follow to illustrate different aspects of these roles in practice.

HIGHER EDUCATION OVERVIEW
Pat Spoor

Introduction
Health librarians, in a university context, are the academic liaison librarians who work closely with departments to develop and manage access to information, deliver academic skills training, support research and ensure that the university library is aware of, and responsive to, the needs of different disciplines. Information provision is one of their core functions but the range and complexity of resources and providers means that they depend increasingly on input from colleagues in e-resources, acquisitions, cataloguing, IT and customer services to provide the complex network of resources that library users need and expect. This role is illustrated with a case study by Lorie Kloda later in this chapter.

The role of academic librarians in general has changed significantly in recent years, driven by a combination of educational, political, technological and financial developments. These changes are elaborated below and are relevant for all academic librarians, whatever their subject domain. However, for academic health librarians the growth of evidence-based practice (EBP) and the need to take account of changes in health policy and practice add an extra dimension to their role as they endeavour to meet the information needs of the students, academics and NHS staff who use HE libraries.

Collection development
Traditionally, academic librarians had an in-depth knowledge of subject collections, but this is changing as the concept of collections gives way to one of access. The advent of 'big deal' journal packages has hugely expanded the range of journals available to

HE. This, and the plethora of subscription and open access e-resources available, has shifted the emphasis for librarians from collection development towards providing seamless access to integrated digital and physical resources. The growth of consortial purchasing, where negotiations with publishers are done via an intermediary, has also changed the nature of the librarians' relationship with resource provision, though this type of cross-institutional co-operation may diminish with the proposed changes to student fees (Browne, 2010).

The prevalence of online journals means the potential for better usage statistics, and thus the opportunity for a more evidenced-based approach to resource purchase. Shrinking budgets and pressure to ensure value for money means librarians spend considerable amounts of time analysing usage data to inform purchasing decisions but the information available is often inadequate, inconsistent and hard to compare between providers.

The current financial climate may result in a reversal of the trend towards aggregation in journal purchasing. Universities are looking more closely at the cost-effectiveness of journal packages and may cancel subscriptions in favour of purchasing a smaller number of heavily used individual titles.

When purchasing resources, health librarians have to take account of changes in the way users access information. For example, the availability of smartphones and difficulty in accessing a personal computer (PC) in clinical settings means that students on placement are increasingly using resources via mobile phones (Coughlan, 2010).

Students are increasingly being encouraged to think of themselves as consumers and, with limited funds, there is a tension between balancing the demands of undergraduates for multiple copies of textbooks and providing researchers with access to the resources they need. E-books could provide a partial solution but a recent report (Research Information Network, 2010) found 'publishers' policies on pricing and accessibility are inhibiting take-up'. Technological and licensing changes enable libraries to digitize chapters and articles and make them available in Virtual Learning Environments (VLEs) but the development of on-demand services could lead to a scenario where students and academics purchase the information they need directly from suppliers, circumventing the library altogether.

Supporting varied audiences

VLEs makes it easier for university libraries to embed information in the curriculum and push it towards students at the time they need it to support their academic work. With increasing student numbers and a diverse student population, including health students who are combining study with work or clinical placements, adopting blending learning techniques also helps meet demand for information literacy (IL) training, accommodates different learning styles and ensures that support is available at the point of need. For online IL skills delivery to be effective, librarians need to be able to create pedagogically sound e-learning resources.

For much of their academic work, health students are expected to be able to find and use primary sources, but, unlike most other students, they also need to master secondary sources like clinical guidelines that will support evidence-based practice after graduation. One of the major aims of academic health librarians is to equip students with appropriate information skills but the extent to which we are successful is often hard to ascertain (Brettle, 2003).

Information literacy

Whilst health faculties increasingly recognize that for EBP to thrive, graduates must have the skills to access and interpret the knowledge base, and finding time in a busy curriculum to teach these skills has always been difficult. In some institutions the approach to IL training is still bottom up and piecemeal, but a number of universities have taken a more strategic approach (Corrall, 2008). For example, the University of Leeds (2003) adopted an institution-wide IL strategy that has made it easier for librarians to work with academics to embed IL more systematically within the curriculum.

Many university libraries are experimenting with federated search tools that make the process of searching simpler but more opaque to the library user. In addition, full texts of university library holdings are now often linked from Google or Google Scholar. Universities are also developing institutional repositories, digitizing their own collections and reading list items to maximize access for students. At undergraduate level, academic librarians are spending more time teaching students to critically evaluate the information they find. This trend is likely to continue as more sophisticated Google-style discovery tools eventually make using traditional bibliographic databases a thing of the past for these students.

Despite improvements in resource discovery tools, lack of integration between the resources available to health students and health professionals is problematic. Ideally, students learn the principles of database searching at university and should be able to apply these to new interfaces they encounter in their working environment, but many struggle to make this transition. A shared NHS/HE interface for bibliographic databases and journals would make life easier for students, NHS staff and librarians alike.

It's not just health students who struggle with literature searching. Supporting health researchers, particularly in literature searching for systematic reviews, can be a stimulating and demanding part of the academic librarians' role and is an excellent illustration of how professional library skills can support the research mission of the institution. Some of these issues are explored in more detail in Chapter 8.

Changing roles

So how is the role of academic health librarians as information providers and educators changing? The transition from managing physical collections to managing access to digital resources requires a different skills mix, for example an understanding of digitization, e-resource licensing, copyright and the application of mobile technologies. On the educator side, academic health librarians work more closely than ever with academics to ensure academic skills are embedded in the curriculum effectively. An understanding of pedagogy, combined with IT skills, is required to create effective e-learning materials. Librarians need to be up to speed with open access, intellectual property law, and institutional repositories if they are to train researchers how to exploit their research effectively. As well as understanding the HE environment, academic health librarians have to keep abreast of changes in health policy and practice, and collaborate with NHS librarians to facilitate the transition between NHS and HE information resources for NHS staff, students and health academics who work across both sectors.

NHS OVERVIEW
Debra Thornton

Introduction
As information providers and knowledge brokers, NHS libraries are ideally placed to 'grow' doctors, nurses and health care professionals. By offering a professional yet personalized service the NHS library provides knowledge services to practising and trainee health professionals whilst emphasizing the importance of using evidence in everyday practice. As more and more 'Generation Y' students and staff join the NHS it becomes ever more necessary to provide the resources and information in a format that suits their needs: 'need to know now' information, i.e. at the touch of a button or click of a mouse.

However, providing resources is only a part of the story – the NHS library must also be effective in imparting the skills to make best use of this information. This means providing information literacy training, teaching people how to locate, retrieve and organize the necessary material, as well as how to assess its value and relevance and implement the findings into practice.

The library service within a health care setting offers a valued and valuable resource – it can provide study space for individual and group study; organize access to a wide range of resources, along with training in how to use these; offer individualized service and assistance to people embarking on a course of study; but it also has a duty to engender an understanding of and enthusiasm for evidence-based health care practice – for managers as well as clinicians.

The physical library
Libraries are often a sanctuary of calm in a busy NHS (despite being a hive of activity at exam times!). Anyone who has spent time on a ward with clinical staff will know just how busy the day to day work of NHS staff is. It becomes clear, then, that the physical library can be relied on to offer a space for escaping the stress and frenzy of work. A recent information needs survey of 480 health care staff in our organization (Thornton, 2010) demonstrated that the traditional role of the library as an educational

resource is still necessary – over 74% of respondents said that they need information for education or a training course (see Figure 6.1). The same survey showed that books are regarded as an important source of information (see Figure 6.2) and feedback from users has indicated the value they place on the library as an important place for study, as well as for 'escaping from the stress of the job for 20 minutes' (Foundation Doctor commenting on the 'Quick Reads' fiction collection).

'I really appreciate the knowledge and expertise of the library staff – they have helped me greatly with all the research needed for my course' (Clinical Nurse Specialist).

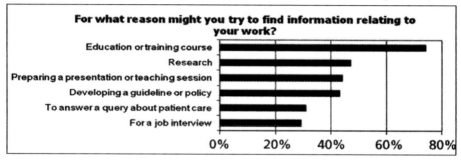

Figure 6.1 *Reasons for seeking information*

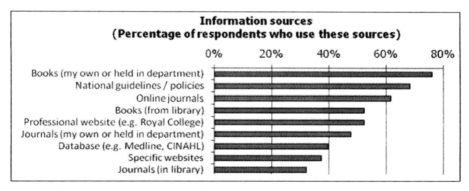

Figure 6.2 *Information sources used by health care staff*

Supporting varied audiences

Regular assessment of user needs is important to ensure that the library staff are able to understand research and study needs and provide the support required by health service staff. Libraries that have an active clinical librarian or outreach librarian service have an ideal opportunity to liaise closely with the very staff who are likely to need the resources of the library. This interaction can incorporate brief education interventions to engender a culture of evidence-based practice by offering to carry out literature searches, advising staff on resources available locally and nationally, and offering training in how to access and use information resources effectively. Research has shown that effective literature searching, carried out by information professionals, can save time and money (Brettle, Hulme and Ormandy, 2006). Literature searching requires not only specialist searching skills – knowledge and understanding of resources, search strategies, the evidence hierarchy, research methodologies – but also dedicated time in which to carry out searches. Busy health professionals simply do not have the time to carry out systematic searches of the literature. PubMed cites over 20 million papers and it is estimated that an 'average specialist' reads 322 articles per year. A new recruit into the subspecialty of diagnostic imaging in cardiology would have to read over 400,000 papers on the subject (five per hour throughout the working day) – and would finish just in time to retire! (Fraser and Dunstan, 2010).

Universities provide extensive reading lists and blended learning facilities for students; therefore liaison between NHS libraries and university partners is essential to ensure that the learning opportunities (online and physical) offered by the university are further supported by the workplace library. This is particularly important as reform of postgraduate medical education and the implementation of the European Working Time Directive (EWTD) have led to difficulties in the provision of training and educational opportunities for junior doctors.

Information literacy

This move from traditional learning methods is increasingly reflected in the workplace as digital technology becomes commonplace and mobile, wireless and personal devices are incorporated into everyday practice. More and more health care organizations are recognizing the value of digital technologies as they redesign services to improve care, reduce error and create more cost-effective pathways of service delivery (Panella, Vanhaecht and Sermeus, 2009). Libraries must make sure they harness new technologies to deliver information at the point of need, incorporating knowledge and educational opportunities into clinical decision making tools. This is still in its infancy in health libraries but some innovative librarians are coming to the fore in testing and reporting on their use (Honeybourne, Sutton and Ward, 2006; McGowan et al., 2010 and Jessie McGowan in Chapter 3).

Changing roles

Libraries in NHS organizations are changing rapidly and have been developing over a number of years. This is largely due to three factors:

1 The explosion in the amount of information available.
2 The emerging technologies being developed to access, generate and share information.
3 The recognition by government and health leaders that learning, development, research and education are major players in the current provision of health care and that the NHS's greatest asset is its staff (Department of Health, 2008).

Libraries must therefore be prepared to offer a much more diverse range of resources and services. Indeed, library managers are being recognized as valuable assets in other parts of the organization and many are being given specific projects quite apart from their role as library professionals. A brief poll of colleagues across the north-west of England has demonstrated some of these diverse roles (some of which are described in the cases in this book) and include: e-learning lead – developing and implementing e-learning packages for health care staff; reader in residence co-ordinator – setting up reading groups within mental health services to improve the health and well-being of service users; web services manager; records management champion; and projects around patient safety, lessons learned, workforce development and staff appraisal, well-being and self-help, patient and public information, equality and diversity, to name but a few. Library staff need the skills to be able to provide whatever is asked of them – whether it be searching for specific information relating to service improvement or designing a new library service.

The relevance and importance of library resources to continuing lifelong learning and professional development of the NHS workforce will remain throughout an individual's professional career. Excellence in education and development activity is necessary to 'drive knowledge creation and new service models through evidence-based research and innovation' (Department of Health, 2010a). Whether library users acknowledge the value of the staff who gave them these skills remains largely irrelevant. If the library can offer a good grounding in accessing, sifting, synthesizing and sorting relevant information, then we can be sure that today's students have skills that will remain with them through their studies and into their professional lives. It is not just a question of delivering the information or the ability to find and manage information – but an enthusiasm for continuing to access and use relevant information. The evidence-based health care movement has had a mixed reception over the years but there is no denying the value of research evidence in improving patient care and delivery of health services, and the NHS reforms continually emphasize the need for high quality evidence to be put into practice (Department of Health, 2010b).

As librarians we are equipping today's learners with the essential information tools and skills they will need as tomorrow's health care professionals. The following case studies illustrate a range of ways that this can be done.

❖❖❖

Case study 6:1 Clinical Information Specialist

Michelle Maden-Jenkins, Aintree Hospital/Edgehill University, UK

Overview

As a Clinical Information Specialist (CIS) I provide a responsive and proactive information service to support the information and research needs of all NHS staff across two acute trusts and one primary care trust. I deliver a responsive literature searching service at the point of need to provide NHS staff with the best available evidence with which to make informed evidence-based decisions relating to patient care or to support their research needs.

Other aspects of the role involve training NHS staff to locate the information themselves and to assess the quality of the evidence found in order to assess its applicability to their practice. In addition the service offers tailored information support/consultancy for specific projects (e.g. Practice Development Unit accreditation) and groups (e.g. journal clubs).

One of the main aims of the CIS service is to save health care professionals' time in locating relevant, quality information to support their needs. The outreach nature of the service means that health care professionals do not have to physically enter the library to use the CIS service. Literature search requests are frequently sent remotely via e-mail, and information literacy training (e.g. literature searching, critical appraisal) can be delivered within the end-user workplace.

Advantages and challenges

The advantage of providing an outreach service is that it allows the opportunity to 'get out of the library' and meet health care professionals in their own environment. In doing so it increases my awareness of the environment within which end-users operate on a day to day basis and provides a chance to learn and understand end-user terminology, which helps with formulating literature searches. Indeed, the variety in the nature of literature search requests keeps the work stimulating: no two searches are ever the same and each one requires a different approach to meet end-user requirements.

Probably the most enjoyable aspect of the role is the appreciation shown by the health care professionals who have used the service. The realization that they have spent so long struggling to locate relevant literature or assess the quality of a paper, when one hour spent learning how to formulate a structured search or use critical appraisal checklists could have saved them valuable time and effort, indicates the value of the service.

One of the main challenges in delivering the CIS service is twofold: effective time management and achieving a balance between actively promoting the service and workload. Requests made for literature searches often require a quick turnaround, especially if they are patient care related. This means that workload has to be prioritized and with only one CIS to support NHS staff across three trusts the difficulty lies in maintaining visibility of the service without being inundated with requests. This requires adopting an organized and strategic approach to marketing the service.

The other major challenge lies in effective marketing of the CIS service to distinguish it from other library services and in making the service relevant to potential users. It is important to be proactive in attending trust directorate/audit meetings to demonstrate *how* the service can help rather than simply detail *what* services are offered. If health care professionals have evidence that the service can save them time and provide them with the skills to locate exactly what information they want and how to assess its quality they will be more likely to use it. The best way this can be achieved is to highlight specific instances of how the CIS service has impacted on health care professionals' working practice.

Finally, as information literacy training is regarded as optional rather than mandatory, encouraging busy health care professionals to attend can therefore be a challenge. It is essential that the training offered is both relevant to the end-user and can be delivered on a flexible basis. Identifying areas in which training can support trust research and development or clinical education objectives is a useful method in marketing and promoting the training.

The biggest change to my role over the last five years has been my increasing involvement with delivering critical appraisal training. Being involved with journal clubs highlighted the fact that the time was often being used to disseminate the results of a paper rather than assess the quality of the research to determine its applicability to practice. It became apparent that many health care professionals were not confident in assessing the quality of research or interpreting statistics.

No other trust departments were running critical appraisal training and I saw this as an opportunity to 'fill a gap' and to promote the library by delivering services beyond those traditionally offered by librarians. Introductory workshops on the critical appraisal of common research designs (systematic reviews, RCTs) were well received and have expanded to include overviews of research methods and interpreting statistics for critical appraisal.

Delivering such training has required me to learn a new set of skills including teaching and learning pedagogy, research methodology, critical appraisal, statistics and writing for publication. The relevancy of the training is reflected in the fact that there is more demand for places on the critical appraisal training than the literature search training.

The future

One of the best ways of ensuring the relevancy of the CIS service is to be aware of and anticipate end-user needs. This can be achieved by taking a proactive approach and immersing yourself within the health care professional environment, for example by attending journal clubs and team/departmental meetings. In doing so, it may require the acquisition of new knowledge and skills to deliver new services/training (e.g. critical appraisal).

In addition it is important to be aware of regional and national developments that may help to make the service more attractive to health care professionals, for example linking in information literacy training outcomes in order to meet national initiatives (e.g. the NHS Knowledge and Skills Framework).

Finally, demonstrating how the service impacts on the working practice of health care professionals and the organization within which they work using specific examples is essential to highlight its value and worth.

Case study 6:2 A librarian's role in e-learning

Valentina Comba, Manager of University of Bologna E-Learning Centre, University of Bologna, Italy

Introduction – communication in the digital age

At the end of the nineties, as medical libraries co-ordinator at the University of Torino (Italy) I was aware of the extraordinary change that the internet and electronic resources were introducing into our profession. For many of us – near the end of our careers – the change was so major that the softest choice was retirement; for others it has been necessary to retrain. I felt the need to read and widen my knowledge and perception about what was happening.

That was the context in which I wrote the book *Comunicare Nell'era Digitale* (Comba, 2000), a set of essays in which, starting from the *Pragmatics of Human Communication* – the very famous book of Watzlawick and his colleagues (1967) at Palo Alto – the differences between face to face and distance communication were discussed and their impact on important library services: information literacy, reference, digital libraries.

Studying and reading in preparation for writing the book helped me to widen my professional view on new distance services for library users; but the most crucial aspect I discovered through the Paolo Alto studies was the importance of active interaction in communication. Active interaction explains the success of digital or virtual reference – and related – services, and the limited use of digital library services where no active guidance is provided. In fact, at the time I wrote the book, very few studies were devoted to the human aspects and social use of digital libraries; a very important study, which is cited in the book, is by Ann Bishop and Susan Leigh Star (Bishop and Star, 1996). Another author, to whom I owe the crucial understanding of communication in the computer/engineering environment, is Rob Kling and his studies around social informatics (see Kling, 1999; Kling, Rosenbaum and Sawyer, 2005). Since 2000, research about human behaviour and digital information systems has grown and continues to develop.

From digital libraries to e-learning

In July 2002 I moved to the University of Bologna, where I was appointed head of the Digital Library Project. Within the scope of this project I supported two subprojects, one about 'digital reference services' and the other about 'information literacy training'. The move to e-learning happened in part by chance and in part because of my new background knowledge about human communication. In November 2003 I invited to Bologna an Italian 'guru' of e-learning, Guglielmo Trentin, to lead a workshop for librarians about the use of e-learning to teach information literacy. On that occasion the Head of Administration of the University of Bologna asked me whether I would be interested in moving to the distance learning field, and my answer was 'yes'.

It has been very hard and, until very recently, I have had frequent difficulties, especially with the academic specialists in the field. The 'traditional librarian stereotype' is hard to overcome; moreover, I moved when I was already at the top of my career of 'digital librarian' and very well known at international level. But I tried to do my best, and eventually attended a master's course on 'Learning Processes' Management', where lessons about planning and evaluation of training courses made me more aware of the basics, around methods of pedagogy and training.

I now work in the University of Bologna E-Learning Centre as manager, and my main tasks involve service development for faculties, the organization and training of the Centre's staff, international marketing of the University of Bologna for e-learning and promotion of e-learning among librarians, especially for use in information literacy training.

The main assumption is always based on the need for active interaction, in distance and face to face learning, in order to teach in an effective way. And this assumption has proven to be true in some recent experiences: during a course for hospital doctors in blended learning (Comba et al., 2009) and University of Bologna's librarians Moodle platform utilization for information literacy courses.

Other important aspects of my present job are the relationships with other university areas, i.e. quality assurance for didactic teaching, student career guidance services and European project support – especially in relation to online training.

The wide experience in international relations has been very helpful: in my librarian career I had the chance to be in contact with many colleagues abroad – I was one of the founding members of the European Association of Health Information and Libraries, and a member of the IFLA (International Federation of Library Aassociations and Institutions) Section of Reference and Information Services. For example, some contacts in the libraries 'milieu' helped me to visit, in the early stages of my new position, the Open University (UK) at Milton Keynes, to find out more about distance learning delivery. In general, the basic approach I have adopted is never to assume that I have a new idea or a new problem without checking what is happening in other countries.

Other important skills and knowledge that are crucial in my present job are competencies in knowledge management and scholarly communication, as well as metadata preparation, intellectual property rights, copyright and basic IT skills. On scholarly communication, I think that awareness about how research content is intertwined with learning materials is essential. One of the most important discussions in the contemporary academic environment is about quality of learning in the distance learning approach (and blended learning), and how to make sustainable the e-learning approach to lifelong learning. When research is not being brought continuously into the teaching content, the quality of the content gets poorer, and there are many negative consequences for the students' own attitudes towards their current and future learning. But, to be honest, the most important skill I acknowledge to be crucial for the present job, is the ability to search – and find (!) – the information I need to carry on the most difficult tasks. Therefore, I still subscribe to academic library and information science mailing lists. The 'information scientist' touch – selecting citations, picking websites, or, nowadays, videos and images, finding the right author who wrote the paper that I need just in time – has been, and currently is, my rescue, my secret weapon. Even approaching the social networking environment I frequently recall those skills: they represent an inherent basic knowledge that I think is essential for my way of working.

Case study 6.3 Liaison Librarian

Lorie Kloda, McGill University Life Sciences Library, Montreal, Canada

Brief role description

As the liaison to several departments within the university's Faculty of Medicine, my role includes the selection of materials, provision of instruction and reference services, as well as access to information through the library website and other media. I also manage projects and collaborate with researchers to conduct thorough literature searches.

Overview

Being a health sciences librarian in an academic setting means doing a lot of things academic librarians typically do on a daily basis: providing a reference service at the desk, on the phone, via e-mail and chat service; designing and delivering information literacy sessions; purchasing materials for the collection; and, of course, attending meetings for various committees. On any given day, however, I may do all or none of these things. It often seems as though providing a traditional reference service or offering hands-on workshops on how to search the literature have become so routine that I sometimes do not notice them. More and more I find myself scheduled for one on one consultations with students or faculty conducting research and requiring more in-depth services. Graduate students hoping to focus their research topic, or researchers preparing for grant applications will often make an appointment, lasting an hour or more, to explore the literature alongside a librarian to ensure they have a good grasp of what is available, how to find it and how to obtain the full text for reading.

These consults frequently follow subject-specific information literacy workshops I have provided in the context of their courses, or as a result of outreach to faculty members. Much of my job relies on ensuring my user groups are aware that I am their librarian (hence the title, 'Liaison Librarian'). As members of the faculty become aware of my expertise, I am invited to provide workshops, and present on various topics such as scholarly communication and evidence-based practice. These workshops and presentations can target students, faculty and sometimes clinicians at affiliated health centres. In designing and delivering these workshops, I collaborate with other university librarians, hospital librarians and occasionally with faculty in order to meet the diverse needs of the different user groups.

An important component of my liaison duties is to ensure the collections for my department are complete and meet the teaching, learning and research needs of current users. An additional challenge is to try to anticipate the needs in the near future, by purchasing monographs and collections of electronic books in sufficient quantities. It is important to balance core texts with items that may be less known, yet relevant to researchers' current agendas and teaching trends. As well, de-selection of older materials, especially in the clinical sciences, is important for maintaining a useful, healthy collection for students of the health professions.

Systematic reviews have become increasingly popular in the health and social sciences. One of the skills librarians typically possess is that of 'expert searcher' and, in the health sciences, this entails not only expertise in information retrieval, but knowledge of sources and of the subject area. With over ten years' experience working as an information professional in health care settings, I can confidently state that I have reached a level of expertise in searching the medical literature that allows me to participate in research teams conducting systematic reviews.

The role of the librarian in the systematic review research process can vary, and at times I may find myself at one end of the spectrum offering advice on a search strategy, and at other times as a full-fledged member of a research team, which involves more time and work, and typically results in co-authorship of any presentations or publications. Systematic reviews are becoming more common as standard, prior to undertaking new trials or in preparation of a grant application, and I am increasingly called on to advise researchers on the methodology.

Advantages and challenges

The best thing about working as an academic health sciences librarian is the constant interaction with faculty and students. New students and new hires mean that every year I am introduced to many new researchers, with new and exciting research agendas. This keeps my job interesting, and satisfies my constant curiosity to learn about new topics and be involved in diverse projects.

Initially, I was hired in the academic setting as a reference and instruction librarian, focusing on information literacy instruction, and teaching several components of a course on evidence-based medicine. Over time, as I gained expertise in searching the medical literature, and as faculty got more acquainted with me and the services I provide, I was asked to collaborate on research endeavours, and to offer more specialized instruction in the faculty development office. In North America, over the past several years, we have seen a shift in academic libraries from the reference and instruction librarian, to the liaison model of librarianship. When my position title changed to that of Liaison Librarian, my existing relationships helped shape the evolving role I play in the health sciences library. Due to my knowledge and skills in evidence-based medicine and systematic review methods, I am now liaison to several health sciences departments, including epidemiology. Nevertheless I maintain my original role by providing reference and instruction services, and I have added collections and departmental outreach to these roles.

The biggest challenge I face in my position is the speed at which I must turnaround literature search requests, and meeting similar research deadlines for users who are already busy themselves. In addition, I find it an entertaining challenge to try to keep current with the technologies available for teaching and learning in higher education. The diversity of tools, and the necessary skills required to make use of these, is almost dizzying, but can also prove a pleasant distraction, and an incentive to try something new when offering a general workshop on searching MEDLINE, for instance.

The future

In the future, I expect the requests for expert searching to increase, as well as the number of sources and tools used to conduct them. Conducting a good reference interview, one of the most important skills I learned in becoming a librarian, remains as important as ever. In order to meet the demands of my user groups on campus and in hospitals, excellent communication and presentation skills are essential. The library's role as an advocate for open access means that I will need to be able to share my knowledge about, and my role in, scholarly communication with faculty and students. Most of all, as a librarian, I need to be familiar with the rapidly changing information needs and behaviour of health sciences students, clinicians and researchers.

Case study 6.4 The librarian as information broker, educator and change manager in primary care

Sue Lacey Bryant, Associate Director of GP Consortia Development/Chief Knowledge Officer, NHS Milton Keynes, UK

Overview

Staffing for knowledge support for primary care in Milton Keynes has expanded in recent years, seeing the consolidation of a first class knowledge team committed to tailoring and targeting knowledge services for primary care. These developments are described in this case, alongside the roles for librarians that have come about as a result.

The Primary Care Trust (PCT) has a Library Service Level Agreement (SLA) with Milton Keynes Foundation Hospital Trust Library for provision of services to primary care, which encompasses both the commissioning and provider arms of the PCT and general practice. Historically, the PCT has made a generous allocation to the Trust for library services, benchmarked across South-central Strategic Health Authority (SHA), and from this the library had appointed a 0.5wte (whole time equivalent) Outreach Librarian post, working with practices out of the library.

The development of local knowledge services, supported by the expansion of staffing, has been enabled through:

1 Optimizing opportunities offered by Quality:MK (a large-scale quality improvement programme funded by The Health Foundation 2007-10) to:
   - pilot role redesign, tailoring services for primary care, and targeting these
   - make visible the ability of librarians to actively manage knowledge, enable evidence-based practice and contribute to efficiency and quality improvement.
2 Innovation in response to a regional decision to allocate per capita library funding by health organization, which allowed the commissioning arm to establish a new 0.8wte role (originally denoted as Commissioning Librarian):
   - Strong contract management by the PCT to prompt service review and assessment of impact and achieve value for money from its Library SLA, leading to the extension of the hours of the outreach post from 0.5 to 1wte.

Beyond this, the development of the vision, confidence and perseverance to perceive and seize the opportunities that have presented over the past four or five years can be traced back to earlier influences on Milton Keynes, notably:

- a strong tradition of collaborative working by committed librarians employed in different parts of the health economy
- the original development of the Outreach Librarian role by the hospital library (using project monies)
- the hosting of the National Library for Health Primary Care and Public Health Librarian Support programme by the Public Health Directorate of the PCT 2004-7
- programme management of Quality:MK by a Chartered Librarian.

An evolving role

As a Chartered Librarian who joined the NHS as a Health Education/Information Officer in Croydon in early 1980s, I later enjoyed a long and varied career as an independent information specialist. Alongside activities to support the professional development for librarians, a portfolio of work as a practice librarian and knowledge manager in the Aylesbury area in the early 1990s served as a springboard to extend my skills and experience, principally into aspects of knowledge service development and health informatics.

My links with Milton Keynes while completing contract work with the National Library for Health afforded an opportunity for local librarians to engage with senior NHS managers, initially via a survey. Primary care leaders articulated their top three priorities for the library service as support for evidence-based practice, alerting services and information skills training. The subsequent launch of Quality:MK opened up opportunities to address these needs.

Invited to take on the role of knowledge manager for Quality:MK early in 2007, the opportunity for me to manage the programme as a whole arose unexpectedly in May.

Seizing the day opened up fresh opportunities to pilot initiatives to support evidence-based practice, and expand knowledge services fully aligned to the priorities of primary care.

Quality:MK was an ambitious change management programme championed by high profile stakeholders. Funded as part of The Health Foundation's initiative on Engaging with Quality in Primary Care, the focus was to deliver a whole system approach to quality improvement. A partnership of the PCT, the Centre for Evidence-Based Medicine at Oxford, the Public and Patient Involvement Forum and *health:mk* (the practice based commissioning collaborative), Quality:MK was committed to three principles: public- and patient-centred care, based on best evidence, driven by primary care.

By leading a core, part-time team of GP champions, librarians and a pharmacist, I managed an ambitious portfolio of projects, supporting a wide circle of project leads. The team experimented with tools and techniques and piloted initiatives, and shaped system and day to day processes. Quality:MK offered professional development opportunities for project staff and leads, and for other NHS managers and GPs interested in the work. These ranged from influencing skills to training in evidence-based practice.

A first class knowledge team to support decision making in primary care

The librarians work together to ensure that information is available and used to support decision making in four priority areas:

1 Strategic decisions about the commissioning and procurement of secondary and specialist care.
2 Revision of local care pathways across the boundaries between acute and primary and social care in Milton Keynes.
3 Changes in practice based on group discussions among primary health care teams to review best evidence.
4 Multiple day to day decisions agreed between doctor and patient.

The virtual primary care knowledge team comprises four posts that serve primary and community care and general practices in Milton Keynes:

1 A full-time Primary Care/e-Learning Librarian post working out of the postgraduate medical library (with 0.8wte focused on community services and general practice).
2 A 0.8wte Knowledge Officer (KO) (developed as a Commissioning Librarian role).
3 A full-time Associate Director post that incorporates the Chief Knowledge Officer (CKO) role.
4 Information support from a freelance information specialist.

The Primary Care/e-Learning Librarian is the only member of the team physically based in a library (and that for only part of the time), while the KO and CKO work within the heart of health care commissioning teams at the headquarters of NHS Milton Keynes. The freelance information specialist works remotely.

Knowledge Officer, NHS Milton Keynes: Anne Gray

This role, as an information broker working as part of the health care team to support pathway review and development, and commissioning changes, was piloted through Quality:MK as a part-time Outreach Librarian. The post was met with some reticence at first, but it was soon recognized that a librarian's input can improve the quality of the evidence used to support decision making, and save valuable time for NHS managers. The role developed into a Commissioning Librarian (0.8wte), charged to embed and support the use of evidence within commissioning processes in March 2009 and then as a KO as part of an organizational restructure in 2010. This was undertaken to anticipate future transitions for PCT staff as its roles and responsibilities are handed on to successor organizations. Working alongside a Public Health Information Analyst, the KO now reports to a Consultant in Public Health, and the role encompasses:

1 Information support – prospectively and on request:
   – Profiling the interests of teams, supporting evidence-based discussions.
   – Supporting commissioners to tackle strategic priorities: bringing information skills and timely support to the commissioning process, contributing as a full member of project teams, enabling evidence-based decision making by programme boards.
   – Compiling updates on evidence for planning groups and local implementation teams, e.g. on respiratory, stroke and neurological condition pathways.
   – Enquiries about models of service and literature searches on key topics are conducted on request backed up by occasional bulletins that highlight new publications.
2 Alerting services – helping staff to keep up to date:
   – Knowledge@lerts tailored for commissioners, GPs and community health teams to highlight top news items relevant to organizational priorities.
   – Signposting staff working within particular programmes to alerting services to help them keep up to date with critical developments in health care.
3 Information skills training – specialist training in information sources and critical appraisal skills to facilitate evidence-based practice.
4 Enabling access:
   – Publicizing resources.
   – Maintaining the knowledge zone, learning zone and Public Health Intelligence portal at www.qualitymk.nhs.uk.

Information Specialist: Ann Skinner

The role began as a freelance post focused on disseminating information from IMPACTE (Improving Medical Practice by Assessing CurrenT Evidence, www.miltonkeynes.nhs.uk/default.asp?ContentID=2988#what) groups, organizing and structuring information in an electronic environment, promotional activities, supporting the development of alerting services and providing back-up searching services, as needed. Now contracted by the Chief Knowledge Officer, the role involves:

1 Working closely with the librarians, the communications team and commercial web service provider to disseminate information via the Trust intranet and the PCT website.
2 Web enable information products – such as the NHS Milton Keynes Commissioning and Contracting Manual.
3 Working with staff involved in different phases of the commissioning pipeline across the Trust, e.g. mapping information flows in order to devise a suitable online architecture.

Primary Care/e-Learning Librarian: Linda Potter

Following a review of the services provided by the hospital library in October 2009, a full-time Primary Care/e-Learning Librarian was appointed to the postgraduate library to work with community health services and with primary health care teams in general practice. The role covers:

1 Informing and supporting best practice:
   – Supporting the implementation of best evidence by working closely with GP champions who lead work on managing GP referrals and peer review.
   – Encouraging the implementation of best practice via IMPACTE – small group, self-education sessions commonly within a single practice or community care setting.
2 Sharing expertise and supporting professional development:
   – Information skills training so that NHS staff can find the evidence for themselves and recognize when it is most cost-effective to hand it over to the knowledge team.
   – Critical appraisal of evidence to support IMPACTE groups.
3 Supporting e-learning:
   – Developing a collection of e-learning resources for clinicians and managers.
   – Ensuring access to the National Learning Management System from library PCs.
4 Enabling access:
   – Publicizing resources.
   – Maintaining the sections on GP referrals and IMPACTE groups, contributing to the knowledge zone and learning zone at www.qualitymk.nhs.uk.

5 Library management:
  - Deputizing for the Library Services Manager as needed.

Associate Director of GP Consortia Development/Chief Knowledge Officer: Sue Lacey Bryant

Quality:MK raised local awareness of the importance of knowledge management as an integral feature of evidence-based practice, quality improvement and change management. This in turn led to the recruitment of a Chief Knowledge Officer (CKO) by NHS Milton Keynes, to which I was appointed in September 2009.

This role focused on:

1 Ensuring relevant experience, evidence, research, information and data were made available to and used by staff to inform commissioning and policy making.
2 Mainstreaming Quality:MK to develop a self-improving system within which learning is made explicit and transferred, and systems and processes improved.
3 Enabling staff to define information needs and make best use of information and data.
4 Developing a whole system approach to service review and care pathway development.
5 Leading the organization to achieve relevant World Class Commissioning competencies.

As part of the organizational restructure in November 2010, I was appointed to a wider change management role as Associate Director of GP Consortia Development, within which knowledge management sits as one component. Responsibilities include:

1 Focusing on the formation, early transitional arrangements and final form of local GP commissioning consortia.
2 Identifying and supporting local clinical leadership and plan the transfer of technical skills in commissioning to consortia.
3 Spreading learning in primary care and embedding good practice for the future.
4 Ensuring robust engagement of the public and clinicians in all processes.
5 Responsibility for knowledge and information management:
  - Ensuring that strategic and operational activity is informed by sound evidence.
  - Managing the following teams as streamlined, forward thinking, externally focused services that support Trust priorities, national imperatives and consortia formation: Business Intelligence and Performance Management; Primary Care Systems Implementation; Referrals Support Service; GP Appraisal Administrative Support.
6 Directing the work on health informatics, and supporting knowledge management, conducted by external specialists on behalf of the Trust:

- Enabling staff to define information needs and make best use of information and data, striving to ensure that good quality data is available and provided in user-friendly formats to inform decision making.
7 Enabling the co-ordination and optimization of relevant tools and mechanisms:
  - Working with colleagues on practical approaches to capturing organizational knowledge, so that 'know-how' is made explicit and transferred as an aspect of system reform.

Pending vertical integration of the PCT's provider services with the Hospital in 2011, I retain responsibility for monitoring our Library SLA and for directing the Primary Care/e-Learning Librarian.

Challenges

Health is a knowledge-based industry. As NHS managers take responsibility for shaping new-style health care organizations that must innovate to provide efficient, productive, leaner and patient-focused services, knowledge becomes an ever more vital asset for the NHS.

Moving through the 2010s the information needs of primary care are changing – partly in response to the reconfiguration of health services in the UK as the NHS seeks to address the growing demands on health care from older and sicker patients. With the integration of community health services into hospitals, the shift of public health into the remit of local authorities, and the focus on delivering care across the health and social care divide, totemic organizational barriers that hold neither meaning nor value for patients become redundant.

The speed of change, and the harsh economic environment in which it is being conducted, raise the stakes for health library and information professionals as public servants whose skill set remains poorly understood by the clientele they serve. Indeed, even the concept of 'the library service' is flawed – for it is innovative new roles in the workplace and effective co-operative working focused on organizational priorities and client needs, irrespective of organizational boundaries, that are making the difference in Milton Keynes.

Those committed to evidence-based practice will need to remain fleet of foot, demonstrating their worth and riding the changes to withstand the cost-efficiency savings ahead. The mission is to be seen as an essential part of the solution to the productivity challenge rather than a budget line competing with front line health service providers.

The future

In Milton Keynes there remains much yet to be done to mainstream evidence-based practice into primary care. However, the development of new roles for librarians, and the current positioning of these posts, points to potential new futures – whether in the local authority or perhaps with the new National Commissioning Board, in PCT clusters or supporting GP commissioners.

More broadly, there is an imperative for all NHS library services to modernize by amalgamating back office functions wherever possible, sharing services across a wider geographical and customer base and also specializing, as appropriate. The mission is to reduce overheads and processing costs and free up the time of qualified librarians so that they can understand priorities, work with clients and develop information products and services that add value to the information they deliver.

This review of the different roles that librarians play in supporting primary care in Milton Keynes points to one way forward in the future – seeing health librarians moving away from the library into the workplace, where they can optimize their people skills as well as their expertise in finding and presenting information, while utilizing electronic access as a tool rather than giving it undue focus.

Part of the success of this experienced team lies in building on long established best practice in health libraries. Beyond that, and right at the heart of their work, lies a strong sense of vocation, a willingness to try different approaches and a shared passion and commitment to evidence-based practice.

Conclusion

This chapter has described the librarian as information provider and educator. Both Pat Spoor and Debra Thornton emphasize the need for health librarians to be involved in both provider and educator roles, although as can be seen from Michelle Maden-Jenkin's and Valentina Comba's case studies, roles in both HEIs and within the health service may focus more on the education than provision side. In terms of education, there is an emphasis on developing 'pedagogically sound e-learning resources' and as Valentina Comba suggests, it is important to develop knowledge and expertise 'around methods of pedagogy and training' in order to be taken seriously and accepted by other academics, with whom it is important to develop strong relationships. Training may not be restricted to literature searching and information literacy, and Michelle Maden-Jenkins has found that developing knowledge and expertise in critical appraisal and research design and adding this to her teaching portfolio was not only an 'opportunity to fill a gap' but has led to 'more demand for ... critical appraisal training than ... literature searching training'. For Lorie Kloda, becoming involved in this type of training has led to increased involvement and collaborations on research projects and systematic reviews (topics that are further explored by Alison Brettle in Chapter 8). Diversification such as this can lead to other opportunities, and Debra Thornton suggests that 'library managers are [increasingly] being recognized as valuable assets in other parts of the organization', a point which is well illustrated by Sue Lacey Bryant who describes how the library service has expanded from one role to four, spanning providing, educating, commissioning and dissemination within primary care.

Anticipating user needs, developing professional relationships and acquiring new knowledge are key factors in developing roles and ensuring the quality of service provided. Michelle Maden-Jenkins suggests that one of the ways this can be achieved is by 'taking a proactive approach and immersing yourself within the health care professional environment, for example by attending [meetings and] journal clubs'. Valentina Comba developed a subject expertise and suggests that 'the move to e-learning happened in part by chance ... because of my new background knowledge' and Sue Lacey Bryant recommends having 'confidence and perseverance ... to seize opportunities'.

Despite this diversification the need for traditional skills does not go away. Lorie Kloda notes that 'conducting a good reference interview, [remains] one of the most important skills I learned' in order to meet the demands and anticipate the needs of her user groups whilst Valentina Comba asserts that 'the information scientist touch – selecting citations, picking websites ... finding the right author just in time ... is my secret weapon'. But how can these skills be used in the future? Sue Lacey Bryant suggests that one way is for health librarians to 'optimize their people skills as well as their expertise in finding and presenting information, while utilizing electronic access as a tool rather than giving it undue focus'. Adopting this approach as well as seizing opportunities as they come along may well stand librarians in good stead for maintaining their professional niche at the same time as ensuring they have a future role.

References

Bishop, A. P. and Star, S. L. (1996) Social Informatics of Digital Libraries Use and Infrastructure, *Annual Review of Information Science and Technology*, **31**, 301–401.

Brettle, A. (2003) Information Skills Training: a systematic review of the literature, *Health Information Libraries Journal*, **20** (suppl. 1), s3–9.

Brettle, A. Hulme C. and Ormandy, P. (2006) The Costs and Effectiveness of Information-skills Training and Mediated Searching: quantitative results from the EMPIRIC project, *Health Information and Libraries Journal*, **23** (4) 239–47.

Browne, J. (2010) *Securing a Sustainable Future for Higher Education: an independent review of higher education funding and student finance* (Browne Report), http://hereview.independent.gov.uk/hereview/report/.

Comba, V. (2000) *Comunicare Nell'era Digitale*, Bibliografica.

Comba, V., De Franco, S., Lori, R. and Reggiani, A. (2009) ILB, an E-learning Course for Hospital Doctors in the Regione Emilia Romagna: regenerating the medical librarian profession. In *Positioning the Profession - International Conference on Medical Librarianship, Brisbane (Australia), 31 August-4 September 2009*, http://eprints.rclis.org/16782/.

Corrall, S. (2008) Information Literacy Strategy Development in Higher Education: an exploratory study, *International Journal of Information Management*, **28** (1), 26–37.

Coughlan, S. (2010) University Gives Students Text Books on iPhones, *BBC News*, www.bbc.co.uk/news/education-11427317.

Department of Health (2008) *A High Quality Workforce: NHS Next Stage Review*, Department of Health.

Department of Health (2010a) *Liberating the NHS: developing the healthcare workforce - a consultation on proposals*, Department of Health.

Department of Health (2010b) *Equality and Excellence: liberating the NHS*, Cm 7881, The Stationery Office.

Fraser, A. G. and Dunstan, F. D. (2010) On the Impossibility of Being Expert, *BMJ*, **341** (7786), 1314-15.

Honeybourne. C., Sutton, S. and Ward, L. (2006) Knowledge in the Palm of your Hands: PDAs in the clinical setting, *Health Information and Libraries Journal*, **23** (1), 51-9.

Kling, R. (1999) What is Social Informatics and Why Does it Matter?, *D-Lib Magazine*, **5** (1), www.dlib.org/dlib/january99/kling/01kling.html.

Kling, R., Rosenbaum, H. and Sawyer, S. (2005) *Understanding and Communicating Social Informatics: a framework for studying and teaching the human contexts of information and communications technologies*, Information Today, Inc.

McGowan, J., Hogg, W., Rader, T., Salzwedel, D., Worster, D., Cogo, E. and Rowan, M. (2010) A Rapid Evidence-based Service by Librarians Provided Information to Answer Primary Care Clinical Questions, *Health Information and Libraries Journal*, **27** (1), 11-21.

Panella, M., Vanhaecht, K. and Sermeus, W. (2009) Care Pathways: from clinical pathways to care innovation, *International Journal of Care Pathways*, **13** (2), 49-50.

Research Information Network (2010) *Challenges for Academic Libraries in Difficult Economic Times: a guide for senior institutional managers and policy makers*, RIN, www.rin.ac.uk/our-work/using-and-accessing-information-resources/challenges-academic-libraries-difficult-economic-.

Thornton, D. (2010) *Information Needs Survey of NHS Acute Trust staff*, www.lihnn.nhs.uk/lihnn-publicarea/bestpractice/.

University of Leeds (2003) *Information Literacy Strategy*, www.leeds.ac.uk/library/strategic/ilstrategy_new.pdf.

Watzlawick P., Beavin J. H. and Jackson, D. D. (1967) *Pragmatics of Human Communication*, W. W. Norton.

7

The librarian who analyses information and manages knowledge

Christine Urquhart

Introduction

Trying to provide a brief introduction to knowledge management, as perceived and practised in the health sector, is a challenge when there are so many books and articles on knowledge management. The computer scientist, the human resources manager, the information manager, staff development and the librarian – all have their perspective on knowledge management and what it should involve. The type of organization also affects the perspective on knowledge management, as an engineering organization or projects run by agencies such as the World Bank may emphasize the know-how, and the 'war stories' that staff relate to help newcomers appreciate how things are done in this organization and why. Storytelling, as it is explained by management thinkers such as Stephen Denning at the World Bank (Denning, 2000), seems very far removed from knowledge transfer and getting evidence into practice in a health service organization. Storytelling – is not that all about anecdotal evidence? That is very low down in the hierarchy of evidence for health service staff, surely. But what about the way many students are taught these days – problem-based learning, around a realistic clinical scenario or story? Clinical journals may have sections for care studies, case reports, as well as reports of research trials, and clinical decision making may be fast as it depends on scripts, outline storylines that professionals remember more easily (Urquhart, 1998).

The structures and systems that information professionals design to support better information management and knowledge management for health care staff need to reflect how people learn, particularly in the workplace. A long-term problem for many health staff is that the systems they use for patient administration just serve current needs, and although it is of course important to ensure that the record systems used are accurate and the record reflects the care provided, it is often difficult to see how the information in the patient record can be used to improve practice (Urquhart et al., 2009). Clinical audit is one step forward, and Helen Seeley (in her case study in Chapter 8) explains how her role spans clinical audit and research support. Most health organizations need to demonstrate quality and productivity and many information managers dealing with the management information statistics of health care are faced with performance improvement (e.g. for Kaiser Permanente in the USA (Schilling et al., 2010), and in England the QIPP (Quality, Innovation, Productivity and Prevention) programme (Department of Health, 2011)). There are, at the time of writing, some examples of QIPP case studies on the NHS Evidence site. An example, requiring information management, focuses on the improvement of care for people with learning disabilities. Such information management work includes: use of a care funding calculator, analysis of activity costs, benchmarking, design of outcome based reviews. The evidence base for the initiative was a guideline, one based on perceived best practice. What the QIPP case studies illustrate is the need for a whole systems approach to making changes for greater efficiency and effectiveness.

Knowledge translation requires getting knowledge accepted, used and evaluated in the complex system of health care provision. Bernstein et al. (2009) report their experience on taking screening and brief intervention programmes from research into wider practice, and they note the need for sustainability planning, which involved administrators, the billing and information technology departments, medical records coders, community service providers and government agencies. They also required local champions to encourage the shift in culture among the staff involved. Several of the case studies in this chapter echo the need for awareness of the culture, the need to be aware of what is considered best practice at present and why. As knowledge managers in health care, librarians have to do much more than simply retrieve and appraise the evidence and send it on to staff – they need to anticipate what the audience will make of the information, how to present the evidence and how to work with other professionals for efficient and effective care pathways.

Boisot's (1995) work on the social learning cycle emphasizes the stage of abstraction of knowledge (the most essential features – think of Cochrane systematic reviews), which is followed by diffusion (which requires a sharing of context – think of ways of explaining evidence insights for groups of different health professionals), absorption (learning by doing – trialling new clinical guidelines) and impacting (embedding in practice). Thornton (2009) describes how the Boisot social learning cycle informed the work of librarians with new roles at a defence research organization. Their information professional roles included Information Specialists (librarians but embedded in the subject domain, with responsibilities for education), Information Scientists (with bibliometric and data visualization expertise), Knowledge Agents (akin to clinical librarians and health informationists) and those with specialist expertise for the Knowledge Research Team (ensuring that the research of the organization is properly disseminated), for example. The titles may be different in the health sector, and the work of librarians with bibliometric expertise may only be emerging (for example, as the UK Higher Education Research Assessment begins to use more bibliometrics), but the functions are still there.

The case studies in this chapter highlight different aspects of knowledge management and include examples of health library and information professionals who are embedded in the work setting (Joanna Dundon, Mandy Beaumont, Rachel Court, for example), and one who helps run the public face of a research organization through its research repository (Anne Webb). The human resources perspective on knowledge management stresses the importance of learning, particularly the learning that takes place in teams and work groups; case examples of these include Rachel Court's virtual community of practice in health (Urquhart et al., 2010), and Mike Raynor's contribution, which considers how librarians learn when expanding their role.

Case study 7.1 NHS Evidence Specialist Collections
Rachel Court, University of Warwick

Overview
'NHS Evidence allows everyone working in health and social care to access a wide range of health information to help them deliver quality patient care' (www.evidence. nhs.uk/aboutus/Pages/AboutNHSEvidence.aspx) and its specialist collections provide topic-focused, high quality evidence. I have worked as an information specialist for 'NHS Evidence – diabetes' (www.library.nhs.uk/diabetes) and 'NHS Evidence – emergency and urgent care' (www.library.nhs.uk/emergency) since August 2003. The small team I have been working with (two information specialists, two clinical leads and an information assistant) interacts with several other groups of people. For example, both collections have an external reference group of representatives from relevant stakeholder organizations, such as professional bodies (e.g. the College of Paramedics), charities (e.g. Diabetes UK) and NHS groups (e.g. NHS Diabetes). 'NHS Evidence – emergency and urgent care' also has an editorial panel of clinicians who assist the clinical lead in selecting content for the collection. We are also part of the larger NHS Evidence team (NHS Evidence, 2011), which at the time of writing is made up of a central team based in Manchester and 30 specialist collections based in several centres around England and Wales. Many working groups and joint 'evidence updates' have been formed or undertaken involving members of this wider NHS Evidence team. Through these and through our interaction with stakeholders and clinicians, we have collectively built up a lot of experience of virtual working, making use of technology such as teleconferences, e-mail and online discussion forums where appropriate.

Much of my time in this role is spent: identifying, appraising, adding and organizing new content as specified in each collection's development policy; managing existing content; undertaking evidence updates on specific topics; and training and supervising the other information staff in our team. Despite it being entirely virtual many of the core information skills relevant to physical libraries, such as cataloguing and classification, are equally relevant to the specialist collections. New records are added to a collection either by linking to records already in the specialist collections' resource management system that have been added by another collection or imported centrally (applies to four core sources) or by creating our own records from scratch, which involves entering relevant information in a number of predetermined fields (e.g. title, URL, publication date, review date, publisher, description, topic(s)). We have developed our abstracting skills to be able to write brief, succinct descriptions of web-based documents as this helps our virtual users to decide whether they want to retrieve the full text in a setting where we are not available to advise them face to face. These information skills and others, such as systematic searching of bibliographic databases and websites, contribute greatly to maintaining a high, consistent standard in our work. Other aspects of my role have included project management, taxonomy development, evaluation of the collections, user needs research, provision of current awareness newsletters, service promotion and awareness raising and developing communities of practice. The role I have is not entirely representative of the information specialist role in all the other specialist collections. In some collections, the tasks I have described above have increasingly been divided between roles (for example, Project Manager, Senior Information Specialist, Junior Information Specialist). In my day to day work I use Microsoft Office, reference management software (ProCite) and NHS Evidence's 'in-house' Resource and Content Management Systems. I am also one of the owners of two mailing lists hosted by JISCmail.

Advantages of the role

There are many aspects to this role that I enjoy. One in particular has been the wide variety of tasks involved, such as presenting at meetings, developing collection development policies and checking sources for new content. I have also enjoyed working with and learning from some very experienced colleagues in other specialist collections.

Whilst many of the tasks we perform on a daily basis are essentially the same as they were when I started in 2003, certain aspects of my role have changed (see Yeoman et al. 2003). One major change for me has been the expansion of my team's information posts from one to three, which resulted in me undertaking people management responsibilities and identifying more routine tasks that can be done by a junior information assistant. Searching a wide range of health bibliographic databases and sifting large numbers of retrieved references for 'evidence updates' is now an essential part of the role. Critical appraisal of systematic reviews has always been part of the role for other specialist collections with a smaller evidence base, but this need is increasing for more teams as specialist collections become more involved in work for the UK Database of Uncertainties about the Effects of Treatments (DUETS) (www.library.nhs.uk/duets). The specialist collections have been asked to help identify uncertainties from research recommendations made in published systematic reviews. In the case of Cochrane Reviews, this is relatively easy as these are supposed to be of a high quality and each review contains a section on 'implications for research'. However, the quality of other systematic reviews needs to be considered before looking for any recommendations. Where critical appraisal has not already been done by others (e.g. for the Centre of Reviews and Dissemination's Database of Abstracts of Reviews of Effects (DARE) database), the specialist collection needs to organize this. Teams vary in their approach, but usually information specialists and/or associated clinicians appraise these reviews using a checklist (e.g. Critical Appraisal Skills Programme (CASP); www.sph.nhs.uk/what-we-do/public-health-workforce/resources/critical-appraisals-skills-programme).

Challenges

One of the biggest challenges in this role has been in understanding the needs of the collections' users and potential users. This has been a challenge particularly because we rarely interact with our users directly. At an early stage we defined our audience for 'NHS Evidence – emergency and urgent care' as health care professionals working for the NHS in England in the field of emergency and urgent care, regardless of setting. To try to overcome this challenge, over the years we have consulted the collection's reference group and editorial panel members, run user surveys and spoken directly to delegates at specialty conferences (e.g. College of Emergency Medicine, Trauma Care UK).

Future developments

The information specialist role for the specialist collections is expected to undergo some change in the spring of 2011, when the model for managing the specialist collections is due to change. At the time of writing, the scope of the role has not been finalized, but it appears likely that there will be more of an emphasis placed on searching, appraisal and cataloguing skills and less on the other skills, such as project management, marketing, stakeholder engagement and administration. To prepare for the future, it seems sensible to focus on these core 'information' skills. In a time of ever increasing numbers of papers, appraisal skills in particular are likely to become more important.

Case study 7.2 Developing the role of the library in setting up and managing an organizational repository

Anne Webb, The Kostoris Library, The Christie NHS Foundation Trust

Introduction

The Christie, based in Manchester, UK, was founded in 1901 and is a specialist NHS trust offering high quality diagnosis, treatment and care for cancer patients, world-class research and education in all aspects of cancer. The trust is one of Europe's leading cancer centres, treating over 40,000 patients a year and has one of the largest early phase clinical trials units in the world. The Christie has a firm base in international research, is one of seven partners in the Manchester Academic Health Science Research Centre and is also part of the Manchester Cancer Research Centre with the University of Manchester and Cancer Research UK.

The Kostoris Library is now part of the newly formed Christie School of Oncology and provides resources and services to support the research, education and the management of patient care provided by trust staff.

The Christie has a rich heritage with over 9,000 papers indexed in MEDLINE and the major research databases. Each year around 350 peer-reviewed papers are published by Christie staff in addition to many conference abstracts and other intellectual output. The library regularly provides the Research and Development (R&D) department with lists of papers and abstracts for reports on an ongoing basis and professors, doctors and researchers often request publication lists. Capturing and demonstrating this intellectual output in an easily discoverable format is a challenge and in late 2007 we embarked on the journey of trying to achieve this in a searchable repository.

In keeping with published research (Allard, Mack and Feltner-Reichert, 2005) we felt that repository management fitted into the library's role of collection development and management. We have the skills, as information professionals, to ensure that the data was consistent by adopting appropriate metadata standards. As librarians we are familiar with the structure of biomedical literature, information retrieval to locate references and best understand the technological aspects of repository software. We are also familiar with the open access movement, publishers' policies, copyright and licensing issues in relation to scholarly communication. The repository also offered the potential to raise the library's profile across the organization and encourage further engagement with the research communities.

We first researched repositories in 2006 (Glover, Webb and Gleghom, 2006), although since then the position has changed considerably as more repositories have come online. In the UK the original Securing a Hybrid Environment for Research Preservation and Access (SHERPA) partnership intended to establish the concept of the open access institutional repository and had seven partners when it was formed (2002–6) (www.sherpa.ac.uk/index.html). It now has 33 partners and affiliates (including 32 HEIs and the British Library). SHERPA also provides a variety of services to support repositories, such as RoMEO (www.sherpa.ac.uk/romeo.html) for publishers' copyright and archiving policies and OpenDOAR (www.opendoar.org) a searchable worldwide Directory of Open Access Repositories. Repositories are increasingly common in HE and specialist institutions but they have yet to be adopted in other organizations such as NHS trusts.

Developing a repository within a hospital library

The development of the Christie repository has been overseen by the library with the backing of the Trust's R&D committee. Initially we implemented our repository project through an in-house solution. With the help of a programmer and a web developer we designed a system to capture research output and deliver the information to a searchable SQL database accessed via the internet. Once we started populating and using this repository we gained valuable insight into developing content and the workflows required. However, further development of the in-house repository had limitations due to demands on interdepartmental time and resources. After examining some university repositories and making a site visit to a local university repository in late 2008 we decided to move forward with an externally hosted solution.

We started using the BioMed Central pilot repository software early 2009 and have now gone live with our permanent repository (the Christie Research Publications Repository) found at christie.openrepository.com/christie/.

Funding for the project came from a variety of sources: the purchase of the repository software was provided by the library and the NHS North West Health Care Library Unit. The annual maintenance fee for the repository is funded by the library and the work for retrospective data extraction is funded by the hospital R&D committee.

BioMed Central's Open Repository (www.openrepository.com/) software was selected as it:

- is web based and easy to use without advanced IT skills
- has a customizable interface that integrates with our web pages
- is easy to populate the database (data can be imported from PubMed)
- displays related articles from PubMed alongside Repository content
- allows control of author information for consistency in naming conventions
- integrates quality checks within submission workflow
- has a mapping feature that allows us to develop collections and departmental hierarchies
- enables us to build communities, develop departmental pages and build Researcher Profiles based on submitted content and links.

Using information skills to add value

For a variety of reasons, many repositories suffer from lack of content (Fried, Foster and Gibbons, 2005). To overcome this, the library staff manage the repository by mediating submission. Many academic organizations tend to focus only on more current literature with a limited time period for display and storage. As we want to reflect all the intellectual output of the Christie we intend our archive to go back as far as possible. We find our information management skills are used to ensure that the quality and usability of the repository is maintained. Mediating submission of content ensures consistency at the outset, whereas self-submission by the author may not.

The work for the submission of content is divided into two components:

1 Current research and research updates.
2 Retrospective and archival data for publications dating back to 1950.

The Assistant Librarian takes on the role of repository librarian and manages the processes for preparation and submission of content as part of her day-to-day role in the library. This involves sourcing current papers on a monthly basis from databases such as PubMed (MEDLINE), CINAHL and the Web of Knowledge plus any recommendations of recently published articles made by staff. Prior to submission the article metadata is quality checked to comply with the repository standards such as citation and author consistency, affiliation, appropriate keywords and inclusion of weblinks such as the article DOI (digital object identifier). Articles are submitted as soon as the quality process is complete. A separate component of the work involves a part-time, R&D funded project to capture retrospective data. The work is done on a rolling programme and at times may have several librarians involved in it on an ad hoc basis!

This has provided an opportunity for more library staff to participate and become familiar with the repository software and the submission of articles. Research articles going back over the past 50 years are sourced from a variety of resources. A part-time member of staff employed specifically on the archive project checks the article author affiliation, applies the same quality standards to the metadata and prepares it for submission to the repository, which is then done in a systematic manner. Any member of the library staff familiar with the submission process is able to undertake this work as and when time permits.

Initially the data is captured in the local in-house database and, before being deposited in the Open Repository database, it is upgraded and enhanced. This ensures authority control on the format of author names and journal names. We also add keyword metadata to the records. If the repository record is sourced using the PubMed Identifier (PMID) any available Medical Subject Headings (MeSH) assigned to the article are automatically added to the record in the repository.

What are the advantages of having a repository?

Although the repository has only been live since 2009 it has raised the library profile in the trust and developed our relationships with R&D. We have had positive feedback from both trust staff and external visitors. It has demonstrated one way in which we can support the dissemination of research and assist in the development of new relationships and collaborations.

By viewing the usage metrics associated with the repository we can see that research from the Christie is being viewed across the world. We have also used the repository to assist others to find key Christie researchers in specialist topics and it has been added to trust study day guides and bibliographies. Cancer Research UK, one of our main funding bodies, supports open access (as does the NHS), so many grant holders will therefore be able to deposit into the repository to meet funding requirements.

The repository also:

- enhances our researchers' profiles and demonstrates the impact of their research
- facilitates the provision of reports on research activity across the organization
- allows researchers to create their own listings and feed them into other collaborations and websites
- provides a facility for all research authors to quickly create their own web presence and make it easier for them to link to other like-minded researchers, and develop new contacts and collaborations

- consolidates the library's position with R&D activities and increases both our interaction with researchers and our understanding of their research.

The biggest challenge

The biggest challenge so far has been developing the workflow for administering the repository. We had an ambitious project to ensure all Christie research output spanning over 50 years was collated in a consistent manner. In the future the challenge is likely to be sustaining content development and ensuring that there are both the financial and human resources to continue.

The future

The involvement of librarians in the management of repositories should help position librarians in the mainstream research activities and consolidate their role as information providers and managers of access to knowledge. Repositories fit well with the information professional's role as a steward of digital content. Our skills in managing content, assigning metadata and understanding authority control blend naturally with repository work. However, several challenges remain for the future development of repositories in general. Having a clear vision of what the organization aims to gain from developing a repository helps. For some it may be that the repository is to demonstrate the research output of the institution and boost its prestige by clearly linking publications to it. For others the focus may be on the researcher, creating a suitable online presence to allow intellectual output to be easily disseminated, allow them to develop a greater presence in the research community or enable discovery to a wider audience.

The organization will need to be supportive both in terms of budget and time. In times of financial constraints and reductions in workforce this may be difficult to balance. There may also be opportunities for organizations to collaborate in the development of joint repositories, easing both the funding and staffing of the project.

Encouraging authors to self-archive remains a challenge for most repository managers with mandating deposit being implemented by some organizations.

Clarity and understanding around ownership of publications, copyright issues and publishers' requirements continue to be addressed by both repository managers and authors. The academic publishing environment is subject to pressures and changes from the economics of subscription models and repositories may have a more significant role to play.

We have also learned that marketing is essential and continuous! A major publicity campaign for the repository was undertaken, including talks, demonstrations and publishing articles about the repository.

Eventually we hope to encourage all our researchers to develop and maintain their profiles; it is amazing how this appeals to those that are research active and belong to multiple networks! Research is competitive and we hope that by seeing the work of other departments in the repository researchers will notify us as they publish. We also hope to move to author submission with the repository librarian overseeing data quality.

Currently we are building the repository around peer-reviewed publications but we foresee this being only part of the story in the future; already we are being asked about other publications, meeting abstracts and submitting documents. The repository is already developing into an essential library function as its benefits are realized.

This section originated from an article published in the Library and Information Health Network North West Newsletter as Webb, A. (2009) Engaging with Research: setting up an organisational repository, *LIHNNKUP*, **32**, 16–18, www.lihnn.nhs.uk/document_uploads/Newsletters/LIHNNK_Up_32_November%202009.pdf.

Case study 7.3 Strategic development of library services

Mandy Beaumont, Knowledge and Library Services Manager, Lancashire Teaching Hospital NHS Foundation Trust

Brief role description

Five years ago, my primary role was to lead on the strategic development of library services within Lancashire Teaching Hospitals NHS Trust and to provide a co-ordinated approach to library service delivery within Central Lancashire. Although this is still part of my remit, the role has expanded to provide and support the information requirements within service improvement projects, to lead on trust-wide projects (unrelated to library service delivery) and to be a member of project teams delivering service improvement or commissioning new services.

The role requires me to network and engage with a wide range of people, who work at all levels and in different specialities both internally and externally to the organization. This interaction provides the basis for effective information and knowledge sharing and has been achieved by becoming a member of strategic committees and project groups with senior management support.

What type of ICT systems do I use?

There is increasing use of ICT systems as well as a greater emphasis on the need to store and archive material to support organizational objectives. These include:

1 The use of targeted electronic current awareness bulletins to ensure that the information provided is relevant to the Trust's business and clinical priorities.
2 The use of databases as information repositories to store and retrieve information, i.e. completed literature searches. Storing information in this way assists with the preservation of organizational memory and is a useful resource to be checked when beginning a new service redesign project.
3 Intranet and internet pages to disseminate information and provide access to services for Trust staff.

4 The use of numerous subject-based databases to extract information to answer literature search requests.
5 The use of online survey tools such as survey monkey for the development of online surveys to collect patient feedback on new and existing services.

What type of data/information/knowledge do I manage?

Previously, the majority of information that I supplied and synthesized was clinical in content and a typical search would comprise clinical articles, systematic reviews and guidelines. Searches have now expanded to include management information and its practical application. This provides a more holistic approach to organizational planning and allows all the relevant elements to be considered, resulting in better planned and more effective patient care.

One of the most useful sources of information is comprehensive case studies. These provide a breakdown of the various stages of a project and include: a list of the problems encountered during implementation, the lessons learnt, any patient benefits and whether the changes resulted in any cost savings. Other information sources such as documents on QIPP, patient pathways and cost–benefit analysis are also valuable to project teams and managers.

Where do my information professional skills add value?

Librarians have a wide range of specialist skills that can add value to the delivery of the organization's business objectives. These include:

1 The ability to carry out methodical literature searches, which benefits the organization by:
  — Locating evidence on proposed trust developments. This preparatory work helps to flag up issues and lessons learnt by other organizations who have already implemented these changes and identified any potential problems in advance, resulting in there being less chance of costly mistakes being made due to insufficient knowledge or experience, thus saving both time and money.
  — Providing in-depth information on a specific planned improvement or innovation that could lead to working smarter and more efficiently, therefore reducing costs.
  — Providing evidence-based information to improve quality and productivity by allowing better problem solving and decision making.
2 The ability to organize and classify information so that it can be stored and reused, saving the organization time and supporting organizational memory.
  — The ability to synthesize and present the relevant information in a clear and straightforward manner saves time and allows managers and project leads to concentrate on their main roles.

— Skills such as questionnaire design and the statistical analysis of the results can be used in generic contexts such as patient information surveys. In my role this expertise has been called upon in designing, co-ordinating and then providing reports on surveys sent out to patients regarding the redesign of a service. Librarians can bring a layman's perspective to this work that benefits the patient.

There have been positive benefits with my role for the library service including the ability to demonstrate to senior management that information professions have skills that are valuable to the organization and that these skills have a part to play in the delivery of trust agendas and business objectives. Delivering projects successfully, on time and within budget have further enhanced the library's credibility, providing us with senior level champions in the organization and ensuring we are viewed as an integral part of the organization.

Where do I see this role going?

Although the strategic delivery of library services will still be key, the role will continue to integrate knowledge management principles to assist with the delivery of organizational objectives and the retention of organizational memory. Involvement will continue with service improvement projects and the Lean agenda and there will be a closer working relationship with the Trust's IT department to provide integrated information systems via the intranet and internet. However, the infrastructure to support the work generated by this role will continue to be dependent on the library service evolving and being able to adapt to the changing information landscape.

What is the biggest challenge in my role?

The biggest challenge has been to change the perceived stereotype of information professionals within the organization. Initially the role was seen as one that supported the delivery of the Trust's educational agenda rather than the provider of information to support the delivery of the organization's business objectives. However, this perception is changing and both the role and the library service are now valued as an integral part of the organization.

How can I prepare my role for the future . . .?

To prepare my role for the future, I will need to continue to broaden my experience and knowledge of the clinical and political agenda of the Trust, gain a deeper understanding of knowledge management issues, develop a clear understanding of the wider political health agenda and develop a greater competence in project management.

Case study 7.4 Information Specialist

Mike Raynor, National Institute of Health and Clinical Excellence

Overview

Founded in 1999 the National Institute for Health and Clinical Excellence (NICE) is an independent organization responsible for providing national guidance on promoting good health and preventing and treating ill health.

NICE guidance is based on the best evidence, which includes 'published evidence and evidence-based on real life experiences' (NICE, 2008, 7). NICE has three guidance producing centres that work in collaboration with health professionals, patients and charity groups. They are: the Centre for Public Health Excellence (CPHE,) which develops public health guidance; the Centre for Health Technology Evaluations (CHTE), which produces appraisals of devices and drugs as well as guidance on interventional procedures, other medical technologies and diagnostics; and the Centre for Clinical Practice (CCP), which produces clinical guidelines on the appropriate treatment and care of people with specific diseases and conditions.

My job title is Information Specialist working in Information Services (IS). As guidance production relies heavily on the best available evidence, IS performs a central function within NICE and supports the work of all of the guidance centres. Information Specialists conduct in-depth and systematic literature and evidence searches and contribute to methodological developments in the guidance development and review processes.

Information Specialists are required to identify the best sources to search, from a wide range of medical, health, sociological and economic databases, registries and websites. After searching, Information Specialists will select relevant evidence and pass this to the guidance centres as bibliographic databases, web pages or summary reports. All results are accompanied by fully documented search strategies to ensure transparency and reproducibility. Often an iterative process, this initial stage of development requires close working with technical analysts whose role involves critical evaluation of a range of evidence (e.g. submissions from manufacturers, published academic papers, information received from patient and professional groups), on the clinical and cost-effectiveness of health technologies in order to produce draft guidance.

Information Specialists also provide training in information skills for colleagues within NICE. This includes developing and delivering courses covering searching for pharmaceutical information, using Web 2.0 to manage information, and evaluation of health information on the internet.

Time management is an essential skill as guidance development is tightly project managed. This was a daunting prospect when I first started work at NICE as searching is often a project prerequisite. However, I have found that there is a sense of satisfaction in meeting a deadline and seeing a project move forward. Working in this way has also enhanced my project management skills and I think this is an essential part of an Information Specialist's skills.

Advantages and challenges

One of the best things about my role is working in project teams with diverse skills sets. For example, I am currently part of a CPHE team developing a piece of obesity prevention guidance. The team includes technical analysts, a health economist, a project manager and a member of the Centre's senior management team. This is a very stimulating group to work with who pose interesting and challenging questions about searching for evidence. Many members of the team are subject experts and are a crucial source of keywords and key papers to inform the searching.

A particular feature of working at NICE is the Institute's location in different parts of the country. 'Face to face' meetings (including reference interviews) are often conducted via video conference, which poses interesting challenges and was initially a curiously detached experience! However, this soon becomes normalized and still leads to close working relationships.

The diversity of searching is another aspect I enjoy. I work on projects that decide whether appraisals of medical technologies or pharmaceutical treatments require updating. The appraisal may evaluate the efficacy of a pharmaceutical treatment for a particular cancer or a medical technology such as a device for preserving donated organs. Unlike searching for public health evidence, which requires knowledge of a broad range of subject information sources, updating projects require familiarity with complex conditions as well as drug and device names.

My output takes the form of a reference database of new published evidence and a succinct report summarizing ongoing research drawn from trials registers. I also provide a tentative recommendation, based on what I have retrieved, as to whether the guidance should be reviewed. A technical analyst will look at the research I find as well as my recommendation and add a brief summary of the new evidence to produce a collaborative recommendation on how to proceed with the guidance update.

The technical searching skills I have developed are crucial in this role as it is important not to miss any new evidence. Additionally I am required to make decisions about the relevancy of research, therefore my judgement and appraisal skills are invaluable.

Although searching the public health and medical technologies evidence bases can be markedly different, I feel the two areas highlight what for me is the biggest challenge of my role. Both workstreams require decisions about relevancy and therefore there is a requirement to have an understanding of the research question and be able to interpret results in this context. Update projects require me to sift large numbers of clinical trials articles to decide whether an intervention is for the same class of condition as in the original NICE guidance. Public health guidance requires scoping searches that help to define major facets of the guidance research questions. Again an understanding of when and why something is relevant is essential.

Production of quality health care guidelines requires evidence from service users, health care professionals and the scientific literature. Although questions of the relevancy of results are ultimately team decisions, in their role as searchers of the evidence base Information Specialists at NICE often have a significant 'steering' role to play at the outset of a guidance development project.

The future

Ten years ago Davidoff and Florance (2000) spoke about 'the informationist', a hybrid creature that combines information management skills with an understanding of health and medical research. I think the role of information specialist has come close to this vision and will continue to develop as a hybrid as the boundaries between searching and evaluation begin to blur. This is equally true of information professionals supporting clients who are required to select and synthesize evidence in order to support a decision, for example those who work with students of health and medicine and those employed by pharmaceutical and manufacturing companies.

The future then will require information specialists not only to stay up to date with new methods of information retrieval and dissemination, but also to develop their skills in understanding the efficacy of existing and developing medical, health and sociological research methods.

Case study 7.5 Co-ordinator Clinical Pathways
Joanna Dundon, Aneurin Bevan Health Board

Overview

I am Lead for the Map of Medicine for Aneurin Bevan Health Board on local clinical pathways and National Co-ordinator for Clinical Pathways Tool for NHS Wales Informatics Service (NWIS). Chapter 3 provides further information about the Map of Medicine and Clinical Pathways.

The Health Board is based in South-East Wales covering primary, community, mental health and secondary care services. This is broken down into five localities coterminous with the local authority boundaries, covering a population of 600,000 and over 18,000 staff.

Since March 2008 I have been on secondment for three days per week with Informing Healthcare, now NHS Wales Informatics Service, to co-ordinate the implementation of the Map across Wales. This has meant:

- travelling around the seven Health Boards
- engaging with executives to set up local website views
- presenting and training clinicians and other professionals of the benefits of pathways and hosting stands on wards, in GP practices and hospitals, and at conferences and roadshows, etc.
- ensuring patients and service users are represented in pathway workshops

- hosting visitors from England, Denmark and New Zealand to share our experiences of a clinical pathways tool
- training staff to act as Local Pathway Co-ordinators, Editors and Administrators
- discussing national pathways with National Policy Advisors and Co-ordinators from national organizations such as Welsh Assembly Government, Public Health Wales and the National Leadership and Innovation Agency for Healthcare, Delivery and Support Unit
- facilitating the creation or modification of national pathways and publishing them in a timely fashion
- monitoring implementation and liaising with experts/Clinical Leads to check if there are amendments
- pulling together an all-Wales Order Book of pathways and local Pathways Register to reduce duplication of effort locally in order to get one national pathway rather than seven local pathways and incorporate good practice into national pathways (see Figure 7.1)
- working with suppliers and monitoring their work programme.

My background

I was able to take on this role after developing a range of skills throughout my career. After graduating with a BA(Hons) in Librarianship and Information Studies, I became Abstractor/Indexer at the King's Fund Centre Library in London, a health management charity working on the beginning of the Health Management Information Consortium Database (pooling together the collections of King's Fund, Department of Health and Nuffield Institute for Health). I then was Assistant Librarian – Technical Services where I merged the King's Fund College collection with the King's Fund Centre after cataloguing and classification. I then became Library Services Manager at the Royal Gwent Hospital, Newport, Glan Hafren NHS Trust/Gwent Healthcare NHS Trust, which honed my searching skills. I then moved to the Trust Headquarters as Strategic Health Evidence Manager to support the service redesign programme, Clinical Futures, in searching for new and exciting service models across the world as well as those that had been tried and tested and were evidence-based.

I have also co-authored two systematic reviews (Edwards et al., 2006a, 2006b) and I'm working on a third with Cardiff University nursing lecturers on a Joanna Briggs Institute systematic review on trailblazing consultant nurses.

In June 2006 Informing Healthcare, the National IM&T Programme for NHS Wales, decided to pilot Map of Medicine, an online evidence-based clinical pathways tool, in three areas in Wales, of which Gwent was one. I was asked to be Project Lead because of my knowledge of and interest in evidence-based practice and IT.

My skills have developed from information management in a traditional health library setting to knowledge management, which I find fascinating as it gives me the opportunity to liaise with people and understand what they do at a particular part of a patient's journey, whilst ensuring I link with like-minded experts within one

Health Board Pathways

Condition	Date published	1000 lives	DSU	NHS Wales	ABM	Abertawe Bro	Cardiff and Vale	Hywel Dda	Beta Cardiology	Cwm Taf	Powys	Leeds	National standards and policies	Statements on pathway development
Arthroplasty (hip)			◆											
Hip and knee pain			◆											
Normal births		◆												
Catheterised patient		◆												
Major postpartum haemorrhage														
ICD (Cardioverter defibrillator)														
Tonsillitis/Recurrent sore throat			◆											
Back pain			◆											
Glaucoma			◆											
AMD			◆											
Unscheduled care for eye injuries			◆											
Liver function tests														
Stable angina														
Stroke				intelligent targets										
LUTS														
Mental Capacity Act														
Adult hearing loss			◆											
Antenatal screening x 9														
COPD														
Heart failure		◆		intelligent targets										
Atrial fibrillation				intelligent targets										
Arrhythmias				intelligent targets										
Cardiac rehabilitation														
Familial hypercholesterolaemia														
Female incontinence														
Leg ulcer (PLUS)														
Risk of harm to others														
Substance misuse														
Generic chronic conditions management														
CPA risk assessment														

Figure 7.1 *Health Board Pathways in Wales*
Copyright © NHS Wales Informatics Service

organization or across several in Wales. Nevertheless I still use the abstracting, searching and data extraction skills I have picked up over the years to incorporate synthesized information into pathways. I have also developed presentation, facilitation, negotiation and time keeping skills alongside a knowledge of expert IT systems that make this a challenging (but not impossible) role for a health librarian.

Advantages and challenges

The best thing about this role is working with experts across all specialties and pulling together knowledge management as well as information management. I like the way we can share what we know across boundaries and there is always something new to be learned every day. The biggest challenge is politics – understanding the raison d'être behind some decisions, which might be a power struggle between national organizations or key individuals rather than the product itself. I have learnt a lot about diplomacy and negotiation, which were probably not key skills I considered essential in a library. Having to work with people who are not enthusiastic and are natural pessimists has meant that I have learnt to find other ways to deal with such people, and eventually they come round!

The future

To maintain my role in the future I need to ensure that my project management skills continue to be developed and that I keep up to date with the new direction in NHS Wales and beyond, such as reduction of finance, resources and making best use of what is available without diluting the skills that people have. I want to develop my skills further in managing change. However, I have learnt that communication is key in any process.

Conclusion – Christine Urquhart

Joanna Dundon's work on the clinical pathways project for the implementation of Map of Medicine in Wales shows how skills acquired in systematic reviewing, plus the experience of working at strategic level in service design, made her an ideal person to take on the Map of Medicine role for Informing Healthcare in Wales. Extending your role requires some confidence in your own competence – the vital self-efficacy, or sense of personal mastery. Mandy Beaumont also comments on the need to challenge stereotypes of the role of the information professional as simply there to support education. Joanna may have benefited from cataloguing and classifying all those items for the King's Fund, as that organization is associated with health service management and policy, strategic thinking about health service organization and delivery. Perhaps it depends how much you read of the content of the books that you are processing, or whether you are interested in the content of what you are cataloguing and classifying. It may be more efficient to catalogue quickly, but an awareness of the subject content, and the main issues being debated, may help when talking to library service users.

Joanna comments on how she learnt to do the politics and negotiation, persuading others of the benefits of clinical pathways and a different way of doing things.

Just because some staff do not appear to be using the evidence (as described by Prudence Dalrymple in Chapter 4), there is no need to label them as illiterates in evidence-based practice. They may have knowledge that is not in the literature about practice, what works and does not work, and why. Mandy Beaumont stresses the importance of case study information and the type of project management knowledge that managers need when implementing service improvements. For designing clinical pathways, it is very important that people on the team appreciate the tacit knowledge among the staff, and understand the interaction of the tacit knowledge with the evidence base.

Anne Webb's work on the repository at Christie Hospital also reflects the need for domain knowledge as well as knowledge about metadata standards, in the development of the repository. The team there is adding value to the research output of the clinical researchers by ensuring that the work is visible to other cancer researchers. The choice of repository software was astute, in choosing an interface that the researchers knew, and the decision to take the lead in populating the repository ensures that the management of the content is done properly, and observes copyright legislation. The information specialist's skills are being used in the stewardship of digital content, for the benefit of local and external researchers.

Mike Raynor's role in NICE demands a high level of searching skills, but, like Joanna Dundon, he works in a team where some awareness of the specialist skills and knowledge of others in the team is necessary. Both Mike and Joanna are working in communities of practice that are based around clinical or health problems – this may ease the traditional difficulties of the medical hierarchies. For health information professionals these environments – the multidisciplinary teams – allow the health information professional to contribute to health care organization and delivery in a way that is visible to them, and to the other health professionals involved. Mike comments: 'This is a very stimulating group to work with who pose interesting and challenging questions about searching for evidence.' This suggests that Mike's learning is social learning that takes place within the multidisciplinary team. The questions, challenges and reactions impact on the practicalities of current searching and retrieval work, but there should, we hope, be some feedback into training programmes for health information professionals. Mike also comments on the time management required for his role. Efficiency of library processes is considered in the literature but it is not a common topic, probably tainted by association with time and motion studies. But there is probably a gap here – reflecting on how we organize our work within a library and information environment is particularly important when funding is tight. It is clear from Mike's account that his value to the work of the team depends on getting the searching done as efficiently and effectively as possible. That demands a high level of professional knowledge and judgement in knowing where to draw the line.

Mandy Beaumont and Rachel Court also refer to the co-ordination of different parts of their work as information specialists. Like Joanna, they make use of cataloguing and classification skills in their work, but they have also had to develop skills in abstracting and summarizing. Such skills may always have been part of the repertoire for information scientists working in scientific or commercial environments, but their importance is more obvious now, and Mandy Beaumont stresses that time spent by the information professional in synthesizing information well will save time for many other health staff. Busy people wish to know whether they have to download and read a portable document format file or examine a web page – information scientists can make life more efficient and effective. Rachel comments on one of the challenges in her role as being 'understanding the needs of the collections' users and potential users. This has been a challenge particularly because we rarely interact with our users directly.' And it is a challenge as Rachel's users can be counted in thousands, if not millions. The responsibility for ensuring that information and, more importantly, the evidence, is presented in a format suitable for the users of the service partly lies with the information professional, who has to know who else to ask for advice and consultation. As all the contributors to this chapter note, they need to know about the IT tools that help them provide alerts to those that need them, present information in suitable formats for different audiences and maintain a knowledge base – whether that is national or the local organizational memory.

Anne Webb comments on the skills acquired in using and customizing the repository software. Not all hospital library and information services will develop research repositories, but increasingly librarians need to be prepared to take on the role of ensuring that research publications do reach the audience that need them. For emerging research-based health professions, much of the relevant research may still be hidden within dissertations or theses, which may or may not be easy to find electronically.

The case studies presented in this chapter show how important it is to be able to analyse information (to assess what it is about, to describe the content succinctly, to classify and organize appropriately). To manage knowledge requires an awareness of the impact of the information on the users, and the awareness of the problems – and opportunities – that might be encountered when implementing evidence-based practice.

References

Allard, S., Mack, T. R. and Feltner-Reichert, M. (2005) The Librarian's Role in Institutional Repositories: a content analysis of the literature, *Reference Services Review*, **33**, 325–36.

Bernstein, E., Topp, D., Shaw, E., Girard, C., Pressman, K., Woolcock, E. and Bernstein, J. (2009) A Preliminary Report of Knowledge Translation: lessons from taking screening and brief intervention techniques from the research setting into regional systems of care, *Academic Emergency Medicine*, **16** (11), 1225–33.

Boisot, M. (1995) *Information Space: a framework for learning in organizations, institutions and cultures*, Routledge.

Davidoff, F. and Florance, V. (2000) The Informationist: a new health profession?, *Annals of internal medicine*, **132** (12), 996–8.

Denning, S. (2000) *The Springboard: how storytelling ignites action at knowledge-era organisations*, Butterworth-Heinemann (KCMI Press).

Department of Health (2011) *Quality, Innovation, Productivity and Prevention (QIPP)*, www.dh.gov.uk/en/Healthcare/Qualityandproductivity/QIPP/index.htm.

Edwards, A., Sivell, S., Dundon J., Elwyn G., Evans R., Gaf, C., Iredale, R., Shaw C., Thornton H., Gray J., Clarke A. and Atkinson P. (2006a) Report on Systematic Review: effective risk communication in clinical genetics, Cardiff University, Centre for Health Sciences Research.

Edwards, A. G. K., Evans, R., Dundon, J., Haigh, S., Hood, K. and Elwyn, G. J. (2006b) Personalized Risk Communication for Informed Decision Making About Taking Screening Tests, *Cochrane Database of Systematic Reviews*, 4, CD001865, DOI: 10.1002/14651858.CD001865.pub2nd.

Fried Foster, N. and Gibbons, S. (2005) Understanding Faculty to Improve Content Recruitment for Institutional Repositories, *D-Lib Magazine*, **11** (1), http://dlib.org/dlib/january05/foster/01foster.html#4.

Glover, S., Webb, A. and Gleghorn, C. (2006) Open Access Publishing in the Biomedical Sciences: could funding agencies accelerate the inevitable changes?, *Health Information and Libraries Journal*, **23**, 197–202.

NHS Evidence (2011) www.evidence.nhs.uk/frequently-asked-questions.

National Institute for Health and Clinical Excellence (2008) NICE: our guidance sets the standard for good healthcare, www.nice.org.uk/media/888/38/ourguidancesetsstandard.pdf.

Schilling, L., Chase, A., Kehrli, S., Liu, A. Y., Stiefel, M. and Brentari, R. (2010) Kaiser Permanente's Performance Improvement System, Part 1: from benchmarking to executing on strategic priorities, *Joint Commission Journal on Quality and Patient Safety*, **36** (11), 484–98.

Thornton, S. (2009) Supporting Knowledge Discovery in a Research Organisation. In *QQML2009: Qualitative and Quantitative Methods in Libraries, International Conference, Chania Crete Greece, 26-29 May 2009*, www.isast.org/proceedingsQQML2009/PAPERS_PDF/Thornton-Supporting_Knowledge_Discovery_In_Research_Organisation_PAPER-QQML2009.pdf.

Urquhart, C. (1998) Personal Knowledge: a clinical perspective from the Value and EVINCE projects in health information services, *Journal of Documentation*, **54** (4), 420–42.

Urquhart, C., Currell, R., Grant, M. J. and Hardiker, N. R. (2009) Nursing Record Systems: effects on nursing practice and healthcare outcomes, *Cochrane Database of Systematic Reviews*, 1, CD002099, DOI:10.1002/14651858.CD002099.pub.

Urquhart, C., Brice, A., Cooper, J., Spink, S. and Thomas, R. (2010) Evaluating the Development of Virtual Communities of Practice that Support Evidence Based Practice, *Evidence Based Library and Information Practice*, **5** (1), http://ejournals.library.ualberta.ca/index.php/EBLIP/article/viewFile/6879/6426.

Yeoman, A., Urquhart, C. and Sharp, S. (2003) Moving Communities of Practice Forward: the challenge for the National electronic Library for Health and its Virtual Branch Libraries, *Health Informatics Journal*, **9** (4), 241–52.

8
The librarian within research and evidence-based practice

Alison Brettle

Introduction

This chapter discusses the librarian's role in research and evidence-based practice. Whilst Chapter 4 describes how evidence-based practice has provided health librarians with a range of opportunities to demonstrate their skills, this chapter outlines these roles in more detail with five case studies describing roles that support research and evidence-based practice, and in some cases become actively involved in those activities.

What is research?

Research is about the discovery of new knowledge or facts. It may involve investigation or enquiry, discovering causes, understanding activities or behaviours, exploring perceptions or testing hypotheses. Robson (2002) describes research that may be carried out in a 'real life' context, such as a workplace, which often involves some form of evaluation. Evaluation is a term familiar to most health librarians and is defined as 'a study with a distinctive purpose, it is not a new or different research strategy but it is often used to assess the effects or effectiveness of something (an innovation or service for example) ... whilst not necessarily research, evaluation profits from the principled systematic approach that characterizes research' (Robson, 2002, 203). The skills, techniques and methods used in research, evaluation and evidence-based practice are often the same and to an extent there is some degree of overlap between the three concepts, therefore it makes sense, particularly when talking about librarians' roles, that the three are considered together.

Supporting research and evidence-based practice

As noted and described in Chapter 6, librarians play an important role in supporting other people's research and evaluation activities. The National Institute for Health Research has produced a flowchart describing a ten-stage research process (www.rdinfo.org.uk/flowchart/Flowchart.html) that clearly states where libraries and librarians have a role to play. This includes a key role in the second stage of research – the literature review, by providing advice, training and guidance on literature searching and reviewing or conducting searches on behalf of researchers. In health service research this may well be to researchers based in academic institutions or to clinicians who conduct research within the health service. In a range of ways librarians facilitate access to the resources that researchers need to conduct their research (see Chapter 6). This may involve facilitating access to online databases, obtaining documents from their own collections or interlibrary loans or access to reference management tools and software. At the end of the research process, the report writing and dissemination stage, librarians can often help researchers with proofreading, citation checking as well as advising on where to publish. As is noted in the case studies below (Booth, Brettle) this could be at a general level – to the individual researcher – or at a strategic institutional level, for example in relation to the Research Excellence Framework, the system used for assessing the quality of research within HEIs. Librarians have also become involved in the creation and promotion of institutional repositories, an important means of promoting and providing access to research at an institutional level (described by Anne Webb in Chapter 7).

Undertaking research and evidence-based practice

'Real life' research or research taking place in the workplace context may also be conducted by health librarians, so as well as providing a supportive role to the health research community, health librarians may well be actively engaged in research or evaluation of their own profession or service. This makes sense when you think that skills used for research are those that, as librarians, we use in everyday life – including reading, listening, questioning, watching, summarizing, organizing and reflecting – and that the benefits of conducting research are manifold and include personal and professional development as well as promoting our own library service. Journals such as *Health Information and Libraries Journal* or the *Journal of the Medical Library Association* are at the forefront of publishing such research or evaluation studies (see case studies below for examples). Evaluation of library services is an activity that librarians may well be involved in, as part of routine practice or as a response to the current financial climate, and in recent years it is an activity that has been encouraged at a strategic level (Hill, 2008; SCONUL, 2010).

The librarian's role in evidence-based practice

Evidence-based practice (EBP) (explored in more detail in Chapter 4) revolves round finding and using research evidence and requires search skills and an understanding of research methodology. Becoming an evidence-based practitioner (even by reading and appraising research) is a good way of developing research skills and understanding.

The EBP movement has become entrenched within health care provision and has presented librarians with a means of demonstrating their expertise in literature searching (Medical Library Association, 2005) and opportunities to be involved in a range of roles in the evidence-based process (Palmer, 1996; Scherrer and Dorsch, 1999; Falzon and Booth, 2001; Harris, 2005; McGowan and Sampson, 2005). Furthermore, health information professionals, with their background and experience in evidence-based health care, have promoted and developed 'evidence based library and information practice' (EBLIP), which is seeing a gradual uptake by other areas of the profession (Booth and Brice, 2007).

A review of the literature (Brettle, 2009) suggests that health librarians or health information professionals (HIPs) play four roles within EBP:

1 A supportive role using traditional skills and expertise (their knowledge of health resources and search skills) to train clinicians to find evidence for practice, to find evidence on behalf of clinicians or to provide expert searching and guidance in relation to systematic reviews.
2 A supportive role using their knowledge of critical appraisal to teach critical appraisal or critically appraise search results of the research literature to support health professionals in their EBP.
3 An active role using critical appraisal and research skills to conduct systematic reviews or engage in EBLIP in the library or health information domain (their own comfort zone).
4 An active role using research or critical appraisal skills outside the library and information domain, perhaps within health care teams by working as an informationist or by taking a more substantive role in systematic reviews in health or social care. This active role represents an area where librarians can not only use their skills but further develop their roles.

Figure 8.1 represents these roles in a model that provides a snapshot of how these are currently developing and shows how they relate to the evidence-based process.

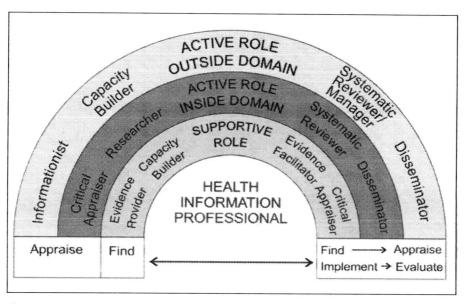

Figure 8.1 *Roles played by health information professionals within an evidence-based context*

The case studies below show many of these roles in action, in some cases illustrating how HIPs may work in one or more 'layers' of the model in one particular job or at different times in their career.

Case study 8.1 Reader in Evidence-Based Information Practice & Director of Information, School of Health and Related Research (ScHARR)

Andrew Booth, University of Sheffield

Overview – ScHARR Information Resources

The last 15 years may have witnessed significant changes to our activities, the supporting technologies we use and the boundaries of our roles but there remains something reassuringly familiar about the portfolio of activities that fill a typical day. The Information Resources Section was set up to support the research activities of health services researchers at the University of Sheffield, to develop research capacity amongst local health service (NHS) staff and to deliver teaching and training activities within the School of Health and Related Research (ScHARR) and these essentially remain the pillars of our practice (Hicks, 1998; Paisley, 1998; Beecroft et al., 2009). The ScHARR Library and Enquiry Service operates outside the University Library network and is funded from research and consultancy income. This not only provides the opportunity for the information team to collaborate in research led by others but also requires that the service keeps closely attuned to the needs of the researchers who secure the income. Our involvement in such multidisciplinary research collaborations has provided a platform for establishing the team's own portfolio of research within health information management. Meanwhile the scope of our research support continues to expand with information professionals now involved in undertaking systematic reviews and delivering e-learning and face to face courses in addition to providing bulletins on funding opportunities, conducting literature searches to underpin funding proposals and offering guidance on getting published. The team maintains contacts with health service staff (local and national) through short courses and longer programmes such as doctoral projects or the Master's degree in Health Informatics. We also interact with many different types of organizations that require systematic reviews, although NICE provides by far the majority of our commissioned work. Naturally, the administrative function has grown accordingly to the extent that participation in executive, research, teaching or marketing committees within the School typically commands most of the morning. Faculty roles, in co-ordinating future research assessment submissions, planning internal and external communications or negotiating information technology or library provision, add significantly to this administrative workload albeit while offering a welcome change of scene. It can thus be seen that although research and evidence-based practice remains the focus for our activities other roles covered by this book continue to figure prominently.

Teaching role

The day typically begins with responding to e-mails from students involved in dissertations, in a PhD or in the various modules that the information team runs within the Masters in Public Health, as part of the MSc in Health Informatics (with the i-School, formerly the Department of Information Studies) or for the Doctoral Development Programme. Supervision of systematic reviews or information management projects provides a welcome test bed for developments in methodology as well as supplying valuable context to our work with the health service. Responses to these e-mails will often require interaction with the student administration system, the virtual learning environment, bibliographic databases or with online full-text journal collections.

Research support

Other e-mails may feature requests for support for costing a review proposal or feeding into a fellowship application from a junior member of staff. The team has devised a template as a prompt for including all elements to be considered when costing a planned review. Judgements on the final cost and timescales will be informed by information retrieved from scoping searches. Requests for a brief curriculum vitae or details of key relevant publications are common to both activities. Invariably peer review activity, for a funding agency, for a journal or for a pre-submission manuscript from a colleague or collaborator, will require extensive time in providing feedback. Fellow researchers will also solicit advice on target journals for their proposed papers, acknowledging our expertise and the associated corporate responsibility to monitor, support and stimulate the School's publications portfolio. Lunchtime may involve delivering an online lecture in a virtual learning environment or attendance at one of many lunchtime health research seminars given by visiting speakers.

Research

After lunch comes project activity, with the information team frequently informing systematic review methodology in addition to conducting the associated literature searches (White et al., 2005). This role particularly has seen expansion in recent years with information specialists increasingly involved in the subsequent stages of sifting abstracts for relevance, appraising research papers, and conducting the synthesis and analysis for the review. Projects may now involve mapping or scoping the literature or synthesizing the qualitative research literature. The last of these has led to our involvement with the Cochrane Collaboration's Qualitative Research Methods Group. Customers for our range of evidence synthesis products include local managers of health and social services, national and regional commissioners of research as well as governmental policy makers (Beverley, Booth and Bath, 2003; Booth, 2004; Carroll et al., 2006; Wilkinson et al., 2009).

Professional development

A brief hiatus before the next appointment allows a check of current awareness e-mail alerts or access to RSS feeds via a personalized iGoogle web page. Useful articles will be tagged using social networking software such as Citeulike or shared with others using Mendeley. Information skills, acquired from years of delivering research support to others, reap rich dividends when used to facilitate one's personal portfolio of research or to share information with collaborators. Items identified via such mechanisms will feed into our Systematic Review or Information Academic Development Groups where we discuss methodological advances and our own plans for projects and publications.

Following a snatched cup of tea the Facilitated Online Learning Interactive Opportunity (FOLIO) team meeting becomes the setting for planning our e-learning course activities (Sutton et al., 2005). Such activities are still a comparatively recent addition to our team's work programme although they represent a natural extension to our long history of delivering face to face courses. Our team of information specialists will design each course, author and produce activities and materials, and take turns in facilitating course delivery. Follow-up from this meeting will require us to produce or revise e-learning materials or to mark portfolio submissions.

Finally there may be a brief opportunity to work on lecture materials for one of the short courses we run, either through our internal Short Course Unit or in conjunction with external partners. Topics include Developing a Successful Systematic Review Proposal, Writing for Publication or Facilitating Critical Appraisal. Our usual model is for a senior member of the information team to lead on delivering each course alongside less experienced team members who are mentored and developed for future involvement. Other routes for staff development include attendance at systematic review courses, week-long evidence-based health care events (Bexon and Falzon, 2003), in-house training and university-sponsored teaching certificates. Twice a year the School runs its own major residential workshops on systematic review methodology, which offer an opportunity for information specialists and research staff across all the sections to collaborate as members of the course faculty.

Of course it would be reassuring to imagine that the working day ends here. In reality, later that same evening may witness a return to work-related tasks that supplement the day's activities and which provide payback in terms of professional involvement and recognition. These may involve correspondence or collaboration with others involved in the evidence-based library and information practice movement, planning international workshops or conferences or working on a book chapter, journal article or regular column feature. If the next day happens to be our day of the week for working from home we might eagerly anticipate protected time to produce papers, reports or new lecture materials. In the past these might be based on our own primary research or evaluation projects of evidence-based health information or clinical librarian initiatives within the health service (Falzon and Booth, 2001; Booth and Falzon, 2003; Booth, Sutton and Falzon, 2003; Booth, Booth and Beecroft, 2010). Equally they may reflect problems or issues encountered when fulfilling our roles in searching in support of systematic reviews (Harrison, 1997; Booth, 2006; Papaioannou et al., 2010). Increasingly, however, such outputs are a natural by-product from our own systematic review activities as both subject experts (for example in clinical librarianship or e-learning) and methodologists (in qualitative systematic reviews) (Winning and Beverley, 2003; Beverley, Bath and Booth, 2004; Booth et al., 2009; Carroll et al., 2009).

Challenges and future directions

The above combination of academic and service roles epitomizes a tension present in the work of most of the School's information specialists. On the one hand support for the research of others is a core aspect of the team's business. On the other hand team members are encouraged to seek academic recognition through their own publication, teaching and research activities. Where there is synergy, for example in providing a specific and identifiable contribution to a multidisciplinary research project or in delivering a module within a wider teaching programme, this may be achieved relatively smoothly. Where it may require more advocacy, and indeed ingenuity, is in maintaining a connection with research that relates to our information professional skills. Evidence-based information practice provides one such mechanism as a portmanteau that involves supporting the evidence-based practice of others, through systematic reviews and critical appraisal, as well as examining the evidence base for our own profession. However, as we have collectively found, hybrid roles, those that mix research, teaching and service delivery, are valued within our School but sit uncomfortably within university systems for academic progression. Routes to recognition include gaining a PhD, pursuing a teaching qualification or taking on a significant level of management responsibility. Each of these routes may be pursued only at the expense of a perhaps unwelcome degree of specialization. Success from within a hybrid role may ultimately be best achieved by leaving such a role behind!

Case study 8.2 Information specialists
Olwen Beaven and Andrea Lane, BMJ Evidence Centre

Overview

We are currently employed as Manager and Deputy Information Specialist Manager at the BMJ Evidence Centre (a department of the BMJ Group – a publisher of medical information and evidence-based resources) based in central London.

We work as part of an information specialist team comprising seven information specialists and an administrative assistant. We occupy an unusual role in the publishing business, in that we, rather than our authors, undertake the literature searching and appraisal of studies for use in a number of the Centre's publications.

Searching and appraising the literature

The main focus of the BMJ Evidence Centre is on evidence-based medicine resources, so most of our day to day work involves the updating of searches and feeding the relevant appraised results onto the appropriate authors or editorial staff – so our principal role is to keep the evidence base of the medical research literature, used in our publications, up to date. Due to the nature of publishing, there is a strong focus on meeting deadlines and our regular update searches are planned out in advance, on a yearly schedule, to ensure that we complete the search and appraisal of references so it fits in with the overall updating requirements of each product. We work on a monthly cycle, so each month we have our assignment of search and appraisal to complete.

The two main products for which we undertake routine search and appraisal at present are Clinical Evidence (a database of best evidence for effective clinical research and decision making) and Best Practice (a collection of expert opinion, guidelines and evidence for use at the point of care), although we also assist with other products and undertake searching for ad hoc consultancy-style projects as required. Our routine searches are divided into medical conditions/illnesses and we look for systematic reviews, randomized controlled trials and guidelines in key databases such as MEDLINE, Embase, the Cochrane Library and guideline collections/resources on the internet, although we do supplement these with additional searches for harms, observational studies, aetiology, treatment rationale, etc. when required (e.g. when providing information for our patient website 'Best Health').

As each product, or project, has its own criteria for what subject matter (specific interventions, population, etc.) is to be covered, we are required to apply different appraisal criteria, (defined through consensus by authors, editors and peer reviewers) to ensure that only material relevant for that publication is forwarded on to authors or editors. As we provide the literature for evidence-based products, we have to maintain consistency across all the different searches and so follow standard procedures to ensure that all the information specialists work in the same transparent way.

Advantages

One of the main things about the role of the information specialist that keeps it interesting is the constant change and new challenges that we face. A small team was originally created solely to support the needs of Clinical Evidence (approximately 250 medical topics). Since then we have expanded to also cover Best Practice (1000 medical topics) and have had regular reviews of our search processes to ensure that we search pragmatically and yet maintain rigour, but are also efficient and able to deliver the differing search requirements to our authors/editors. As the range of work the Evidence Centre undertakes is currently diversifying, we are also now involved in formulating tenders, planning and modifying our work schedules, developing new software to enhance work processes, as well working on ad hoc consultancy projects. So although in essence there is a very methodical, deadline-orientated, production line approach to delivering our searches, every day seems different and it has never been dull or boring!

Challenges

Due to these developments, the information specialist team has had to become very flexible, adapting to the differing needs of products, implementing changes and devising strategies to increase efficiency, whilst all the time maintaining a steady flow of search and appraisal to keep publication schedules on track. We have had to cope with change and learnt to work in a pragmatic way to deliver good quality literature searches within the necessary constraints on time and resources.

Increasingly, our role in appraising studies is seen as important in shielding authors from the overwhelming volume of new research being published, so we have become more involved in planning and understanding the requirements of different products.

The nature of our working environment has also transformed over time and now have three team members who work predominantly from home and we also use freelancers who are home based, so we have had to adapt to less face to face contact and the management of staff remotely.

The biggest challenge for our team is the same as most library and information services in the current financial climate – trying to do more for less. There is more pressure to ensure and demonstrate that you are providing value for money and are not undertaking unnecessary tasks, or expending effort in non-priority areas. There is more scrutiny over the use of resources and the need to employ extra staff. The emphasis is on incorporating additional work into the current workflow and practices, so one expanded search may support the needs of multiple products, thus enhancing efficiency and minimizing the need for extra procedures.

The future

Over the longer term, a key challenge is to 'future proof' the role of the information specialist team in the company. Currently, we are seen as providing searches for specific products, but ideally we need to enhance our profile beyond that, so we are seen as able to provide information of interest to the BMJ Group as a whole. Possibly supplying business-related information on developments in medical/scientific publishing or competing products, or on new developments in evidence-based medicine. It would be useful to utilize more extensively the range of skills that we have as information professionals, so finding opportunities to be involved in training customers on BMJ resources, promoting/marketing products to libraries, or helping with the development of company websites, would all be beneficial. We currently try to submit abstracts to conferences, so that if successful we can practise our presentation skills, whilst also learning and sharing experiences with fellow librarians. In order to secure a continuing role for information professionals in this unusual publishing environment, it will be important to broaden our sphere of influence, so that we do not rely solely on the success of one or two products for our future survival.

Case study 8.3 Senior Lecturer/Information Specialist

Alison Brettle, School of Nursing, Midwifery and Social Work, University of Salford, UK

Overview

I'm currently employed as a Senior Lecturer within the School of Nursing and Midwifery and Social Work, a large school of approximately 158 staff, responsible for training 2700 nurses and midwives at all levels (i.e. in order to obtain their professional qualifications and for continuing professional development purposes). As a member of academic staff, there are three main elements to my role: teaching and learning; research; leadership, management and engagement.

Teaching

I teach information literacy and evidence-based practice on a range of postgraduate courses. As leader of the postgraduate evidence-based practice module, I am responsible for developing module content and ensuring its quality and delivery as well as teaching, supervising and assessing students. As new curricula are being developed within the School, I try to ensure that skills for information literacy and evidence-based practice are appropriately represented, reinforcing, facilitating and providing a link between the role provided by the academic library and staff within the School of Nursing. Increasingly, since obtaining a PhD, my teaching role also includes supervision of doctoral students in a range of topic areas, one on one sessions with students who are struggling with the literature review element of their thesis and teaching on the School's doctoral training programme.

Research

Research has a number of strands. It involves obtaining funding to undertake research projects, conducting research or evaluation projects in-house and disseminating the results of the research in a number of ways (e.g. writing academic papers, presenting at conferences or local events, writing in practitioner journals), networking with other researchers and becoming involved within the research structures within the School of Nursing, Midwifery and Social Work. Initially my involvement in research was at the information retrieval stage of systematic reviews but over the years (after mentorship, support and encouragement from the health research staff around me), this has developed and expanded into involvement in critical appraisal, project management and leading bids as a systematic review methodology specialist. Confidence and knowledge developed through working in systematic reviews has led to the development of my own portfolio of research where I manage to combine my own knowledge and interest of library practice with topics of relevance to my employer, for example evaluating information literacy programmes in health (Brettle 2003, 2007; Brettle, Hulme and Ormandy , 2006, 2007) or the evaluation of clinical librarian services (Brettle et al., 2011). Invariably teaching and research becomes intertwined, with research ideas and publications developing out of my practice, for example developing and evaluating an online tutorial to teach information literacy skills to clinicians (Grant and Brettle, 2006), a project that arose as students kept forgetting what had been taught in class, but also provided an opportunity to adopt an evidence-based approach to my own work. These projects or their results can then be fed back into teaching and learning, providing real examples for students and also ensuring that teaching is kept up to date and is evidence based.

Leadership

Management, leadership and engagement is more difficult to define and can cover a wide range of activities, which will be illustrated with examples that make use of my background in health information or my research and information skills. As part of the research structure within the School I co-lead a programme of research on 'health technologies and evidence-based practice'. This is a grouping of research interests and a way of bringing together research on a similar theme to develop and undertake research in order to achieve the School's targets (e.g. research income generation, contribution to the Research Excellence Framework (REF)). The REF is a means of assessing research at a national level, which in turn provides centralized funding to higher education institutions. Research is assessed by a range of factors (income, postdoctoral students and publications) and as I have a good knowledge of publications, publication practices, organizing information and critical appraisal skills, I am a member of the committee within the School that makes strategic decisions in relation to the REF. All research within the University and the health service needs to be conducted in accordance with good ethical practice. To ensure this occurs, a committee within the College of Health and Social Care oversees all postgraduate research projects and approves them before they can take place. Sitting on this committee provides a good insight into standards required for conducting good quality research as well as broadening my knowledge about different research designs. A range of my professional development activities also fit into this area of my work. As Editor of the *Evidence Based Library and Information Practice Journal*, from its early days, I have been part of a team that has tried to make research evidence available to library practitioners. This has not only opened my eyes to open access publishing, but I've also learned about library research and practice in all sectors. Editorial meetings are via Skype and most editing is done via e-mail. Hosting and organizing an international library conference has also provided opportunities to work internationally with librarians from all sectors. It has also required re-acquaintance with a set of organizational and marketing skills that I learned in life before becoming a librarian!

Role evolvement

My role has evolved over 13 years. I was initially employed as an information specialist to support research in a specialist unit on a research (or academic-related) contract. Although the research element was the main focus, I have always sought to maintain the elements of teaching and academic leadership that make up an academic role. The evolvement has been due to a number of factors: primarily as an information specialist working outside a library I always felt a personal need to 'fight my corner' and justify my position within the institution; and as more or less a 'lone worker' I did not easily fit the structures and organizational policies. I believed that the best way of justifying my position was to demonstrate my competency in the same way as other academics (e.g. by publishing) and I constantly looked for opportunities to be involved, demonstrating the value of my skills. I believe I have been successful in doing this, as I have survived various organizational restructures and have recently transferred to an academic contract. One way of demonstrating my competency was to undertake a PhD, a qualification being increasingly demanded of academic staff. I did this via a non-conventional route, by publication (or portfolio), which involved drawing together and critiquing my own research publications. Although this took a number of years, it was something I was able to achieve part-time, whilst maintaining my publication profile and demonstrating academic credibility with my colleagues and peers.

Advantages and challenges

The best thing about the role has been the constant evolution and the opportunity to become involved in a wide range of activities with an ever increasing network of professionals. These opportunities were often initially outside my comfort zone, but a supportive mentor in my early career encouraged me to take on new things and make me believe that I had skills and qualities that made a difference to health professionals suffering from information overload. This volume of opportunities is also one of my greatest challenges, 13 years on: each day is different and there are always conflicting deadlines and projects. I still think it is important to demonstrate the value of information professionals. As the financial climate becomes more difficult and both the higher education and the health sectors face cuts and reorganization, demonstrating this value and looking for areas where my skills can be utilized becomes even more crucial. Ensuring that I keep up to date with professional development is important, but time-consuming, and, as an information professional working in the health sector and higher education, where should I focus my energies?

The future

Finally, this role could move in a range of directions. As time-pressed health professionals become more overloaded with information, students still struggle with information literacy and huge organizational restructuring in both higher education and the health setting takes place, new developments in teaching technology (e.g. online learning) or teaching methods will be needed. With generic research skills that can be applied both within health or the library and information sector it would be possible to specialize and move forward in either area. Alternatively, developing a more administrative or management role within the School or the University would be another way forward, for example there are opportunities in leading doctoral programmes or the wider management of research within the University. Ensuring that your skills are up to date, thinking out of the box on how to use them and having the confidence to seize opportunities is the way forward for any role.

Case study 8.4 The health information professional role in a clinical research setting
Helen Seeley, Addenbrooke's Hospital, Cambridge

Introduction
Literature shows health information professionals need to respond to change, build on the past and re-engineer themselves to meet the information-intensive demands of the future (Lewis, Urquhart and Rolinson, 1998). Nowhere is this more apparent than in a clinical research setting that is focused on encouraging and engineering changes in delivery of health care. Changes need to be aligned with the best evidence, but it is not enough to supply the evidence, in the traditional librarian role of information provision (Gray, 2001). Instead, the health information professionals' skills need to encompass awareness of the social and economic factors that affect how health care is provided. The culture of multidisciplinary team working affects how information is sought and shared. Technical solutions to information systems need, ideally, to support and enhance best practice, rather than being a burden to professional staff.

Setting
I describe my role as a health information professional in a research partnership aimed at improving the effectiveness and efficiency of regional head injury service provision in the East of England. Head-injured patients have complex needs demanding a co-ordinated service response across disciplines, organizations and specializations. As we covered tertiary (specialist centre) care, secondary care (in district general hospitals) and primary care (family/GPs, community health services) a holistic approach was necessary. To research, develop and evaluate the improvement, a multiple-phase action research process was used. My responsibilities as a health information professional stretched across the research strategy, and involved collaborative working with university researchers in a world-class teaching hospital, managers, commissioners and multi-agencies (Figure 8.2 on the next page).

The research partnership provided strategic direction through a steering group, in which my experience and skills in data cataloguing, health information management, and development and application of database systems were recognized as essential (Figure 8.3 on the next page) (Seeley et al., 2001, 2006a, 2006b; Pickard et al., 2004; Seeley and Hutchinson, 2006; Seeley, 2007; Seeley and Urquhart, 2008).

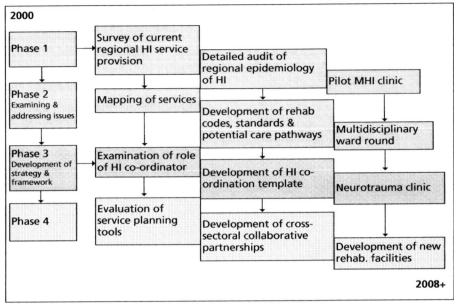

2000

| Phase 1 | Survey of current regional HI service provision | Detailed audit of regional epidemiology of HI | Pilot MHI clinic |

| Phase 2 Examining & addressing issues | Mapping of services | Development of rehab codes, standards & potential care pathways | Multidisciplinary ward round |

| Phase 3 Development of strategy & framework | Examination of role of HI co-ordinator | Development of HI co-ordination template | Neurotrauma clinic |

| Phase 4 | Evaluation of service planning tools | Development of cross-sectoral collaborative partnerships | Development of new rehab. facilities |

2008+

Figure 8.2   *The Eastern Head Injury Group study action research cycles*

Planning and action – review
Collaborative development of service tools

1   Role of Principal Researcher
2   Groups: Research Group, focus groups, HI Working Groups, Neurosciences Strategic Group.
3   Partnerships
4   Literature reviews
5   Initial survey (2000)
6   Reviews a) A&E b) Neurorehabilitation
7   Questionnaires (A&E, Neurorehabilitation)
8   Interviews and visits (A&E, Rehabilitation Units)
9   Retrospective audit: Head Injury admissions to Addenbrooke's + as many other hospitals as possible in region (numbers, categories, pathways/initial mapping, resources, data quality); prospective audit of HI transfers; prospective regional audit of HI pts with disruptive behaviour
10 Assessment of impact and implications of new resource/technology/role/work patterns/change
11 a) Observation ward b) Minor HI clinic c) TBI follow-up clinic d) CT scanning, image transfer e) HI co-ordinator role > Business Plan: HI co-ordinator post
12 Evaluation/outcome studies
13 Piloting of HI standards
14 Piloting of rehabilitation codes
15 Detailed mapping
16 Development of standards
17 Development of rehab. codes
18 Development of Head Injury Co-ordination template

Figure 8.3   *Specific methods used*

Reflection and learning – planning

Dissemination and knowledge/information-sharing

19 Multidisciplinary conferences
20 Workshops
21 Working groups
22 Reports
23 Study days: HI training day for A&E staff; Aggression in HI seminar; Neurorehabilitation meeting
24 Working documents
25 Presentations at key professional bodies conferences (BAEM, SBNS, RCSE, BSRM, DOH 3rd Committee, BSR,BIRT, ERSCG, Headway)
26 Liaison with DOH, NICE, NSF, NHS Modernisation Agency, UKABIF, BrICS
27 Links created with other regions: Trent, Oxford, Lincs., London, Wales
28 Publication of papers: EMJ, JRSM
29 Development of reg

Figure 8.3 *Continued*

The role

I was multitasking, at a project management level, but I also had to take on a knowledge management leadership role within the research and collaborative continuum (Figure 8.4). The role is similar to the informationist in its continuous learning, but with essential domain knowledge and awareness of how to encourage change management in service delivery at all levels. The role therefore incorporates all aspects of knowledge management including clinical and policy literature review, data collection and analysis, collation and comparison of evidence, development of tools for change, and devising dissemination strategies for diverse groups (Figure 8.4).

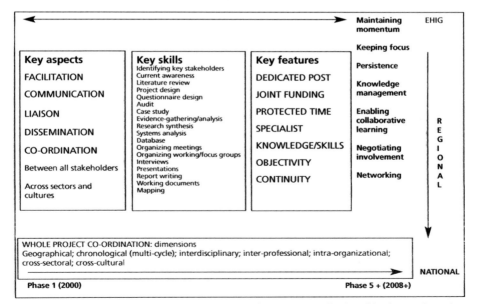

Figure 8.4 *The role and scope of the health information professional in the EHIG study*

As the health information professional, I also co-ordinated and maintained an overview of requirements, timescales and formats needed. In turn, that required developing and maintaining a communications network at the multiregional level and paying attention to different organizations' cultures, as some methods of communication worked better for some groups than for others.

Another aspect of the role was to act as gatekeeper to the research and stakeholder group, providing feedback and research that enabled practitioners to take part in the learning process, and I was also responsible for the development of improved information systems and defining new knowledge.

Results

This work has produced a replicable service framework, service planning tools, a regional head injury database and a model for strong leadership (that notably includes a health information professional) in a flexible collaborative learning network. Table 8.1 summarizes the strategies, methodologies and models. As can be seen, it was important to have evidence for why things were done in the way they were done. The

Table 8.1 *Research outcomes*	
Head Injury Services	**Strategies, methodologies and models**
Developed/created the systems for a comprehensive, co-ordinated responsive and flexible and sustainable service framework for Head Injury	Established a model of collaborative cross-cultural working, including a model for effective and innovative partnership working
Service planning tools to plan, develop, implement and evaluate an effective and comprehensive regional service for Head Injury	Developed a whole systems approach to knowledge transfer and dissemination
• Standards for the management of Head Injuries in Acute hospitals • Rehabilitation definitions and codes • Head Injury Co-ordination template	Established a collaborative cross-cultural Research Leadership model
Templates • Evaluating a new facility • Evaluating a new technology • Evaluating new evidence/research • Contextual mapping process	Developed a model for the role of a Health Information Specialist in an academic and clinical setting Developed a methodology for developing and sustaining networks
Resources • Regional Head Injury network, including named Leads in HI amongst all key stakeholders, including PCTs • New and innovative posts: Brain Injury Liaison Officer linking acute and community sectors and NHS and voluntary sectors • New facilities • Funding through partnerships with private/voluntary sectors	Contributed towards a theory of large scale transformational change in the health sector Whole systems approach, drawing strength from cultural diversity, defining alternatives, looking at root causes, pushing the debate, broadening the agenda, creative direct action, contextual research leadership, approach to and theory of knowledge/evidence, comprehensive dissemination, sustaining networks

clinical evidence suggested what should be done, but we needed a feasible and acceptable method of making the necessary changes.

Availability of good, accurate information systems was essential. This is self-evident, perhaps, but the systems were deficient in many ways at the start. This study developed initiatives and strategies to address the gaps and variability in services, as well as creating new information systems. One of the aims was to document the process and provide other head injury services with systems and a methodology they could use and adapt themselves for innovative change.

In this project, a need for change in service delivery helped fund a dedicated health information professional who proved key to the development of the successful, cutting-edge knowledge network, and a key component of the effectiveness of the research programme was the innovative information professional role that developed.

Discussion

On reflection, what developed was a network of practice. Networks of practice (Cox, 2007) may be viewed as a looser arrangement than communities of practice (Cox, 2005) yet the research leadership plus health information professional enabled an effective learning network that sustained improvement in health service delivery.

The 'neutral stance' of the health information professional role helped in communication among different professional groups. Awareness of the needs of different professional groups helped when disseminating information to all those involved, and the health information professional role had a 'helicopter' view of what was required, by whom, when and in what format. The importance of the neutrality and the different skills were appreciated as essential to the effectiveness of the team, the research and the collaborative continuum.

The flexible nature of the post was important, allowing development of a variety of skills – organization, administration, research methods and analysis and dissemination.

I was not working alone, and discussion and reflection with other members of the team helped address some limitations in experience and knowledge. The regular input of the research leadership group and the Collaborative Action Research (CAR) approach, enabled triangulation of different types of evidence, and thorough evaluation of the various cycles of the action research.

For a health information professional to be accepted by a clinical and research team, their work must be credible to the health professionals. There are four dimensions to credibility (Jacobson and Goering, 2006): scientific credibility; the expertise of the communicator; the authority of the communicator; and the neutral stance of the communicator. In this study, there was an emphasis on obtaining and generating accurate data and information for planning, with regular collaborative discussion and comprehensive feedback. The health information professional role included the responsibility of accurate data capture, interpretation and intelligent dissemination (i.e. communicating it in an appropriate, meaningful and accessible format). Working with the research partnership (a source of expertise) helped to put a stamp of authority on the information analysis. The neutrality of the role, whilst important in data analysis, did not necessarily contribute to the credibility of the research, but as the project progressed the credibility of the health information professional probably increased, as responsibilities became greater. Rankin, Grefsheim and Canto (2008) also conclude that an embedded informationist is more likely to provide a credible, acceptable and sustainable service.

Conclusions

My role in a clinical research setting of aiming to implement changes in service delivery has similarities to the informationist role of working in context, as continuous learning and domain knowledge are important (Bailey and Rudman, 2004). In this case some domain knowledge had been gained in clinical audit, prior to starting in the principal co-ordinator role, but more domain knowledge was gained throughout the research (continuous learning, while working in context). Interestingly, the evaluation of the National Institute of Health informationist programme also showed that domain knowledge was deemed more important (second to expertise in searching) in 2006 than in 2004 (Grefsheim et al., 2010).

More general research skills were also developed, partly as I was undertaking doctoral research based around the role, but these would have been necessary in any case, and some informationist roles stress these (Detlefsen, 2004). Although part-time doctoral research may seem a very long process, in this case the five-year timescale suited the nature of the research work.

The innovative health information professional role that developed in this project has some features of the role of the 'boundary spanner' in that it fulfilled an important boundary role between a number of organizations and cultures, receiving, filtering and disseminating the flow of information between the research group and the wider collaborative network. This seems critical to sustainability and the spread and implementation of innovative change. The health information professional was proactive in this role in finding, sorting, processing, applying, negotiating, transmitting and reframing and sharing knowledge.

Costs of specialist health information professionals need to be justified (Hill, 2008). In this project, there was a definite need for change in service delivery and specific funding was allocated. It is difficult to say that without the health information professional role, the project would not have been successful, but the extent of changes made and the success of the learning networks certainly indicate that the heath information professional role was important and probably vital.

Case study 8.5 The integration of informationists into advanced roles

Rebecca N. Jerome, Taneya Y. Koonce, Annette M. Williams and Nunzia Bettinsoli Giuse, Vanderbilt University Medical Center, USA

Introduction

In the mid-1990s, Nunzia Bettinsoli Giuse MD, MLS, the director of the Eskind Biomedical Library (EBL) at Vanderbilt University Medical Center (VUMC) in Nashville, Tennessee, USA, began developing a new model for librarian integration into patient care teams. Challenging the idea that librarian skills should be used primarily for searching the literature, EBL librarians began expanding their roles by collaborating with patient care teams, attending bedside rounds and synthesizing evidence from the literature to address complex patient-specific questions that arise during team discussions of diagnostic, treatment and other management decisions (see Giuse et al, 2005). This effort, the Clinical Informatics Consult Service (CICS) (Mulvaney et al., 2008), is predicated on the idea that librarians who have developed appropriate skill sets in the clinical subject area and in critical appraisal of research are able to serve as information consultants. Such librarians aid the clinical team by identifying and synthesizing the most relevant and high quality evidence for integration into patient care decisions. The CICS has expanded significantly since its inception, growing to encompass a number of librarians and involving inpatient areas throughout the Medical Center.

Expanding EBL's evidence appraisal and synthesis collaboration efforts

With the growth of Vanderbilt's internally developed electronic medical record (EMR) system, StarPanel, in the early 2000s, EBL identified an important opportunity for extending librarian consultation to VUMC's outpatient clinics. Though the clinics do not have bedside rounds, the EMR allows EBL to adapt its consultation model to the outpatient area. Through the EMR's secure messaging feature, clinicians send evidence requests to the library, with linkage back to the patient case prompting the question (Jerome et al., 2008). This allows the tailoring of information based on relevance that serves as a key principle of EBL's evidence provision efforts (Giuse et al., 2010).

With a cadre of librarians who have advanced skills in reading and interpreting the literature, informationist roles at EBL have also expanded into several other important VUMC efforts, including:

1 Order set development: teams charged with authoring and updating order sets for use in Vanderbilt's computerized order entry system consult with EBL librarians to identify relevant evidence; as the CICS supports patient-specific decisions based on evidence, the order sets effort allows the library to aid with embedding evidence in health care practices at the institutional level.

2 MyHealthAtVanderbilt: in this EMR portal for Vanderbilt patients, librarians utilize their skills in critical appraisal of information and patient-focused customization to create health topics tailored to a patient's ICD-9 codes and demographics. At each log-in to the portal, a patient sees educational links relevant to his/her condition and other characteristics. Librarians have also linked explanatory text to lab test and other results in the portal to aid patients in educating themselves as needed.

3 Systematic reviews: in 2007, Vanderbilt was awarded an Evidence-Based Practice Center (EPC) contract with the US Agency for Healthcare Research and Quality (AHRQ); this Center is charged with developing topics for comparative effectiveness review and authoring systematic reviews to evaluate evidence on various health topics. EBL librarians have been an integral part of the EPC team since its inception, participating in all steps of the systematic review process, including authoring content in the final report.

4 Molecular biology and clinical genetics: most recently, EBL has begun preparing for meeting clinician and researcher needs prompted by the continuing growth of personalized medicine. With the increasing importance of genotype-driven care and research at Vanderbilt, librarians are working to build skills to serve as intermediaries for this complex set of resources, including molecular biology data and databases that play an important role in such endeavours.

Built on a firm foundation

None of these services would be possible without EBL's strong infrastructure of training; this model provides both a firm foundation of initial skill development for all librarians involved in these projects, as well as mechanisms for ongoing growth and quality assurance practices. The library's training model also provides extensive training for paraprofessionals, equipping them with skills to support the reference desk, allowing librarians to expand their institutional involvement beyond the physical walls of the library.

Changing users' views of the library and librarians

By developing and applying advanced skills in this variety of collaborations throughout the Medical Center, EBL librarians function in highly visible roles that are changing how clinicians, researchers and patients view the capabilities and skills of the profession. The evolution of EBL's efforts strategically positions it for ongoing success, aligning with the Medical Center's vision by anticipating trends in medicine and health care to poise the library for continued integration and success in the organization. Its current focus on developing skills to support the growth of personalized medicine at VUMC is one key example of this forward thinking approach.

In sum, EBL's infrastructure of training and ability to anticipate and prepare for challenges in clinical care and research keep the librarians continually engaged and excited about their contribution to the institution and the profession, while also ideally positioning the library to keep pace with an ever-changing health care environment.

Conclusion

This chapter began with a model derived from the literature of the different roles that health librarians can play in relation to evidence-based practice. The case studies illustrate this model in action, particularly focusing on those roles where health librarians have become embedded, integrated or become key players in multidisciplinary teams and have developed skills in analysing and synthesizing information as well as being the experts in finding information. These key features have been promoted as the cornerstones of the 'informationist role', which was described by Davidoff and Florance but exploited in particular at Vanderbilt University and has been described here by Rebecca Jerome who describes how the services are 'predicated on the idea that librarians who have developed appropriate skill sets in the clinical subject area and in the critical appraisal of research are able to serve as information consultants'.

These features are predominant, however, in the other roles described in this chapter, such as that described by Helen Seeley, who as part of a multidisciplinary team, used her information skills, knowledge of the different user groups within the team and the ability to synthesize to have a 'helicopter view' of the project that was essential in ensuring team collaboration and driving the project forward. Similarly both Andrew Booth and Alison Brettle use analysis and synthesis skills in order to become key players in multi-professional systematic review teams, extending their role from that of expert literature searcher to one that also involves critical appraisal, synthesis and the provision of methodological support and guidance.

Olwen Beaven and Andrea Lane also note the increasing use of appraisal skills in their work at BMJ Evidence. Primarily their focus is on the use of their expert searching and information management skills in an evidence-based context, albeit in the private sector. However, they note the increasing need for appraisal skills in 'shielding authors from the overwhelming volume of new research'. This experience is similar to those described by Michelle Maden-Jenkins and Lorie Kloda's case studies in Chapter 6, who have become increasingly involved in systematic review or appraisal activities in their provider and educator roles.

But how do health librarians gain skills important for research and appraisal? After time to conduct research and writing, skills and confidence have been acknowledged as the second largest barrier for librarians conducting research (Clapton, 2010). If health librarians lack skills and confidence to conduct research themselves, are they also reluctant to develop appraisal and research skills? The case studies described above do not support this view, and instead provide ideas for librarians to gain skills in research and appraisal, and relate back to the concepts of self-efficacy and communities of practice that Christine Urquhart describes in Chapter 5. Jerome describes how a strong infrastructure for training at Vanderbilt provides a firm foundation of initial skill development as well as a mechanism for ongoing growth and quality assurance. Andrew Booth describes how more experienced and senior librarians within the ScHARR team offer mentorship and development opportunities for less experienced members of the team to enable them to develop their skills. Alison Brettle also describes how a strong mentor and a supportive environment encouraged her to become involved in research and develop research skills. Eventually this led to PhD study – formal recognition of research training and skills, a route also mentioned by Andrew Booth and Helen Seeley as a means of gaining credibility and recognition amongst academic peers. PhD study, however, is not the only means of gaining credibility amongst members of the multidisciplinary team. Helen Seeley emphasizes that health information professionals must demonstrate their credibility to be accepted by the team – but this can include showing expertise, authority and neutrality. This perhaps explains why involvement in systematic reviews and other areas of evidence-based practice have become such important roles for health librarians – they are able to demonstrate and use their expertise of searching rather than the subject area to maintain an authoritative and neutral stance within the evidence-based process.

Another way of becoming involved in research and appraisal activities is to adopt an evidence-based approach to your own library and information practice. Library practice often generates questions of interest that may involve engaging with evidence-based practice at a range of levels. A question or problem may lead to a literature search to find evidence that may help determine a way forward. Inevitably this evidence will need appraising, and appraising the literature on a known subject area is inevitably easier than on an unknown one. The same question may lead you to conduct an evaluation or small piece of research relating to your own practice (gaining research skills and confidence along the way). As the cases described above suggest, having research and appraisal skills (however they are obtained) can lead to a wealth of roles and opportunities for health librarians.

References

Bailey, J. and Rudman, W. (2004) The Expanding Role of the HIM Professional: where research and HIM roles intersect, *Perspectives in Health Information Management*, 1 (7), 1–6.

Beecroft, C., Booth, A., Otter, M. E., Keen, C. and Lynch, C. (2009) Supporting 'Best Research for Best Health' with Best Information, *Health Information and Libraries Journal*, 26 (4), 307–15.

Beverley, C. A., Bath, P. A. and Booth, A. (2004) Health Information Needs of Visually Impaired People: a systematic review of the literature, *Health and Social Care in the Community*, 12 (1), 1–24.

Beverley, C. A., Booth, A. and Bath, P. A. (2003) The Role of the Information Specialist in the Systematic Review Process: a health information case study, *Health Information and Libraries Journal*, 20 (2), 65–74.

Bexon, N. and Falzon, L. (2003) Personal Reflections on the Role of Librarians in the

Teaching of Evidence-based Healthcare, *Health Information and Libraries Journal*, **20** (2), 112–5.

Booth, A. (2004) In Pursuit of e-Quality – the role of 'communities of practice' when evaluating electronic information services, *Journal of Electronic Resources in Medical Libraries*, **1** (3), 25–42.

Booth, A. (2006) 'Brimful of STARLITE': toward standards for reporting literature searches, *Journal of the Medical Library Association*, **94** (4), 421–9.

Booth, A. and Beecroft, C. (2010) The SPECTRAL Project: a training needs analysis for providers of clinical question answering services, *Health Information and Libraries Journal*, **27** (3), 198–207.

Booth, A. and Brice, A. (2007) Prediction is Difficult, Especially the Future: a progress report, *Evidence Based Library & Information Practice*, **2** (1), 89–106.

Booth, A., Sutton, A. and Falzon, L. (2003) Working Together: supporting projects through action learning, *Health Information and Libraries Journal*, **20** (4), 225–31.

Booth, A., Carroll, C., Papaioannou, D., Sutton, A. and Wong. R. (2009) Applying Findings from a Systematic Review of Workplace-based E-learning: implications for health information professionals, *Health Information and Libraries Journal*, **26** (1), 4–21.

Booth, S. H., Booth, A. and Falzon, L. J. (2003) The Need for Information and Research Skills Training to Support Evidence-based Social Care: a literature review and survey, *Learning in Health and Social Care*, **2**, 191–201.

Brettle, A. (2003) Information Skills Training: a systematic review of the literature, Health Information & Libraries Journal, **20** (suppl. 1), 3–9.

Brettle, A. (2007) Evaluating Information Skills Training in Health Libraries: a systematic review, *Health Information & Libraries Journal*, **24** (suppl. 1), 18–37.

Brettle, A. (2009) *Exploring the Roles and Impact of Health Information Professionals Within Evidence Based Practice*, unpublished doctoral dissertation, University of Salford.

Brettle, A., Hulme, C. and Ormandy, P. (2006) The Costs and Effectiveness of Information Skills Training and Mediated Searching: quantitative results from the EMPIRIC project, *Health Information & Libraries Journal*, **23** (4), 239–47.

Brettle, A., Hulme, C. and Ormandy, P. (2007) Effectiveness of Information Skills Training and Mediated Searching: qualitative results from the EMPIRIC project, *Health Information & Libraries Journal*, **24** (1), 24–33.

Brettle, A., Maden-Jenkins, M., Anderson, L., McNally, R., Pratchett, T., Tancock, J., Thornton, D. and Webb, A. (2011) Evaluating Clinical Librarian Services: a systematic review, *Health Information & Libraries Journal*, DOI:10.1111/j.1471-1842.2010.00925.x.

Carroll, C., Cooke, J., Booth, A. and Beverley, C. (2006) Bridging the Gap: the development of knowledge briefings at the health and social care interface, *Health & Social Care in the Community*, **14** (6), 491–8.

Carroll, C., Booth, A., Papaioannou, D., Sutton. A. and Wong, R. (2009) UK Health-care Professionals' Experience of On-line Learning Techniques: a systematic review of qualitative data, *Journal of Continuing Education for Health Professionals*, **29** (4), 235–41.

Clapton, J. (2010) Library and Information Science Practitioners Writing for Publication: motivations, barriers and supports, *Library and Information Research*, **34** (106), 7-21.

Cox, A. M. (2005) What Are Communities of Practice: a comparative review of four seminal works, *Journal of Information Science*, **31** (6), 527–40.

Cox, A. M. (2007) Beyond Information? Factors in participation in networks of practice: a case study of web management in UK higher education, *Journal of Documentation*, **63** (5), 765–87.

Detlefsen, E. (2004) Clinical Research Informationist, *Reference Services Review*, **32** (1), 26–30.

Falzon, L. and Booth, A. (2001) REALISE-ing Their Potential?: implementing local library projects to support evidence-based health care, *Health Information and Libraries Journal*, **18** (2), 65-74.

Giuse, N. B., Koonce, T. Y., Jerome, R. N., Cahall, M., Sathe, N. A. and Williams, A. (2005) Evolution of a Mature Clinical Informationist Model, *Journal of the American Medical Informatics Association*, **12** (3), 249–55.

Giuse, N. B., Williams, A. M. and Giuse, D. A. (2010) Integrating Best Evidence into Patient Care: a process facilitated by a seamless integration with informatics tools, *Journal of the Medical Library Association*, **98** (3), 220-2.

Grant, M. J. and Brettle, A. J. (2006) Developing and Evaluating an Interactive Information Skills Tutorial, *Health Information & Libraries Journal*, **23** (2), 79–88.

Gray, M. (2001) *Evidence-based Healthcare*, Churchill-Livingstone.

Grefsheim, S. F, Whitmore, S. C., Rapp, B. A., Rankin, J. A., Robison, R. R. and Canto, C. C. (2010) The Informationist: building evidence for an emerging health profession, *Journal of the Medical Library Association*, **98** (2), 147–56.

Harris, M. (2005) The Librarian's Roles in the Systematic Review Process: a case study, *Journal of the Medical Library Association*, **93** (1), 81–7.

Harrison, J. (1997) Designing a Search Strategy to Identify and Retrieve Articles on Evidence-based Health Care Using MEDLINE, *Health Libraries Review*, **14** (1), 33–42.

Hicks, A. (1998) Developing Information Skills Training for National Health Service Personnel: experiences at the Trent Institute for Health Services Research, *Program*, **32** (2), 123–36.

Hill, P. (2008) Report of a National Review of NHS Library Services in England: from knowledge to health in the 21st Century, www.library.nhs.uk/nlhdocs/national_library_review_final_report_4feb_081.pdf.

Jacobson, N. and Goering, P. (2006) Credibility and Credibility Work in Knowledge Transfer, *Evidence & Policy*, **2** (2), 151–65.

Jerome, R. N., Giuse, N. B., Rosenbloom, S. T. and Arbogast, P. G. (2008) Exploring Clinician Adoption of a Novel Evidence Request Feature in an Electronic Medical Record System, *Journal of the Medical Library Association*, **96** (1), 34–41.

Lewis, R., Urquhart, C. and Rolinson, J. (1998) Health Professionals' Attitudes Towards EBM and the Role of the Information Professional in the Exploitation of Research Evidence, *Journal of Information Science*, **24** (5), 281–90.

McGowan, J. and Sampson, M. (2005) Systematic Reviews Need Systematic Searchers, *Journal of the Medical Library Association*, **93** (1), 74–80.

Medical Library Association (2005) Role of Expert Searching in Health Sciences Libraries: policy statement by the Medical Library Association adopted September 2003, *Journal of the Medical Library Association*, **93** (1), 42–4.

Mulvaney, S. A., Bickman, L., Giuse, N. B., Lambert, E. W., Sathe, N. A. and Jerome, R. N. (2008) A Randomized Effectiveness Trial of a Clinical Informatics Consult Service: impact on evidence-based decision-making and knowledge implementation, *Journal of the American Medical Informatics Association*, **15** (2), 203–11.

Paisley, S. (1998) Intelligent Purchasing in Trent: information for decision-making in the region's health authorities, *Health Libraries Review*, **15** (2), 87–95.

Palmer, J. (1996) Effectiveness and Efficiency: new roles and new skills for health librarians, *Aslib Proceedings*, **48** (10), 247–52.

Papaioannou, D., Sutton, A., Carroll, C., Booth, A. and Wong, R. (2010) Literature Searching for Social Science Systematic Reviews: consideration of a range of search techniques, *Health Information and Libraries Journal*, **27** (2), 114–22.

Pickard, J., Seeley, H., Kirker, S., Maimaris, C., McGlashan, K., Roels, E., Greenwood, R., Steward, C., Hutchinson, P. and Carroll, G. (2004) Mapping Rehabilitation Resources for Head Injury, *Journal of the Royal Society of Medicine*, **97** (8), 384–9.

Rankin, J. A., Grefsheim, S. F. and Canto, C. C. (2008) The Emerging Informationist Specialty: a systematic review of the literature, *Journal of the Medical Library Association*, **96** (3), 194–206.

Robson, C. (2002) *Real World Research*, 2nd edn, Blackwell Publishing.

Scherrer, C. and Dorsch, J. (1999) The Evolving Role of the Librarian in Evidence Based Medicine, *Bulletin of the Medical Library Association*, **87** (3), 322–8.

SCONUL (2010) *SCONUL Vision 2010*, www.sconul.ac.uk/publications/pubs/vision%202010.

Seeley, H. (2007) Developing Services for Head Injury: obtaining the data, *Health Informatics Journal*, **13** (2), 135–53.

Seeley, H. and Hutchinson, P. (2006) Rehabilitation Following Traumatic Brain Injury: challenges and opportunities, *Advances in Clinical Neurosciences and Rehabilitation*, **6** (2), 22–8.

Seeley, H. and Urquhart, C. (2008) Action Research in Developing Knowledge Networks, *Health Informatics Journal*, **14** (4), 279–96.

Seeley, H. M., Maimaris, C., Carroll, G., Kellerman, J. and Pickard, J. D. (2001) Implementing the Galasko Report on the Management of Head Injuries: the Eastern Region approach, *Emergency Medicine Journal*, **18** (5), 358–65.

Seeley, H. M., Hutchinson, P., Maimaris, C., Carroll, G., Kirker, S., Tasker, R., Haynes, K. and Pickard, J. D. (2006a) A Decade of Change in Regional Head Injury Care: a retrospective review, *British Journal of Neurosurgery*, **20** (1), 9–21.

Seeley, H. M., Maimaris, C., Hutchinson, P. J., Carroll, G., White, B., Kirker, S., Tasker, R. C., Steward, C., Haynes, K., Hardy, D. and Pickard, J. D. (2006b) Standards for Head Injury Management in Acute Hospitals: evidence from the six million population of the Eastern region, *Emergency Medicine Journal*, **23** (2), 128–32.

Sutton, A., Booth, A., Ayiku, L. and O'Rourke, A. (2005) e-FOLIO: using e-learning to learn about e-learning, *Health Information and Libraries Journal*, **22** (suppl. 2), 84–8.

White, C., Booth, A., Cooke, J. and Addison, F. (2005) SCISTER Act: delivering training in information skills for social-care professionals, *Health Information and Libraries Journal*, **22** (1), 54–62.

Wilkinson, A., Papaioannou, D., Keen, C. and Booth, A. (2009) The Role of the Information Specialist in Supporting Knowledge Transfer: a public health information case study, *Health Information and Libraries Journal*, **26** (2), 118–25.

Winning, M. A. and Beverley, C. A. (2003) Clinical Librarianship: a systematic review of the literature, *Health Information and Libraries Journal*, **20** (suppl. 1), 10–21.

9
The librarian as decision maker

Jackie Cheeseborough

Introduction

Managers of library and information services have always based their decisions on professional judgement, experience, and knowledge of their users' and employers' requirements. However, constant change makes the current situation different. A manager and leader of a health information service needs to be sensitive to their environment and comfortable with constant change. As health information professionals, we need to keep up to date with new technology and new ways of delivering information services. We also need to be aware of the external political situation and the impact that this will have on the information needs of our users. In addition, it is important to understand both the changing needs of the clients using our services, and the directors of our organizations. Management decisions need to be made in context, using our organizational knowledge (Cortada, 2009). It is crucial that the decisions that library managers make are relevant to the current needs of their employers and service users and that services are developed in line with changes. A professional judgement made out of context will not be the right one and will lead to the information service being irrelevant and superseded. If possible, library decision makers need to be anticipating changes in their organization, and to be ready with ideas and proposals. The need for decision making is becoming much more rapid, with quicker turnaround expected by employers.

Forward thinking

Health librarians need to scan the external environment, and also be aware of changes taking place within our own organizations. Our information management skills are a great strength. Library managers should be clear about their strategic direction, but strategy is likely to have to be more flexible than it used to be as external circumstances change. It is important to have a strategic framework, and to be clear of the direction of travel, for example from print to digital, from quiet to lively, from physical to outreach, and the steps that are needed to achieve this. Strategic goals should be underpinned by operational plans but we need to be aware of external developments, and changes in direction may be needed. Local strategies must be linked to our organizations' overarching strategies. Good decision makers need to be alert to changes in thinking in their organizations. If library managers are asked to make changes that they are uncomfortable with, ensuing decisions must be based on a firm understanding of the needs of their organization. Alternatives should be suggested as long as it helps with the objectives of the organization.

Evidence for decision making

Decisions should be made with an understanding of the available evidence. Evidence-based library and information practice (EBLIP) brings together three ingredients for decision making: best available evidence, professional judgement and knowledge of users' needs and preferences, whilst recognizing the challenges, particularly in understanding the knowledge needs of our users and non-users (Booth, 2008). Once again, our professional skill set places us in a good position. Managers of large services can use the skills of their own team to provide literature reviews of the evidence, or managers of smaller services can provide their own. However, decision making also relies on the instincts of the leader, based on a thorough understanding of their own organization and the users of their services. We have to act at a subconscious level applying both explicit and tacit knowledge (Cortada, 2009). Successful decision making will lead to health information managers being respected by their employers, which will give them greater influence. The leader has to steer their ship safely through sometimes treacherous waters, holding true to their own strategic principles and information values, whilst ensuring that they meet the changing needs of their users and employers. Sometimes this can mean performing a skilful balancing act. Managers of large services need to surround themselves by good advisers, experts in particular fields, knowledge management, digital libraries, archives, information literacy and then be able to listen to advice and make the correct decision. Managers of smaller services may need to have many of these skills themselves.

Knowing your users

It is necessary to have up-to-date knowledge of the information needs of users on which to base decisions. Sometimes large scale surveys that seek to incorporate both current users and non-users (Bertulis and Cheeseborough, 2008, 186–97) and sometimes much quicker surveys can be useful as indicators of need. Data gathering can take different forms: paper-based surveys, online surveys, focus groups and interviews. Evaluation of services and projects is also important. Library managers have traditionally been successful at gathering data, but qualitative data is increasingly necessary, being able to judge the customers' satisfaction with services, as can be measured using rigorously tested instruments such as LibQual+TM (Russell, 2010).

Understanding change

Successful decision makers need to be able to experiment with new ideas as it will not be possible to have creative and innovative services otherwise. This may mean being prepared to make mistakes, but changing our attitude towards them and seeing them as a learning experience (Cufaude, 2002). This requires courage and the ability to be flexible and responsive.

Making decisions in changing environments, and based on users' needs and those of employers, requires leadership skills in health library managers, and an understanding of the management of change. Library and information services staff are currently having to experience regular cycles of change, for example taking on new roles such as eHealth (the use of information and IT in clinical practice) policy advisers, or moving from working in quiet health sections of academic libraries to working in lively, noisy, social spaces that require retail skills as well as information specialist ones. Whatever the changes that are being experienced, the health librarian as leader will need to motivate their team, enthuse them about the changes, openly and honestly explain what will be happening, and communicate constantly. The team should be invited to be involved in the decision making where appropriate, which is likely to lead to better results, as long as the leader is clear about the direction of travel and is able to articulate the vision, strategic framework and boundaries in which decisions will be made. In a changing environment decisions should not be made separately and out of context and both small as well as large decisions need to be made within a clear strategic and management framework.

Health librarians as managers and decision makers

Management decision making is similar whether it is a hybrid information service or a purely digital service. For managers of hybrid services, the decision regarding the balance between digital and physical services needs to be based on a clear collection development policy. With decreasing budgets, decision making on how and which services should be provided becomes more challenging and the use of cost-effectiveness analysis (CEA) can be a useful decision making tool. CEA provides comparative evidence on cost and effectiveness to inform decision making whilst taking other factors into consideration (Hulme, 2006). Difficult decisions need to be made with a clear knowledge of user and employer needs and in the light of relevant policies. Good project management skills are also necessary.

Marketing and promotion should be an intrinsic part of strategic planning. Health information services need to be seen as well as be provided. Marketing is an integral part of any project and any key management decision. As services become increasingly digital, or completely digital, the librarian's role in the provision of them can become hidden. Users often feed back that the health information professionals are the most valued part of the service. Digital libraries need to be able to provide a personal service that promotes the skills of the librarians, for example through virtual enquiry services.

Health librarians are uniquely placed to be great decision makers as information management skills are crucial for good decision making. We have the skills and it is important that we use them effectively and quickly, and in context, to meet the changing needs of users and employers. The following four case studies illustrate these points in practice, demonstrating a range of roles where health librarians act as decision makers.

Case study 9.1 Head of Library and Knowledge Services in Primary Care

Katherine Dumenil, St Helens and Knowsley Teaching Hospitals NHS Trust

Overview

My current job title is Head of Library and Knowledge Services; however, I started my career in the NHS as an outreach librarian, with the role of educating and supporting clinical staff in evidence-based practice. My new role has not changed my aims of educating and supporting staff in evidence-based practice, but it changes the staff I interact with and how I achieve those aims. My main role now is to strategically lead the service and to advise our customers within primary care on how to develop knowledge services and ensure the evidence is central to all decisions, both clinical and management.

Achievements and barriers

I currently work with a range of colleagues, from directors to clinicians, to create services that make evidence-based practice simple, second nature and fundamental to the organizations I work with. Some examples of this would be:

1 I have worked with our Director of Performance who heads up a department focused on data to identify knowledge services that could complement the data his directorate provides to the commissioners. We both identified the need for commissioners to be aware of innovation and best practice while having the ability to learn from others across the world. This is one of the seeds that led to the North West Regional Horizon Scanning Service, which now produces around 20 horizon scanning bulletins for commissioners and service leads.
2 I consulted with all our service leads and commissioners to shape a current awareness service that was tailored to each staff groups needs. This led to our localized Knowledge Service, which brings together local and national information in a format they wanted.
3 I was asked to advise on the policy for the development of corporate documentation and then to sit on the group that approves policies and guidelines. My purpose was to ensure all organizational documentation was driven by evidence. The library service took this opportunity to not just comment on the final document but to offer support to those staff developing this documentation in finding the evidence.
4 The Head of the Research Team and I worked with the Head of Commissioning to embed the message that evidence did not just mean data but encompassed a wide range of sources. This lead to a local Evidence Directory and an evidence template for all business cases.

In the last couple of years we have been successful in integrating our service in the business of PCTs, but there have been many barriers to developing a successful library service over the years. In primary care the first obstacle to providing a library and knowledge service is the geographical spread of and time pressure upon staff. A traditional physical library could not succeed in primary care, you simply would find no one has the time to visit a library. We have developed two solutions to this: outreach and online services.

The outreach service provides education and support at the point of need, be it in a one to one session with a GP at their practice, a training session for district nurses at their base during lunchtime or attending a commissioning meeting to make sure you capture the evidence needs. The point of the outreach service is for the library to become integrated into the daily practice of health staff and not be a physical building that has barriers to being visited.

The website we developed has two core functions: the first is to provide access to all resources and the service we provide at the point of need and, secondly, as a platform to our new Knowledge Service. The Knowledge Service, as mentioned above, was developed with commissioners, service leads and clinical staff to provide a single point for local, regional and national information, with the ability to be alerted to the specific information they want. A nurse can go to the cancer page and find information relating to their role, from the PCT's guidelines to the latest research; while a commissioner can go to the cancer page and will have a different view and find the latest local health profile/data to the national commissioning tool kits.

Another barrier is the constantly changing NHS, which acutely affects primary care, and our challenge is to have the ability to change our strategic direction in line with the NHS.

Over recent years a key change for our service is the type of staff we support; we continue to support students and clinical staff as we always have, but we have had to develop (both within the service and professionally) the capability to support management and commissioning within the NHS. The electronic development has been essential, as in all sectors and professions; however, the focus of the service and the professional development to achieve the expertise and confidence in me and the staff within my service to support management and commissioning decisions has ensured our survival.

We have been successful in ensuring our customers recognize the importance of the services librarians can provide in evidence-based practice, not just for clinicians but for commissioning as well.

Advantages and challenges

The best thing about my role is breaking down these barriers and seeing where you make a difference: a commissioning decision based on evidence that has saved the organization money; a clinical decision that has improved patient care; the support to a nursing student, not just in their current course but in their future career.

The biggest challenge ahead for all health librarians is yet again in ensuring we have a place in a changing NHS who, as with all public sectors, are facing cuts to spending. To do this we need to provide a modern, cost-effective library service and again prove the need for the library and the library professional role within an NHS organization, whatever it may look like.

Case study 9.2 Programme Director for Knowledge Management
Ann Wales, NHS Scotland

Overview

As the Programme Director, I aim to ensure effective use of knowledge across Scotland's health and social services. The principles of health care quality mean that knowledge needs not only to be available but to be applied to delivery of safe and effective care, centred on the needs of the patient or client. My role is about getting knowledge into action, to deliver high quality care. Practitioners can only improve their performance and patient outcomes if they can find, share, create and use knowledge. Improving patient care requires embedding effective use of knowledge in organizational processes, workforce skills, behaviours and values, and in online information systems. My responsibilities include:

1 Development and delivery of the national strategy for knowledge management.
2 Delivery of online knowledge services – principally The Knowledge Network (www.knowledge.scot.nhs.uk) – as a platform for finding, sharing and using knowledge. It combines a comprehensive range of content from over 100 providers with tools for communication and collaboration, and for measuring impact of use of knowledge.
3 Empowering and enabling the workforce through developing the skills, behaviours and values of using knowledge effectively.
4 Building organizational capacity for knowledge management through knowledge action plans that focus on building culture, leadership, processes, tools and capability for better use of knowledge.

A typical day

An early start to have some time for thinking, writing and planning before the business of the day begins. Office hours are absorbed by back to back meetings, in person and remotely using technology. Sometimes it is necessary to travel across the country, but all the meetings, face to face or remote, help to influence policy makers and build the relationships that are essential to getting knowledge used through our services. Interactions are with:

1 Partners in health and social care to identify needs for knowledge services and to progress collaborative projects. Development of our services is generally in partnership with a 'customer' – representatives of different staff groups and needs.
2 Senior strategic leads in health and social services provider organizations, and in government to engage their support for knowledge services and identify new ways to gain uptake and impact.
3 Our key partners in knowledge management – leads nationally and locally in library and knowledge services, quality improvement, organizational development, e-health/information, communications and technology, research and development, training, education and practice development. While these are partners in service provision and development, our sponsors are the clinicians and practitioner leads in health and social services who need to use our services and advise us on whether they are fit for purpose.
4 Team project managers to monitor and support work on a wide range of knowledge management projects – ranging from complex software development and information system design to supporting organizations to develop organizational knowledge action plans, outreach and workforce training in knowledge management skills, and developing new approaches to better use of knowledge – for example through tools for capturing tacit knowledge and disseminating knowledge within the health and care system.
5 Commercial partners – providers of subscription content, system providers and software developers. Working with major commercial suppliers with a limited budget to get value for money through negotiation, a solution-focused approach, and positioning our service as 'loss leader' for new developments is key to service development.

Evenings are generally occupied with catching up with e-mail, dealing with problems that arise during the working day, and defining headlines for business plans and reports that need to be written up in the precious early morning space.

The Knowledge Network
As Scotland's national knowledge service for health and social care, The Knowledge Network provides an enterprise knowledge management system covering the key aspects of getting knowledge into action:

1 A comprehensive index of around 15 million information and learning resources, from some 150 providers in public, voluntary and commercial sectors, using a 'Google-style' search and indexing technology.
2 A range of tools for communication and collaboration, with a strong emphasis on social networking and building communities of practice. These approaches to knowledge exchange and dissemination are key to getting knowledge into practice. They focus equally on capturing and sharing tacit knowledge – 'stories' – about

experience of using knowledge in practice and on sharing published or explicit knowledge to support colleagues working on similar areas of practice.

3 Access to tools and measures for improving performance and outcomes – i.e. measuring whether use of knowledge has made a difference in practice. These tools focus largely on data recording and analysis, and are beginning to extend the support of the Knowledge Network into the full spectrum of data, information and knowledge.

Health information professional role

Our knowledge services are founded in the core information professional skills of sourcing, acquiring, analysing, organizing and disseminating knowledge. The focus on getting knowledge into action extends our scope beyond traditional information sources to capturing and sharing of tacit knowledge, synthesizing knowledge from both textual and data sources, and embedding knowledge in day to day practice and learning.

Since first taking up this post in 2003, it has evolved beyond its original focus on providing an online library for the NHS, to become a more integrated knowledge management role with a 'whole system' perspective, reaching across health and social services boundaries (see Wales, 2004, 2005; McLeod, Thain and Wales, 2005; Thain and Wales, 2005; NHS Education for Scotland, 2006, 2010; Caldwell et al., 2008). I now emphasize the translation of knowledge into practice. That means that the Knowledge Management service increasingly operates through relationships with the services that support, deliver and monitor the 'action' – quality improvement, e-health, scrutiny bodies, health improvement, front line practitioners and reaching out to social services as well as health.

Case study 9.3 Knowledge Services Lead
Kim Montacute, NHS Yorkshire and Humber

Overview

As the Knowledge Services Lead for an English NHS region, I support the workforce and education function whose key objectives are to improve workforce productivity, workforce planning systems and knowledge, information and library services.

The core function of my role includes acting as the professional lead to the knowledge, information and library services workforce and supporting collaborative networking, continuing professional development (CPD) and library service modernization. I also ensure that library, information and knowledge services are fit for purpose to support the clinical, research and management objectives of the health and social care sector by developing a multi-professional learning infrastructure.

Across the region I co-ordinate and quality assure a network of 25 library, knowledge and information services to ensure that all NHS staff (in Yorkshire and Humber, 140,000 people) have access to high quality resources. I do not have any managerial responsibility for the library service staff though. Similar roles operate in other regions and this network promotes library and information services, supports research and evidence-based practice, innovation and evaluation as well as the professional development of health library staff across the country.

A typical day

My role is very varied and on a typical day I can be taking decisions about any or all of the following. In acting as professional lead, I am a habitual horizon scanner and am always trying to ensure that library and knowledge services are involved at the heart of services to ensure constant improvements in patient care. Recruiting staff, I am frequently invited to be on interview panels for appointing NHS library staff, as senior line managers for library services often have no specialist knowledge. It is a pleasure to bring new blood into the NHS and to support current staff moving forward in their careers. I'm responsible for mentoring candidates who are applying for Chartership or Fellowship to the Chartered Institute of Library and Information Professionals (CILIP), the UK professional body for librarians. Each mentee is different and decisions about how to help them develop to achieve the membership level being applied for are vital and need to be carefully considered relating to their work environment and personality. A constant decision is how to ensure good cross-fertilization between the projects I am involved in, linking the right people up and disseminating knowledge appropriately. Even though I trained in librarianship over 25 years ago I still find some of the basic skills in demand. Most recently this has been when working on the installation of a new document storage and retrieval system, where I provided a key role in decisions regarding indexing terms and building the taxonomy.

In terms of CPD and library service modernization I procure electronic resources for the region, to supplement the resources available nationally to NHS staff. To assure the quality of library services, I receive and analyse annual statistics and quality assurance framework submissions from NHS libraries in the region. I also conduct mystery shopper visits and regional/national moderation to ensure that compliance standards are equitable across the country. To ensure that library staff within the region receive appropriate CPD I commission a range of opportunities, from subsidized places on key conferences to postgraduate studies courses, through to specific skills such as applying Web 2.0 technologies to promote services.

New challenges

To ensure that library, information and knowledge services are fit for purpose to support the clinical, research and management objectives of the health and social care sector I have to constantly reconsider my budget priorities and frequently seek to achieve more outputs with fewer resources. As there is a huge push for health information to be easily accessible for patients, carers and the public I have worked with the public library sector to develop a Memorandum of Understanding that enables NHS library staff to train public library staff about health resources as well as acting as a backstop for health-related enquiries received in public libraries. There is a need for constant communication with the national groups and my regional network so that library service managers are up to date with government polices and can develop their services accordingly.

The best things about this role include never knowing what you are going to be asked to be involved in next and knowing you make a difference, to colleagues, wider NHS staff and by implication to improvements in patient care. There are a variety of decisions I take every day that I know have made an impact on how people work, improved their skills or changed practice. As a key player in a truly multi-professional team of senior managers, I know that there is respect for my professional abilities amongst my peers. The organization values my core skills so I am often a key player in evidence gathering and writing submissions for a variety of corporate governance and assurance programmes. Finally, seeing constant service development and making decisions about which innovations to encourage, for example the use of net vibes for current awareness services, developing knowledge management activities or new roles such as clinical librarian services, or working on the national Embedding Informatics in Clinical Education programme, makes me realize how valuable our professional skills are to the NHS.

New aspects of the role

One of my most challenging roles at the moment is being the external 'expert' on a PhD supervision panel. I am enjoying this very much and am learning as much as I am supporting. It is also lovely at this stage of my career to be involved with groundbreaking research into our profession and being involved in writing for publication.

In line with the changing nature and structures within the health service and technology, the role has evolved in several ways. Structurally my employers' name has changed three times in seven years even though the basic functions remain the same and I have worked in many teams ranging from education commissioning through to workforce planning. Geographically the area for which I am responsible has expanded from West Yorkshire to the whole of Yorkshire and the Humber. More recently I have been able to use my more specific evidence searching, assimilation and publication skills set in a one day per week secondment to our Quality Observatory, which is working to improve quality and effectiveness by looking at referral thresholds for certain clinical conditions as well as the evidence base for the implementation of new technologies in patient care. We are also using knowledge management techniques to evaluate programmes and support the quality and productivity agenda. Changes in technology and the unique nature of NHS networks mean there is always a requirement to learn new applications and present materials differently, but I have always found the theoretical grounding for the capture, storage, organization and retrieval of information stands me in good stead.

Maintaining visibility

The biggest challenge within the role is trying to maintain the visibility of library and knowledge services across the ever-changing NHS landscape. For example, we need to encourage clinical staff to use our services as first port of call when starting a new project or programme of study instead of in desperation at the eleventh hour. Library services have many champions including chief knowledge officers at board level but there is always an untapped pool of potential users who would benefit from our support. Beating the 'everything is electronic now' myth is a huge challenge. Many users are very happy with the wealth of materials available via their intranet or web portal but do not see the connection between these resources and the staff who develop them. There is also a huge education and training need for people to be able to critically appraise the literature they can so easily find, and apply it to their specific work environment. Finally it is essential to keep up to date with ever changing policies and new political priorities. NHS structures are constantly evolving so keeping the library 'brand' visible is a constant challenge.

Preparing for the future

Throughout my career I have always been a member of CILIP. Achieving my lifelong ambition to become a Fellow has helped my credibility with colleagues, especially clinical professionals. The advocacy and career structure provided by our professional association has always supported my role and my personal development. Acting as a champion for the skills and expertise of our profession is vital as this will ensure that commissioners are aware of the need for our services and will include them in future planning.

There will be a need for wider involvement in the health information for patients agenda, working with a range of public sector and charitable organizations to support patients to make informed choices about their lifestyle and health needs.

I think knowledge harvesting will become a crucial activity in the ever changing health and social care environment: ensuring that key knowledge areas are identified and that the relevant documentation and expertise is 'harvested' and then packaged so that future staff can access it easily.

There will also be an even greater need for utilization of my business planning skills to ensure that more resources are targeted towards knowledge services and that best use is made of them to support patient care.

Case study 9.4 Head of Information and Public Relations
Lotta Haglund, Karolinska Institutet University Library, Stockholm, Sweden

Overview

Karolinska Institutet (KI) is a single faculty medical university in Stockholm, Sweden, and Karolinska Institutet University Library is the on-campus medical library, with our target groups being students and staff. It is my responsibility to plan and organize KI library marketing efforts to present the library mission, services on offer and operations to our stakeholders. My main objectives are to increase dialogue with target groups to strengthen their knowledge about library services; to increase the use of librarian competencies, library services and information sources; and to increase the librarian's knowledge of our user groups.

Role

To accomplish these objectives, I interact with library staff, other information professionals at KI, staff and students, and the staff paper editor within KI; other librarians (national and international); and international guest students and researchers. My work relies heavily on ICT systems, for example software for writing, presenting, calculating, scheduling and making mind maps. Additionally, I use the internet for finding and circulating information via our web page, the library intranet, the KI intranet and many social media sites, for example Google groups, wikis and Facebook.

Of the more than 110 staff in the library, I am the generalist, with little in-depth knowledge but good general knowledge about the entire library. I add value to library operations in my role as a communication professional by working strategically with information/communication planning through applying marketing activities, and as an internal consultant, helping colleagues to plan and execute communication strategies. It is becoming more common for Swedish university libraries to have someone in this role, and I am part of a network of approximately 15 colleagues from other university libraries, most of them librarians with a special interest or knowledge in marketing. In this role one requires marketing and communication skills, something I have acquired by attending courses, seminars and conferences, but mainly through 'learning by doing', and studying relevant marketing literature.

My role demands a variety of tasks and skills, from an accomplished administrator to having an extrovert personality for the more glamorous aspects (i.e. hosting social functions). One also needs to have good interpersonal skills, be creative (think outside the box), pedagogical and, occasionally, diplomatic. One of the best things about this role is the opportunity to meet numerous people, and to continuously learn new things about KI and different aspects of librarianship. Since I am not one for routine work, this suits me perfectly – no two days are alike!

When I began working with library promotions 15 years ago, users had to physically visit the library to search databases and access journal articles. Over the past ten years, we have seen a dramatic change in user behaviour, supported and promoted by librarians, where staff and faculty today access scientific information from the web-based library from their own computers. Most visitors to the physical library are students, who use it as a common area to study and meet friends, with little need for librarian expertise. Reference questions are scarce. This shift in use has made it difficult for librarians to interact with users, to promote library services and to learn about user needs. Those staff and faculty old enough seem to have forgotten what they once knew about the value of librarian expertise, and now have little idea of the potential of involving the library in their work.

Some years ago, we interviewed a number of researchers about their information needs and search habits. The librarian asked what approach they used when looking for a known article in PubMed that they could not find. None of the researchers suggested contacting the library, even though a librarian was asking the question, but instead said they would ask a colleague, a supervisor or give up. I am convinced that libraries have to change their marketing strategies from focusing on promoting use of library resources, to educating users about how a librarian's skills can help them.

Because of this shift in user behaviour, there has also been a shift in marketing channels and tools, from printed folders and brochures, to web, e-mail and social media. Additionally, many libraries are working on embedding themselves in the work of the users (primarily faculty).

Challenges

The biggest challenge in this role is looking at the library from the user's viewpoint. This should result in a different message from the library – instead of promoting what we do, we should promote what we achieve for users. Another challenge is getting the attention of our target groups: when they have less time, think they do not need the library and are suffering from information overload. This challenge demands much creativity and a strong customer focus. To accomplish this I need to look outside the library environment for new ideas, and to acquire theoretical and practical marketing knowledge.

For future success, I will need to work even harder to understand the fundamentals of science and the working conditions of researchers, to be able to tailor marketing efforts to their needs. One potential future scenario is that education and research will become more fragmented, reducing the role of universities in favour of international research groups or communities, where students will assemble their tailor-made education from a selection of shorter courses offered by many organizations internationally. This could lead to decreased loyalty to, and reduced payment for, the university library services, in turn leading to increased competition for the library by publishers, information brokers or other providers of scientific information.

As the library takes on more non-traditional tasks, I will need to understand complex new activities, such as the curation of scientific data, bibliometry and nano-publications, and their implications for the library and research, to be able to pedagogically explain library operations to our users.

With new communication technology evolving, the future holds increased competition for the attention of our users, and increased demands on me to understand and use these tools. One example is social media, which today already places different demands on my role – users expect fast interaction, and there is the need to handle both praise and criticism. Will the library soon have a 24/7 online librarian?

Lastly, we are seeing an increased demand to show library stakeholders value for money, placing pressure on libraries to evaluate library operations. As I am responsible for library marketing, the question of investment return is potentially on the agenda of every staff and faculty meeting, who prefer to see their money being used for research.

Conclusion

Katherine Dumenil's case study emphasizes the need for a 'finger on the pulse'. It is important to know what matters to the decision makers, and probably even more important to be able to predict what might happen in the future, and be prepared with Plan A and Plan B. Another message from this case study is the importance of marketing, not only in the sense of promoting the service, but understanding the needs of market, building relationships with customers (customer relationship management) and providing services that meet the needs of users – within the budget available. To do that, the market needs to be segmented or profiled. That principle is illustrated by the way the website is designed so that a nurse visiting the web page obtains the information they need, and a commissioner obtains what they need. Visit a supermarket and look at the organization there – there will be a quick stop area for picking up sandwiches, snacks and drinks for lunch. The same snack biscuits will appear on the shelves elsewhere, in a greater range of choices and pack sizes. Some users only have time for the overview, others want to have more in-depth information. More information is not necessarily better.

Lotta Haglund also emphasizes the importance of thinking about library services from the user perspective – getting away from trying to emphasize what we do and what skills we have, to appreciating what can be done to make the work of the user easier and more effective. This is a point emphasized by Jackie Cheeseborough in the introduction. Katherine Dumenil's marketing activities focus on a discrete group of users, all working for or with the health service. Lotta Haglund points out that researchers increasingly collaborate across organizational boundaries – why ask the library for information when an e-mail to a colleague in another country might provide the information faster? But that exchange of information brings in the need for data curation on research projects – sharing is fine, but who is the owner of the information? Who has rights of access, which version is the authentic version and who provides an audit trail of approved amendments? Who is responsible for providing continuing access? Many of the informationists (see the case study by Rebecca Jerome in Chapter 8) now assist researchers keep track of their research data, and information professionals now need to persuade researchers that the skills of information management are required in data curation. As Lotta points out, one cannot rely on users dropping into the library for a brief chat – the library service has to go out to meet users, to find out what they need, to remind users of what is provided and to negotiate new services. Ann Wales describes a national strategic role, which involves working with a range of policy makers, developing projects to meet the needs of knowledge management. This role involves liaison not just with representatives of health and social care staff, and health policy makers, but also with the technologists who can review, provide and adapt the tools that enable knowledge management activities across Scotland's health service. The case studies in Chapter 7 illustrate individual projects, Ann's contribution in Chapter 9 shows what needs to happen to make knowledge management happen across a national health service.

For health librarians in the UK, the new challenge, as indicated by Kim Montacute is working with new groups to ensure that patients and the public are informed properly about health and lifestyle decisions, and the services that are available to them. Other organizations may offer such information and advice to patients and the public – public libraries, charities and patient support groups, to name just a few of the obvious examples. Other services may provide added value services – decision support and analysis – just as insurance comparison websites let you compare the best price and offerings available on car insurance. Strategy is not just about having a vision of where you are going, but how you are going to get there. (That is very apparent from Ann Wales's description of the structures within which she works.) Everyone might agree that patients need to be better informed about health and lifestyle decisions, but we need to work out how we get there. What should health libraries do? How do they work with public libraries? Where do national telephone and internet advice services fit in? What additional skills are needed by those working in the traditional health libraries – and what additional skills are needed by those working in public libraries? Sometimes the additional skills are not really additional skills at all, the requirement is to practise and extend existing skills confidently in a new environment. Kim Montacute emphasizes how her role encompasses supporting continuing professional development, and senior library managers often need to have this vision of where the service needs to go and how they must get there. As Jackie Cheeseborough emphasizes in her introduction to the chapter, that requires using evidence.

Decisions about service delivery options need to be made on the evidence of what works and what is less effective. Ann Wales stresses the importance of continuous learning from the knowledge management development projects. Library services need to monitor and evaluate their own services – evidence is information collected internally as well as that available externally. One of the faulty models of decision making is that of continuing to collect information but failing to make a decision – the pattern of behaviour that is associated with students photocopying article after article in the hope that the information will somehow hop on to the page of their assignment without the need for internal processing. As Jackie emphasizes, it is often better to act, try out a solution and if it does not work well, then there is learning to be gained from the experience.

References

Bertulis, R. and Cheeseborough, J. (2008) Royal College of Nursing's Information Needs Survey, *Health Information and Libraries Journal*, 25 (3), 186-97.

Booth, A. (2008) Using Evidence in Practice, *Health Information and Libraries Journal*, **25** (3), 233–6.

Caldwell, L., Davies, S., Stewart, F., Thain, A. and Wales, A. (2008) Scottish Toolkit for Knowledge Management, *Health Information and Libraries Journal*, **25** (2), 125–34, DOI:10.1111/j.1471-1842.2007.00747.x.

Cortada, J. (2009) Power and Use of Context in Business Management, *Journal of Knowledge Management*, **13** (3), 13–27.

Cufaude, J. (2002) Laying the Foundation: the architecture of great ideas, *Information Outlook*, **6** (1), 6–9.

Hulme, C. (2006) Using Cost Effectiveness Analysis: a beginner's guide, *Evidence Based Library and Information Practice*, **1** (4), 17–29.

McLeod, L., Thain, A. and Wales, A. (2005) Influence of Strategic Direction for NHS Scotland Knowledge Services on Indexing Policy for the NHS Scotland E-library, *Health Information and Libraries Journal*, **22** (1), 44–53, DOI:10.1111/j.1471-1842.2005.00550.x.

NHS Education for Scotland (2006) From Knowing to Doing: transforming knowledge into practice in NHS Scotland, www.elib.scot.nhs.uk/news/documents/nhss_knowledge_strategy.pdf

NHS Education for Scotland (2010) *Enabling Partnerships: sharing knowledge to build the mutual NHS*, www.knowledge.scot.nhs.uk/uploads/Enabling_Partnerships.pdf.

Russell, P. (2010) Measuring Up: the experience of LibQual at ITT Dublin library, *SCONUL Focus*, **49**, 47–51.

Thain, A. and Wales, A. (2005) Information Needs of Specialist Healthcare Professionals: a preliminary study based on the West of Scotland Colorectal Cancer Managed Clinical Network, *Health Information and Libraries Journal*, **22** (2), 133–42, DOI:10.1111/j.1471-1842.2005.00570.x.

Wales, A. (2004) Developing Integrated Knowledge Services for NHS Scotland: managing continuity and transition within a new collaborative dynamic, *Health Information and Libraries Journal*, **2** (1), 52–4.

Wales, A. (2005) Managing Knowledge to Support the Patient Journey in NHS Scotland: strategic vision and practical reality, *Health Information and Libraries Journal*, **22** (2), 83–95, DOI:10.1111/j.1471-1842.2005.00572.x.

Conclusion

Christine Urquhart and Alison Brettle

In the first part of the book we attempted to describe some of the changes that are taking place in education and in the health service. The emphasis was on events within the UK, but it is also important to remember that the UK is influenced by political initiatives from Europe and elsewhere. Globalization affects the organization and funding of health and education everywhere. We hope, therefore, that the case studies presented in the second part of the book provide some transferable lessons for library and information professionals working in different settings. One of the themes of knowledge management is the power of the story, to explain, through the story of an event, how problems were viewed, structured and solutions found. The stories are memorable, and provide a good memory aid for those seeking solutions to new problems that arise. Some of the case studies may not be immediately useful to you but, nevertheless, we hope that they will spark interest in finding creative solutions to current problems, or perhaps guide you in the design of a new service in the future.

The case studies, inevitably, represent (mostly) the success stories. We do not deny the value of learning from failure, and some of the most interesting and useful lessons for practice can come from reflections on what did not work. Research projects often provide a fund of useful experience on personal learning from failure, but we all know that it is very difficult to find a publication outlet for failed research projects or projects with negative findings. Similarly, it is much easier to find examples of success stories and good practice examples than to find contributors prepared to confess to the reasons why projects or ideas did not work out in practice. That is a drawback for further development of the profession and perhaps we need to be prepared to analyse failures in more detail, and do more careful 'accident investigation' in the future. Such accidents often provide the best learning experiences, after all. In the meantime, we can only urge you to read the case studies with some critical reflection on what might have been left out.

One of the reasons why a case study service model may not work so well in your setting is the unknown factor (or factors) to do with the organization or the power structures. Some of the contributors to the case studies have mentioned the history, briefly, of previous related activities. Often a plausible reason for the speedy development of a new role of the health library and information professional was that the seed idea for the role fell into very well prepared ground. Sometimes you need to be prepared to deal with the rocks and the weeds of unprepared ground first, before planting your seeds. There are organizational barriers to shift, and people to cultivate! Occasionally, you need to be prepared to move to a setting that will suit you, or to work with groups of staff that are willing to support your ideas, or spend a certain amount of time persuading those around you of your value. One of the incidental lessons that one of us learnt on a large project involving many higher and further education institutions in the UK was the great variety of cultures and different ways of doing things that existed in these institutions. When people talk about evolutionary progress they often and wrongly associate it with the idea of gradual progress towards a better future. In fact, what survives is what was the best adaptation at a time in the past, for the prevailing conditions. Some of the case studies describe how the contributors moved, possibly from an evolutionary dead end, to a situation where they could develop their role more successfully.

With changes to the way health and social care is being delivered, there are opportunities on the horizon (an optimistic viewpoint) or threats to your current post (a pessimistic viewpoint). We hope that the book has provided you with some ideas that you could use to make your own post more secure, or which you can take to a different role, and one not necessarily in the health sector. Many of the case study contributors stressed how they were applying skills they had, but in a different way and for different, less traditional purposes. With the development of new partnerships and new administrative structures in health and social care, there are places for people with good information management and networking skills.

Librarians offer both transferable skills and specialized knowledge, alongside a combination of implicit curiosity and commitment to the power of informed decision making, user focus, an understanding of information sources and of the information preferences of their clientele, attention to detail combined with the ability to listen, a desire to communicate and a strong service ethic. These characteristics provide a strong base from which librarians can develop and establish new roles. According to Phillipe Kahn (founder of Borland International and Starfish Software):

> The key word is flexibility, the ability to adapt constantly. Darwin said it clearly. People thought that he mainly talked about survival of the fittest. What he said was that the species that survive are usually not the smartest or the strongest, but the ones most responsive to change. So being attentive to customers and potential partners is my best advice –after, of course, perseverance and patience.   (www.quotationreference.com/)

Many, but not all, of the case studies developed out of library work, and this of course reflects the scope of our publisher. If you read carefully, you should find many examples of the way health library and information professionals are liaising and working with other professionals in the health sector - health professionals, the managers and administrators, the IT staff, as well as the staff working in information management departments dealing with routine patient data collection and analysis.

Evidence-based practice involves all these roles and there are more opportunities to work with and across other departments now.

We have stressed the professional role and professionalism in the book, and one limitation is the fact there was no space to examine changes in paraprofessional roles. Professionals may be expensive to employ and support for continuing professional development, paraprofessionals or library technicians may be a more attractive option for organizations wishing to develop a particular specialist, but narrowly specialist, role to support professionals. An example is the health information assistants employed by NHS Direct to deal with the information aspects of an enquiry. They receive training, and work to a protocol, but in other respects this is the reference enquiry of traditional library and information work. The lesson is to be watchful and be prepared to delegate, with training and support, some aspects of your current role to the paraprofessional or assistants. That should free up time to develop your own role. We trust that we have provided you with plenty ideas for that.

Index